Communications
in Computer and Information S

Editorial Board

José Cordeiro   Slimane Hammoudi
Marten van Sinderen (Eds.)

Software and
Data Technologies

7th International Conference, ICSOFT 2012
Rome, Italy, July 24-27, 2012
Revised Selected Papers

 Springer

Volume Editors

José Cordeiro
INSTICC and IPS, Department of Systems and Informatics
Rua do Vale de Chaves, Estefanilha, 2910-761 Setúbal, Portugal
E-mail: jcordeir@est.ips.pt

Slimane Hammoudi
Université d'Angers
10 Boulevard Jeanneteau - CS 90717, 49107 Angers Cedex 2, France
E-mail: slimane.hammoudi@eseo.fr

Marten van Sinderen
University of Twente
Information Systems Group, Department of Computer Science
P.O.Box 217, 7500 AE Enschede, The Netherlands
E-mail: m.j.vansinderen@utwente.nl

ISSN 1865-0929   e-ISSN 1865-0937
ISBN 978-3-642-45403-5   e-ISBN 978-3-642-45404-2
DOI 10.1007/978-3-642-45404-2
Springer Heidelberg New York Dordrecht London

Library of Congress Control Number: 2013956130

CR Subject Classification (1998): D.2, D.3, I.6, I.2.4, H.2.8

Typesetting: Camera-ready by author, data conversion by Scientific Publishing Services, Chennai, India

Printed on acid-free paper

Springer is part of Springer Science+Business Media (www.springer.com)

Preface

The present book includes extended and revised versions of a set of selected papers from the 7th International Conference on Software Paradigm Trends - ICSOFT 2012. The conference was held in Rome, Italy, and sponsored by the Institute for Systems and Technologies of Information, Control and Communication (INSTICC).

The purpose of ICSOFT 2012 was to bring together researchers and practitioners interested in information technology and software development. This seventh edition had four tracks focusing on the four main paradigms that have been intensively studied during the last decade for software and system design, namely: models, aspects, services, and context. These four paradigms will drive the design and development of future software systems encompassing a large number of research topics and applications: from programming issues to the more abstract theoretical aspects of software engineering; from models and services to the most complex management information systems; distributed systems, ubiquity, data interoperability; context understanding and many other topics included in the scope of ICSOFT.

ICSOFT 2012 received 127 paper submissions from 41 countries. To evaluate each submission, a double-blind paper evaluation method was used: each paper was reviewed by at least two internationally known experts from the ICSOFT Program Committee. Only 14 papers were selected to be published and presented as full papers, i.e., completed work (10 pages in proceedings / 30-minute oral presentation). Additionally, 41 papers were accepted as short papers (6 pages / 20-minute oral presentation) - for a total of 55 oral presentations – and 15 papers as posters. The full-paper acceptance ratio was thus 11%, while the total oral paper acceptance ratio was 43.3%.

The quality of the papers herewith presented stems directly from a successful and solid conference, which would not have been possible but for the dedicated effort of a complex organizing structure, from the steering and scientific committees to the INSTICC team responsible for handling all secretariat and logistical details. A word of appreciation is also due to the conference keynote speakers and to the many authors and attendants who gave us the honor of helping present their ideas and hard work to the scientific community.

We hope that you will find these papers interesting and consider them a helpful reference in the future when addressing any of the research areas mentioned above.

September 2013

José Cordeiro
Slimane Hammoudi
Marten van Sinderen

Organization

Conference Chair

José Cordeiro   Polytechnic Institute of Setúbal / INSTICC,
                 Portugal

Program Co-chairs

Slimane Hammoudi   ESEO, France
Marten van Sinderen   University of Twente, The Netherlands

Organizing Committee

Helder Coelhas   INSTICC, Portugal
Andreia Costa   INSTICC, Portugal
Bruno Encarnação   INSTICC, Portugal
Vitor Pedrosa   INSTICC, Portugal
Cláudia Pinto   INSTICC, Portugal
Susana Ribeiro   INSTICC, Portugal
José Varela   INSTICC, Portugal
Pedro Varela   INSTICC, Portugal

Program Committee

Muhammad Abulaish, Saudi Arabia
Hamideh Afsarmanesh,
   The Netherlands
Markus Aleksy, Germany
Rafa E. Al-Qutaish, UAE
Daniel Amyot, Canada
Kenneth Anderson, USA
Toshiaki Aoki, Japan
Keijiro Araki, Japan
Farhad Arbab, The Netherlands
Bernhard Bauer, Germany
Fevzi Belli, Germany
Alexandre Bergel, Chile
Jorge Bernardino, Portugal
Marcello Bonsangue, The Netherlands
Marko Boškovic, Canada

Mark Van Den Brand,
   The Netherlands
Lisa Brownsword, USA
Manfred Broy, Germany
Dumitru Burdescu, Romania
Fergal Mc Caffery, Ireland
Olivier Camp, France
Gerardo Canfora, Italy
Mauro Caporuscio, Italy
Cinzia Cappiello, Italy
Jorge Cardoso, Portugal
Cagatay Catal, Turkey
Sergio de Cesare, UK
Krzysztof Cetnarowicz, Poland
Kung Chen, Taiwan
Shiping Chen, Australia

Marta Cimitile, Italy
Peter Clarke, USA
Rem Collier, Ireland
Kendra Cooper, USA
Sergiu Dascalu, USA
Steven Demurjian, USA
Giovanni Denaro, Italy
Brian Donnellan, Ireland
Juan C. Dueñas, Spain
Philippe Dugerdil, Switzerland
Jürgen Ebert, Germany
Maria Jose Escalona, Spain
João Faria, Portugal
Cléver Ricardo Guareis de Farias,
  Brazil
Rita Francese, Italy
Nikolaos Georgantas, France
Paola Giannini, Italy
J. Paul Gibson, France
Itana Gimenes, Brazil
Athula Ginige, Australia
Cesar Gonzalez-Perez, Spain
Slimane Hammoudi, France
Christian Heinlein, Germany
Markus Helfert, Ireland
Brian Henderson-Sellers, Australia
Jose Luis Arciniegas Herrera,
  Colombia
Jose R. Hilera, Spain
Jang-eui Hong, Korea, Republic of
Milan Ignjatovic, Switzerland
Ilian Ilkov, The Netherlands
Ivan Ivanov, USA
Bharat Joshi, USA
Yong-Kee Jun, Korea, Republic of
Sanpawat Kantabutra, Thailand
Dimitris Karagiannis, Austria
Roger (Buzz) King, USA
Mieczyslaw Kokar, USA
Jun Kong, USA
Dimitri Konstantas, Switzerland
Walter Kosters, The Netherlands
Martin Kropp, Switzerland
Tei-wei Kuo, Taiwan
Konstantin Läufer, USA

Yu Lei, USA
Hareton Leung, China
Frank Leymann, Germany
Hua Liu, USA
David Lorenz, Israel
Ricardo J. Machado, Portugal
Leszek Maciaszek, Poland/Australia
Ahmad KamranMalik, Austria
Eda Marchetti, Italy
Katsuhisa Maruyama, Japan
Antonia Mas, Spain
Tommaso Mazza, Italy
Stephen Mellor, UK
Jose Ramon Gonzalez de Mendivil,
  Spain
Marian Cristian Mihaescu, Romania
Dimitris Mitrakos, Greece
Valérie Monfort, Tunisia
Mattia Monga, Italy
Sandro Morasca, Italy
José Arturo Mora-Soto, Spain
Paolo Nesi, Italy
Rory O'Connor, Ireland
Pasi Ojala, Finland
Flavio Oquendo, France
Marcos Palacios, Spain
Vincenzo Pallotta, Switzerland
Patrizio Pelliccione, Italy
Massimiliano Di Penta, Italy
Pascal Poizat, France
Andreas Polze, Germany
Rosario Pugliese, Italy
Jolita Ralyte, Switzerland
Anders Ravn, Denmark
Arend Rensink, The Netherlands
Werner Retschitzegger, Austria
Claudio de la Riva, Spain
Colette Rolland, France
Gustavo Rossi, Argentina
Gunter Saake, Germany
Krzysztof Sacha, Poland
Francesca Saglietti, Germany
Sreedevi Sampath, USA
Maria-Isabel Sanchez-Segura, Spain
Luis Fernandez Sanz, Spain

Tony Shan, USA
Beijun Shen, China
Marten van Sinderen, The Netherlands
Harvey Siy, USA
Yeong-tae Song, USA
Cosmin Stoica Spahiu, Romania
Peter Stanchev, USA
Davide Tosi, Italy
Sergiy Vilkomir, USA
Gianluigi Viscusi, Italy
Florin Vrejoiu, Romania
Christiane Gresse von Wangenheim,
  Brazil

Martijn Warnier, The Netherlands
Dietmar Wikarski, Germany
Jongwook Woo, USA
Qing Xie, USA
Bin Xu, China
Haiping Xu, USA
Tuba Yavuz-kahveci, USA
I-Ling Yen, USA
Hong Zhu, UK
Amal Zouaq, Canada
Elena Zucca, Italy

Auxiliary Reviewers

Narciso Albarracin, USA
Rodrigo Garcia-Carmona, Spain
Mark Johnson, USA
Michael McMahon, USA
Joseph Kaylor, USA
Dae S. Kim-Park, Spain
Bernardi Mario Luca, Italy

Sohei Okamoto, USA
Maria Saenz, USA
Alexander Serebrenik,
  The Netherlands
Carine Souveyet, France
Tom Verhoeff, The Netherlands

Invited Speakers

Stephen Mellor
Daniela Nicklas

Fabio Casati
Jan Dietz

Freeter, UK
Carl von Ossietzky Universität Oldenburg,
  Germany
University of Trento, Italy
Delft University of Technology,
  The Netherlands

Table of Contents

Invited Paper

Data, Context, Situation: On the Usefulness of Semantic Layers for Designing Context-Aware Systems

Daniela Nicklas and Nils Koppaetzky

Carl von Ossietzky Universität Oldenburg, Department of Computing Science
26111 Oldenburg, Germany
dnicklas@acm.org,
nils.koppaetzky@uni-oldenburg.de

Abstract. Context-aware applications adapt their behavior according to the current situation of their user or their (often physical) environment. This adaptation could be the change of the user interface, the performance of actions (like sending messages or triggering actuators), or the change of used resources (like network bandwidth or processing power). To determine relevant situations, many heterogeneous data sources could be used, ranging from sensor data over mined patterns in files to explicit user input. Since most sensors are not perfect, context quality has to be considered. And since many context-aware applications are mobile, the set of data sources might change during runtime. All this issues make context management and reasoning, and the development of correct adaptations within context-aware applications a challenging task. This paper is based on a keynote given at ICSOFT 2012 that introduces a layered model to separate different tasks and concerns in designing data models for context-aware applications. It shows how existing works map to this layered model, and how the model can help in designing context aware applications that are better to maintain and safer to use.

Keywords: Context-aware applications, Situational awareness.

1 Introduction

Many applications adapt their behavior according to their situation: navigation systems that change the proposed routing based on current traffic information, enhanced coffee mugs detect spontaneous coffee breaks and inform the other colleagues, or, more seriously, mobile context-aware business processes support workers in the field by up-to-date environmental information, to name a few. The design of this class of applications is difficult since the behavior depends on changing situations that have to be derived from lower level context information (e.g., sensor data), or given by the user. A commonly used context definition by A. Dey [1] states that context is "any information that can be used to characterize the situation of entities". This shows the great variety of context information.

In the domain of software engineering, other notions of context have emerged. Some work takes the context of a software developer into account that occurs during programming [2, 3]. Obviously, this is fundamentally different from the context of the developed application's user. However, tools and systems for programmers that adapt their behavior according to the software developer's context are again context-aware applications.

J. Cordeiro, S. Hammoudi, and M. van Sinderen (Eds.): ICSOFT 2012, CCIS 411, pp. 3–18, 2013.

In this contribution, we highlight the challenges that arise when dealing with the development of context-aware applications. This not only means that the context of the application has to be considered during requirement analysis and design, but also that the deployed application has to be aware of its context and adapts to it. Thus, it needs means to detect relevant context parameters (e.g., a smart phone application that gets the location of the user by a GPS sensor), needs to decide whether a relevant context change has happened, which often requires additional knowledge (e.g., the user entered the factory premises), and then performs the adaptation (e.g., switching from a private account to a business account, or displaying relevant work tasks that could be only done here).

Early work on software engineering for context aware applications already motivates the need for new techniques and architectures when dealing with context-aware applications. A first challenge arises from the processing of sensor data. Due to the heterogeneity of sensor technologies and sensor data protocols, this task should be decoupled from the application logic. Within the context toolkit [4], so-called context widgets hide the gathering of the sensor data and provide a first abstraction for the application. However, this is only a first solution for the tasks of a context-aware application. When sensor data is gathered and interpreted as a relevant context parameter, it has to be combined with other knowledge to determine if a relevant context change had happened. The representation of this knowledge is typically referred as the *context model*. While in early applications, this model remained informal or part of the application logic itself, soon researchers found that it should be modeled separately, in a formally defined way, to ease the correct definition of relevant context parameters, the development and the maintenance of the resulting application [5]. From this on, a multitude of context modeling techniques have been developed, since a good context information modeling formalism reduces the complexity of context-aware applications and improves their maintainability and evolvability. In addition, since gathering, evaluating and maintaining context information is expensive, re-use and sharing of context information between context-aware applications should be considered from the beginning. The existence of well-designed context information models eases the development and deployment of future applications [6]. This also helps in developing model-based middleware systems and frameworks for context-aware applications, and context management platforms [7–10].

The remainder of this paper is structured as follows: we first introduce two applications that act as examples for complex context-aware applications throughout the paper in Section 2. We illustrate common challenges in Section 3. In Section 4 we introduce the layered system model and the anatomy of context-aware applications. Finally, we show how the design of the sample applications can benefit from this system model in Section 5 and conclude in Section 6.

2   Sample Applications

In this section, we introduce two sample applications that depend on live context information. One is a machine maintenance process within a smart factory that provides condition based monitoring and maintenance, and the other is a flexible assistant system that should make maritime offshore operations safer. We derive common challenges and tasks for the design of such applications in Section 3.

2.1 Smart Factory Maintenance Process

In [11], a machine maintenance scenario with in a so-called smart factory is described. Sensors monitor the state of all machine tools used in a company, and the maintenance process should make sure that these tools are replaced before their attrition limits are exceeded and they are worn out. If they are not replaced in time, machine failures can occur, which can be very costly because they can cause a production breakdown. In the machine maintenance process, sensors in machines measure the attrition of the installed tools. This context data about the tools is managed in a context model, and a smart workflow is started to arrange the replacement of worn out tools based on context events. As we can see in Figure 1, the introduction of this context model decouples the application – here modeled and executed by a smart workflow – from the actual sensors and their heterogeneity. It provides higher-level information and notifies the application about relevant context changes.

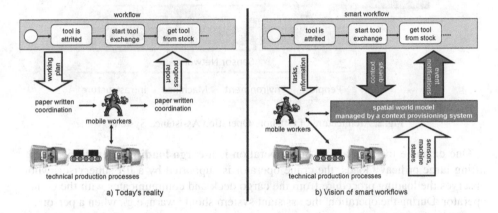

Fig. 1. Smart workflows: Incorporate context information into workflow technology [11]

2.2 Safe Offshore Operations

The other sample application is an assistance system for offshore operations. Offshore operations, like construction or maintenance of wind power plants, are due to their complexity and their hard environmental conditions risky and prone to accidents. Within the project *Safe Offshore Operation* (SOOP) [12] we develop tools and methods for risk analysis, human behavior modeling, operation planning [13], training, situation recognition, and sensor technology [14] to support crews and carriers during planning and undertaking these operations. One goal of SOOP is to increase the safety of these operations by observing the status of safety relevant entities with a context aware assistant system. It supports the crew by displaying an overview of the situation and triggering warnings when critical situations occur.

Figure 2 shows the planned architecture of the assistance system. The relevant context covers the state of people (e.g., location of crew members), the environment (e.g., wind and weather), machines (e.g., a heavy-lift crane) and the infrastructure itself (e.g., communication network or sensor systems). These parameters are observed using a sensor network on-board of the ship. Within the assistance system, a configurable situation recognition component determines whether a relevant context change happens and communicates this as warnings and aggregations. To configure the situation recognition, the relevant combinations of context parameters are represented in so-called situation models. As we see later, the proposed semantic levels help in designing such a system in a flexible and maintainable way.

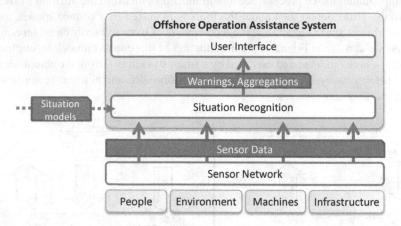

Fig. 2. Architecture of Offshore Operation Assistance System

One example for such an offshore operation is a **cargo loading operation**. When lifting large or heavy loads, the crane operator is supported by a lift supervisor, who observes the loading procedure from the cargo deck and communicates with the crane operator. During the operation, the assistant system should warn, e.g., when a person is to close to the lifted cargo or under it, or when the lift supervisor does not keep sufficient distance to the cargo.

3   Challenges in Developing Context-Aware Applications

In this chapter, we present three major challenges that occur when dealing with complex context-aware applications:

Representation of Context Information. As Dey stated, context can be anything that can be used to characterize the situation of an entity [1]. Thus, the data types and characteristics of potential context information may vary a lot. In particular, we have to deal with the following types of context:

- *Geographic context:* spatial data of all kind. Since most context-aware applications depend on their physical context as well, the context model typically needs to model the physical environment. In the smart factory example, this would be the shop floor layout and the location of installed machines, in the offshore operations example the ship layout and maritime maps. Such context information comes from map services or (spatial) databases and is typically obtained prior to the operation of the application. However, some sensors (like laser scanners or camera-based systems) are able to detect and obtain geographic context; using simultaneous localization and map building (so-called SLAM) techniques [15], this information as a map or add it to dynamic evolving map.

- *Dynamic context:* movement and change. This context type covers all kind of rapidly changing parameters, like location of mobile objects, weather measurements, or communication delays. For dynamic context, sensor data has to be processed, and depending on the amount and the update rate of the incoming sensor data, specialized infrastructures like data stream management systems might be a good design choice for managing this context type.

- *Information context:* documents and virtual objects. Beside physical phenomena, many context-aware applications also rely on information context that comes from the "digital world". This could be documentation or tutorials for the machine maintenance task, relevant e-mail notifications, or any other non-physical information object that might be relevant for the current situation.

- *Technical context:* the infrastructure. In addition to the aforementioned context types, information about availability and state of the infrastructure itself might be part of the context model. For the offshore operation assistance system, it is of crucial importance whether the sensor network is still in operation, or if part of it might be down due to communication problems or weather conditions. Mobile applications also might change the infrastructure they use when they are on the move: they might discover new services (e.g., wireless connection, a projector, or some load speakers) and connect to them. This re-configuration of applications typically depends on some technical context model.

- *User context:* activities, plans, and preferences. Finally, the state of the user herself might be important for assessing the situation, and be thus part of the context model. Depending on the application, this could include activity monitoring (is she standing, running, sleeping?), the interpretation of plans (it seems that she is up to walk towards this machine), and preferences (when a critical situation occurs, this user prefers to be warned by vibration, not by sound). This type of context is the most sensitive one: when dealing with user context within applications, it is of utterly importance to design a thorough privacy concept.

Stemming from the different context types, we have to deal with both discrete values and continuous values, with multi-dimensional data, multi-media data, spatio-temporal data, and with heterogeneous data sources. Within the context model of Henricksen and Indulska [16], these data sources are annotated of being "sensed" (coming from sensors), "static" (modeled once), "profiled" (given by the user) and "derived" (derived from other context data). When dealing with non-static context, the temporal characteristics (i.e., the freshness of the data) has to be taken into account. Finally, since sensors do not present fully accurate data, the information might highly differ in information quality. To deal with this heterogeneous context information, a variation of context modeling techniques have been developed, ranging from simple key-value-based approaches over spatial models to full-fledged ontologies [6].

Context Reasoning and Situation Recognition. Some information can be directly sensed, but often the context information needed to determine the situation has to be derived from the observable facts. And for this, many different options may exist, as was illustrated by Loke in his paper "On representing situations for context-aware pervasive computing: six ways to tell if you are in a meeting" [17]. This derivation process is often called context reasoning. Many techniques exist for context reasoning, some rely on logical specifications, other on learning approaches. While there is no exact definition on it, the process transforms so-called "lower-level context" to "higher-level context". Note that depending on the available data sources, they might be already able to directly produce higher-level context. A good review on situation recognition techniques can be found in [18].

Adaptation of Context Management. While simple context-aware applications can be easily implemented with a fixed context management approach, complex context-aware applications like our two motivating examples have to deal with an additional challenge: the context management itself might depend on the situation and thus needs to be adaptable. This covers the selection of available data sources, of context parameters, and of the situation recognition algorithms. In the smart factory example, the context observation of a repair process needs only to be turned on when a machine really needs to be repaired, and might depend on the failure of the machine, the available resources, and the worker's personal context. Similar, during an offshore operation, many different operations are carried out, and each of these operations has their relevant context parameters and their specific situations that need to be observed.

4   The Anatomy of a Context-Aware Application

Based on the key challenges for the development of context-aware applications, we introduce a generic architecture of such applications that can be mapped to many concrete frameworks and solutions. We first explain the overall architecture depicted in Figure 3, and discuss which type of context information could be shared between applications and thus be managed in common components. We then map the architecture to the sample applications and discuss its benefits in Section 5.

4.1   Architecture

In Figure 3, a generic architecture of a context-aware application is depicted. The top layer, *application*, holds the actual application logic. If it is an end-user application, this layer might be further decoupled to separate between application logic and user interface. Some context-aware applications are hidden from the user; they just provide context-aware services, e.g., as part of an operation system. On example would be a mobile phone system that provides network connectivity depending on the context of the user; the context could include technical context (which hotspots or networks are available), user context (user tasks), and geographical context (where is the user now, and where is she heading to? Maybe a free high-speed network will appear soon). Finally, some context-aware applications are not intended for one certain user, but just provide general services to the world, like traffic management for smart cities.

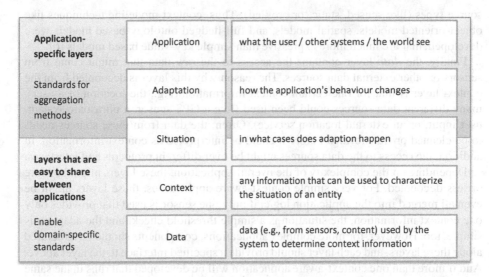

Application-specific layers	Application	what the user / other systems / the world see
Standards for aggregation methods	Adaptation	how the application's behaviour changes
	Situation	in what cases does adaption happen
Layers that are easy to share between applications	Context	any information that can be used to characterize the situation of an entity
Enable domain-specific standards	Data	data (e.g., from sensors, content) used by the system to determine context information

Fig. 3. Anatomy of a context-aware application and "sharability" of context information

On the second layer, *adaptation* covers the logic that determines how the application behavior should change. While the application layer needs the necessary components to implement the changed behavior, the logic for when and how the behavior should change can be decoupled from the application itself. This makes it easier to change this logic; this change is often necessary because of new requirements or a new environment where the application should be deployed. Users might want to configure this logic according to their preferences. And finally, since automatic adaptation of applications might cause irritations on the users side, a context-aware application should be able to explain why a certain change just happened (to support so-called intelligibility [19]).

The *situation* layer contains the situation recognition logic. For situation recognition, various context information has to be combined. This combination could be rather simple, like a formula that checks for certain values or thresholds, or be coded in complex patterns that include temporal characteristics of the context information. Situation recognition techniques have been studied extensively in pervasive computing; while in specification-based approaches, the knowledge about the combination of the context information is specified in formal logic models, in learning-based approaches, a situation recognition model is first trained with hopefully typical context information and then later used for situation recognition. For this, a wide variation of models has been used, like Bayesian derivative models, Hidden Markov Models, Decision Trees, Neural Networks, and Support Vector Machines [18].

The *context* layer represents the data model of the context information. According the the widely used definition of Dey, this data model contains any information that can be used to characterize the situation of an entity. Thus, the set of situations to which the application should adapt determines which context information could be needed and is therefore part of the context model. Due to the heterogeneity of context information (as discussed in Section 3), the context model must be able to represent different data structures (like optional attributes), data types (like spatio-temporal data), and data source types (like sensed, static, or profiled). Thus, context modeling techniques like object-oriented models, spatial models, and full-fledged ontology-based models were developed, that are much more expressive than simple key-value based models [6].

Finally, the *data* layer contains the access to the raw data that might come from sensors or other external data sources. The reason why this layer is decoupled from the context layer is that for one certain context information (e.g., the location of a user), many different data sources could been used (like a GPS sensor, a ultrasonic system, user input, or an external location service). Often, the data from these sources needs to be cleaned or transformed before it could be interpreted as context information. In addition, the access to the data sources might be over different protocols and interfaces.

Depending on the complexity of the overall application, these layers might be more or less decoupled. For very simple context-aware applications, these layers might be even all merged into the application logic: if only one sensor is used that provides only one context information, the situation is a simple threshold check, and the adaption is simple, too. However, for more complex applications, components should be structured along these layers, and each layer should provide a specified interface to the layer above. And if more than one context-aware application will be developed that runs in the same of in overlapping context, the deployed components could be run as shared services.

4.2 Sharing Context Information

To share context information, we have to take a closer look at the semantics of the information that is presented at the various level. In [20], we already referred to Andrew U. Frank's five tiers of ontologies [21], which are used to discuss consistency constraints in geographical information systems.

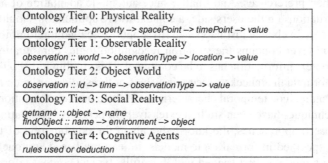

Fig. 4. The five tiers of ontologies according to [21]

Figure 4 gives an overview on these tiers. *Tier 0* is the ontology of the physical reality. It contains the assumption that there is exactly one real world; hence, for every property in the world and for a given point in time-space there is a single value. Note that in context-aware applications, the relevant reality can also includes non-physical entities, like services, web pages, or workflows.

Tier 1 includes observations of reality. This is the first tier that can be accessed in computational systems. Here, a value can be derived at a location with a given observation type. The type determines the measurement scale of the value (e.g. nominal or rational) and the measurement unit (e.g. meters or seconds). For spatial values, also a coordinate systems must be given. Values normally have a limited accuracy due to observation errors. This tier corresponds to the data layer of the generic architecture of context-aware applications (Figure 3).

In *Tier 2*, single observations are grouped together to individual objects that are defined by uniform properties. Now, the value of an observation is the state of a whole object, given by an identifier. Andrew U. Frank only considers physical objects in this tier, i.e. "things which exist in the physical world and can be observed by observation methods". They have a geometric boundary in the world, but it can change over time (e.g. dunes or fluids). In object-oriented context models, this tier directly corresponds to the aforementioned context layer. But even in simpler context models (like key-value pairs), the grouping to objects might be done implicitly, since the might be only one object of interest, or the grouping is done via naming conventions of they keys.

Until now, the ontology tiers cover data that can be seen as *objective reality*—you can send out a team of geographers or students to model physical objects and they will come to an agreement about their observations. In *Tier 3*, the socially constructed reality is represented. Social reality includes all the objects and relations which are created by social interactions. These are properties that are classified and named within the context of administrative, legal or institutional rules. Object names belong to this tier since they are assigned by culture; for many important things (but not all) there are functions to determine the name and to find the object by name in a certain environment. Since a context model in the context layer also would contain names for the objects, this ontology tier also corresponds to the context layer.

Finally, in *Tier 4* the rules are modeled that are used by cognitive agents (both human and software) for deduction. This tier is normally built into database query languages, applications or inference engines of knowledge based systems. This tier would correspond to situation definition, the adaptation logic, and the application itself, thus to the first three layers of the generic architecture of context-aware applications.

In this model, the higher the tier, the more the objective reality is interpreted for a certain application. Thus, this model can be also used to determine, which components could be shared between applications. The data layer is the most objective layer—it just represents single observations of the real world (including the digital or virtual reality). If no application-specific interpretation is made yet, such observations could be easily shared between applications.

For the context layer—corresponding to Tier 2 and 3—sharing is still possible. However, it depends on how overlapping the context information of the applications really is. If the applications all run on the same mobile device, many of them might need overlapping technical context (like network connectivity, energy level, or available external services), user context, or geographical context. Thus, a shared context management might help to reduce the applications complexity and resource usage of the device.

In general, Tier 4 ontologies are not sharable, since they highly depend on the application and thus are the result of a application-specific interpretation. However, there might be some generic situations that could be of interest of more than one application. Thus, the design of an architecture for context-aware applications could contain a library of generic situations which applications can directly use; most likely this set has to be extendable to cover the situations which are more specific.

5   Benefits of the Layered Approach

In this chapter, we have a closer look at the sample applications and discuss how they can benefit from this layered approach.

5.1   Smart Factory Maintenance

The smart factory maintenance application is one of a set of applications that were developed in the Nexus project, which addressed context management for large scale, highly complex, and highly dynamic context information [22]. Figure 5 shows an overview on the Nexus approach, with a mapping to the ontology tiers discussed in Section 4, and the resulting layered architecture.

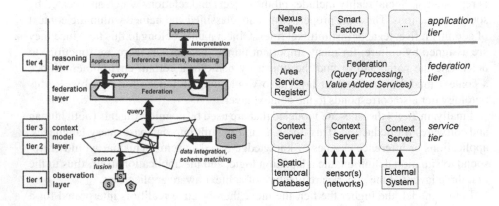

Fig. 5. Nexus approach and federated architecture

On the left side of Figure 5, we see that the Nexus approach is to federate over several context sources, to make the context information available for many context-aware applications. The smart factory maintenance process—and other context-aware applications within a smart factory—can thus benefit from context modeling and context processing effort that has been already carried out. The data model used at the federation layer directly corresponds to the context layer of our generic architecture; the situation layer is implemented on top of that as value added services. Thus, applications could decide whether they want to process their situation recognition within the federation layer or if they want to get the context information from the federation and do the situation recognition within the application.

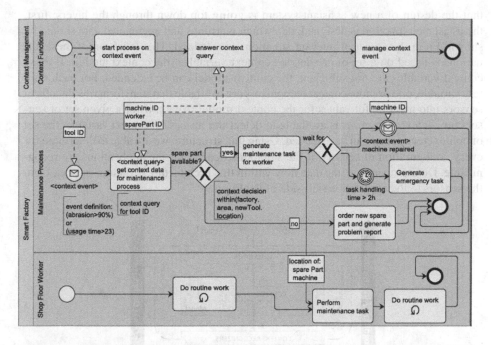

Fig. 6. Smart Factory machine maintenance scenario, modeled as context-aware workflow [23]

For the adaptation layer, the Smart Factory machine maintenance scenario uses business process modeling. Figure 6 shows an simplified version of this model using BMPN[1]. Within this process, the workflow depends on the context; this dependency is realized using so-called context queries (for synchronized communication) and registration and notification of context events (for asynchronous communication). Using this technique, the adaptation process can be partially modeled and reviewed by domain experts and requires no specialized technical knowledge. Also, a workflow execution engine can be used to directly execute these models.

Finally, the application layer itself—i.e., what the user sees—can be implemented with so-called human tasks. For this, many workflow execution engines already provide support, like dashboards and task lists. The allocation of the task can be again context-aware, e.g., only workers who are close to the maintenance tasks, are informed about it and can pick-up the task if they have time to perform it.

5.2 Safe Offshore Operations

For the assistance system for offshore operations, the key challenge is the adaptability of the situation recognition to new operations and to new set of available sensors. Thus, the layered architecture is here used to decouple a set of recognizable context parameters from a se of recognizable situation models. Figure 7 shows on the right side

---

[1] Object Management Group: Business Process Modeling Notation. Final Adopted Specification. http://www.omg.org/cgi-bin/doc?dtc/2006-02-01

that the design of a new assistant system is going top down through the layers: first, the assistance function is designed, i.e., which warnings and aggregated data should be shown. From this, a set of relevant situations are defined. The definition of these situations is based on a set of pre-defined context variables (the context model). If these context variables are not sufficient, the context model can be extended. For each context variable, one or more context recognizers are available that transform raw data from sensors into meaningful values for the context model. Again, if for a given set of sensors no context recognizer is available to detect the necessary context variable, the set of context recognizer can be extended. Using this structure, we are able to determine for every configuration of sensors, if the situations needed for the applications are recognizable. During operation, the data flow within this architecture is bottom-up, i.e., from the sensors to the application (left side of the Figure).

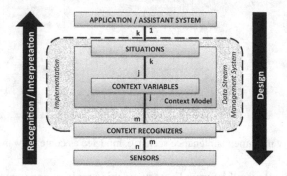

Fig. 7. Generic Assistant System: Design and Operation

In the following, we give short examples for the layers of the assistant system and its situation recognition [24].

Assistant system. The assistant system provides the user interface to display the overall situation and warnings. If an operation shows abnormal situations or changes to a critical situation it should warn the crew, for we observe both, the normal flow of operations as well as critical situations that should be avoided.

Situation description and definition. Analyzing the cargo loading operation described in chapter 1, we find three situations that are safety relevant, such as:

– **PersonToCloseToLiftedCargo**: A person is to close to or under the lifted cargo.
– **LiftSupervisorToFarFromCargo**: The LiftSupervisor who has to follow the cargo does not keep sufficient distance to it.
– **LineOfSightInterrupted**: The cargo interrupts the line of sight between CraneOperator and LiftSupervisor.

Such situation descriptions have been identified by a predated risk analysis. They can be defined using a specification-based approach by a set of values of real world parameters.

For the cargo loading operation, a critical situation would be "a person is to close to the lifted cargo". It could be defined followed:

$$cargolifted = "true"$$
$$distance(cargo, person) < safetydistance$$

Context Model of Cargo Operation. To define the situations as a condition over a fixed set of measurable parameters of real world entities, we describe these entities, their possible parameters, and their relations. Figure 8 illustrates the static context model. In our example, all entities are physical entities and our sensors can gather information referring to the physical character of the entities. The set of relevant parameters of a physical entity are *absolutPosition, relativePosition, geometry* and *size*, with the relative position referring to another physical entity (self-relation arrow).

Context Variables. The j context variables are relevant parameters of an entity in our system that are measureable by sensors or derivable from prior knowledge. They are used to define the situations described above.

Context Recognizers. The m context recognizers are programs to derive values of context variables from raw sensor data, or from values of context variables that are already determined. As the value derivation of context variables can be very complex, the context recognizer can vary from very simple implementations to those with high complexity. Context recognizers are comparable to context widgets introduced in [4].

Sensors. The n sensors are used to perceive and observe the environment by measuring data. In our case a sensor network using wireless ultra wide band technology is used to determine the positions of entities.

Recognition and interpretation. The process of runtime recognition of situations with the introduced system follows figure 7 bottom-up. It increases the degree of abstraction, compression, and interpretation of data with every layer. Raw data, delivered from the sensors is used to derive the context variables with the help of context recognizers. A set of values of context variables is abstracted into situations, which are transmitted to the assistant system and could trigger warnings. Hence a large number of raw sensor data are mapped to few domain concepts during the recognition process.

To enable highly dynamic runtime situation recognition, we implement the situation recognition within a data stream management system (DSMS), a system that allows to manage and process continuous data streams from heterogeneous data sources (e.g., sensors). Similar to a data base management system, queries can be stated and mathematical expressions applied to manage, filter, and process the data. However, in a DSMS these queries are registered in the system and executed continuously. After registration a declarative query is transformed into a so-called query plan. We use the open source DSMS Odysseus [25], which supports query sharing. Thus, if some context recognizers or situation models are already deployed in running in the system, and a new situation model is registered that shares some of the context recognition, this will result in a shared query plan and thus in shared resources. As we can see, the layered architecture can not only help in good structuring and separation of concerns within a software system, but also to save resources like processing time and memory usage.

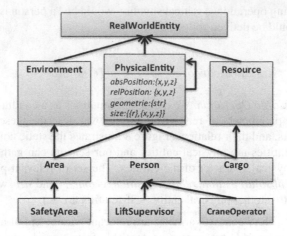

Fig. 8. Context model for the cargo loading operation described in chapter 1, modeled as a class diagram with UML 2.0

6   Conclusion

In this paper, we discussed general characteristics of context-aware applications and which challenges software developers have to face when designing such applications. We presented a generic layered approach that has been implemented in several frameworks and applications. Based on two sample scenarios that cover complex context-aware applications, we show how their design can benefit from this layered approach.

References

1. Dey, A.K.: Understanding and using context. Personal and Ubiquitous Computing 5 (2001)
2. Antunes, B., Cordeiro, J., Gomes, P.: Context modeling and context transition detection in software development. In: Proceedings of the 7th International Conference on Software Paradigm Trends, ICSOFT 2012, Rome, Italy, July 24-27, pp. 477–484. SciTePress (2012)
3. Grambow, G., Oberhauser, R., Reichert, M.: Knowledge provisioning: A context-sensitive process-oriented approach applied to software engineering environments. In: Proceedings of the 7th International Conference on Software Paradigm Trends, ICSOFT 2012, Rome, Italy, July 24-27, SciTePress (2012)
4. Salber, D., Dey, A.K., Abowd, G.D.: The context toolkit: aiding the development of context-enabled applications. In: CHI 1999: Proc. of the SIGCHI Conf. on Human Factors in Computing Systems. ACM Press (1999)
5. Henricksen, K., Indulska, J.: A software engineering framework for context-aware pervasive computing. In: 2nd IEEE Intl. Conference on Pervasive Computing and Communications (2004)
6. Bettini, C., Brdiczka, O., Henricksen, K., Indulska, J., Nicklas, D., Ranganathan, A., Riboni, D.: A survey of context modelling and reasoning techniques. Pervasive and Mobile Computing 6, 161–180 (2010); Context Modelling, Reasoning and Management

7. Yau, S.S., Karim, F., Wang, Y., Wang, B., Gupta, S.K.: Reconfigurable context-sensitive middleware for pervasive computing. IEEE Pervasive Computing 1, 33–40 (2002)

8. Capra, L., Emmerich, W., Mascolo, C.: CARISMA: context-aware reflective middleware system for mobile applications. IEEE Transactions on Software Engineering 29, 929–945 (2003)

9. Hu, P., Indulska, J., Robinson, R.: An autonomic context management system for pervasive computing. In: Sixth Annual IEEE International Conference on Pervasive Computing and Communications, pp. 213–223. IEEE Computer Society, Los Alamitos (2008)

10. Wojciechowski, M., Wiedeler, M.: Model-based development of context-aware applications using the MILEO-context server. In: 2012 IEEE International Conference on Pervasive Computing and Communications Workshops (PERCOM Workshops), pp. 613–618 (2012)

11. Wieland, M., Nicklas, D., Leymann, F.: Managing technical processes using smart workflows. In: Mähönen, P., Pohl, K., Priol, T. (eds.) ServiceWave 2008. LNCS, vol. 5377, pp. 287–298. Springer, Heidelberg (2008)

12. Sobeich, C., Boede, E., Luedtke, A., Hahn, A., Nicklas, D., Korte, H.: Project SOOP: safe offshore operations. In: ISIS - 9th International Symposium "Information on Ships", DGON (Deutsche Gesellschaft fuer Ortung und Navigation) and German Society for Maritime Technology, STG (2012)

13. Droste, R., Läsche, C., Sobiech, C., Böde, E., Hahn, A.: Model-based risk assessment supporting development of HSE plans for safe offshore operations. In: Stoelinga, M., Pinger, R. (eds.) FMICS 2012. LNCS, vol. 7437, pp. 146–161. Springer, Heidelberg (2012)

14. Wehs, T., Janssen, M., Koch, C., Coelln, G.V.: System architecture for data communication and localization under harsh environmental conditions in maritime automation. In: IEEE 10th International Conference on Industrial Informatics, University of Applied Sciences Emden/Leer, Germany (2012)

15. Dissanayake, M., Newman, P., Clark, S., Durrant-Whyte, H.F., Csorba, M.: A solution to the simultaneous localization and map building (SLAM) problem. IEEE Transactions on Robotics and Automation 17, 229–241 (2001)

16. Henricksen, K., Indulska, J.: Developing context-aware pervasive computing applications: Models and approach. Pervasive and Mobile Computing 2, 37–64 (2006)

17. Loke, S.W.: On representing situations for context-aware pervasive computing: six ways to tell if you are in a meeting. In: Proceedings of PerCom Workshops 2006, pp. 35–39. IEEE Computer Society (2006)

18. Ye, J., Dobson, S., McKeever, S.: Situation identification techniques in pervasive computing: A review. Pervasive and Mobile Computing 8, 36–66 (2012)

19. Fong, J., Indulska, J., Robinson, R.: A preference modelling approach to support intelligibility in pervasive applications. In: 2011 IEEE International Conference on Pervasive Computing and Communications Workshops, PERCOM Workshops, pp. 409–414. IEEE (2011)

20. Becker, C., Nicklas, D.: Where do spatial context-models end and where do ontologies start? a proposal of a combined approach. In: Proceedings of the First International Workshop on Advanced Context Modelling, Reasoning and Management, UbiComp 2004, Nottingham, England, University of Southhampton (2004)

21. Frank, A.: Tiers of ontology and consistency constraints in geographical information systems. International Journal of Geographical Information Science 15, 667–678 (2001)

22. Grossmann, M., Bauer, M., Hoenle, N., Kaeppeler, U.P., Nicklas, D., Schwarz, T.: Efficiently managing context information for large-scale scenarios. In: 3rd IEEE International Conference on Pervasive Computing and Communications, PerCom 2005, March 8-12, pp. 331–340. IEEE Computer Society, Kauai Island (2005)

23. Wieland, M., Kopp, O., Nicklas, D., Leymann, F.: Towards context-aware workflows. In: Proceedings of Workshop on Ubiquitous Mobile Information and Collaboration Systems, Caise 2007 Workshop, vol. 2, pp. 577–591. Springer (2007)

24. Koppaetzky, N., Nicklas, D.: Towards a model-based approach for context-aware assistant systems in offshore operations. In: 2013 IEEE International Conference on Pervasive Computing and Communications Workshops, PERCOM Workshops. IEEE (accepted for publication, 2013)

25. Appelrath, H.J., Geesen, D., Grawunder, M., Michelsen, T., Nicklas, D.: Odysseus: a highly customizable framework for creating efficient event stream management systems. In: Proceedings of the 6th ACM International Conference on Distributed Event-Based Systems, DEBS 2012, pp. 367–368. ACM, New York (2012)

Papers

Papers

Fencing the Lamb: A Chart Parser for ModelCC

Luis Quesada, Fernando Berzal, and Francisco J. Cortijo

Department of Computer Science and Artificial Intelligence,
CITIC, University of Granada, Granada 18071, Spain
{lquesada,fberzal,cb}@decsai.ugr.es

Abstract. Traditional grammar-driven language specification techniques constrain language designers to specific kinds of grammars. In contrast, model-based language specification techniques decouple language design from language processing. They allow the occurrence of ambiguities and the declarative specification of constraints for solving them. As a result, these techniques require general parser generators, which should be able to parse context-free grammars, handle ambiguities, and enforce constraints to disambiguate them as desired by the language designer. In this paper, we describe Fence, a bottom-up chart parser with lexical and syntactic ambiguity support. Fence accepts lexical analysis graphs outputted by the Lamb (Lexical AMBiguity) lexer and efficiently resolves ambiguities by means of the declarative specification of constraints. Both Lamb and Fence are part of the ModelCC model-based parser generator.

Keywords: Chart Parser, Context-free Grammars, Ambiguities, Constraints.

1 Introduction

Traditional language specification techniques [2] require the developer to provide a textual specification of the language grammar.

In contrast, model-based language specification techniques [15,24,25,21] allow the specification of languages by means of data models annotated with constraints.

Model-based language specification has direct applications in the following fields: programming tools [1], domain-specific languages [9,10,18], model-driven software development [26], data integration [27], text mining [29,4], natural language processing [11], and the corpus-based induction of models [14].

Due to the nature of the aforementioned application fields, the specification of separate language elements may cause lexical and syntactic ambiguities. Lexical ambiguities occur when an input string simultaneously corresponds to several token sequences [19], which may also overlap. Syntactic ambiguities occur when a token sequence can be parsed in several ways.

The formal grammars of languages specified using model-based techniques may contain epsilon productions (such as $E := \epsilon$), infinitely recursive production sets (such as $A := c$, $A := B$, and $B := A$), and associativity, precedence, and custom constraints. Therefore, a parser that supports such specification is needed.

Our proposed algorithm, Fence [23], is a bottom-up chart parser that accepts a lexical analysis graph as input, performs an efficient syntactic analysis taking constraints into

J. Cordeiro, S. Hammoudi, and M. van Sinderen (Eds.): ICSOFT 2012, CCIS 411, pp. 21–35, 2013.

account, and produces a parse graph that represents all the possible parse trees. The parsing process discards any sequence of tokens that does not provide a valid syntactic sentence conforming to the language specification, which consists of a production set and a set of constraints. Fence implicitly performs a context-sensitive lexical analysis, as the parsing process determines which token sequences end up in the parse graph. Fence supports every possible construction in a context-free language with constraints, including epsilon productions and infinitely recursive production sets.

The combined use of the Lamb lexical analyzer [22] and Fence [23] allows the generation of processors for languages with ambiguities and constraints, and it renders model-based language specification techniques feasible. Indeed, ModelCC [24,25,21] is a model-based language specification tool that relies on Lamb and Fence to generate language processors.

Section 2 explains model-based language specification techniques and lexical analysis algorithms with ambiguity support. Section 3 introduces Fence, our parser with ambiguity and constraint support. Section 4 presents our conclusions and future work.

2   Background

Language processing tools traditionally divide the analysis into two separate phases; namely, scanning (or lexical analysis), which is performed by lexers, and parsing (or syntax analysis), which is performed by parsers. However, language processing tools based on scannerless parsers also exist.

Subsection 2.1 introduces model-based language specification techniques and the model-based parser generator ModelCC. Subsection 2.2 analyzes existing scanning algorithms with ambiguity support. Subsection 2.3 describes existing parsing algorithms.

2.1   Model-Based Language Specification

In its most general sense, a model is anything used in any way to represent something else. In such sense, a grammar is a model of the language it defines. In Software Engineering, data models are also common. Data models explicitly determine the structure of data. Roughly speaking, they describe the elements they represent and the relationships existing among them. From a formal point of view, it should be noted that data models and grammar-based language specifications are not equivalent, even though both of them can be used to represent data structures. A data model can express relationships a grammar-based language specification cannot. A data model does not need to comply with the constraints a grammar-based language specification has to comply with. Typically, describing a data model is generally easier than describing the corresponding grammar-based language specification.

In practice, when we want to build a complex data structure from the contents of a file, the implementation of the mandatory language processor needed to parse the file requires the software engineer to build a grammar-based language specification for the data as represented in the file and also to implement the conversion from the parse tree returned by the parser to the desired data structure, which is an instance of the data model that describes the data in the file.

Whenever the language specification has to be modified, the language designer has to manually propagate changes throughout the entire language processor tool chain, from the specification of the grammar defining the formal language (and its adaptation to specific parsing tools) to the corresponding data model. These updates are time-consuming, tedious, and error-prone. By making such changes labor-intensive, the traditional language processing approach hampers the maintainability and evolution of the language used to represent the data [13].

Moreover, it is not uncommon for different applications to use the same language. For example, the compiler, different code generators, and other tools within an IDE, such as the editor or the debugger, typically need to grapple with the full syntax of a programming language. Unfortunately, their maintenance typically requires keeping several copies of the same language specification in sync.

The idea behind model-based language specification is that, starting from a single abstract syntax model (ASM) that represents the core concepts in a language, language designers can develop one or several concrete syntax models (CSMs). These CSMs can suit the specific needs of the desired textual or graphical representation. The ASM-CSM mapping can be performed, for instance, by annotating the abstract syntax model with the constraints needed to transform the elements in the abstract syntax into their concrete representation.

This way, the ASM representing the language can be modified as needed without having to worry about the language processor and the peculiarities of the chosen parsing technique, since the corresponding language processor will be automatically updated.

Finally, as the ASM is not bound to a particular parsing technique, evaluating alternative and/or complementary parsing techniques is possible without having to propagate their constraints into the language model. Therefore, by using an annotated ASM, model-based language specification completely decouples language specification from language processing, which can be performed using whichever parsing techniques are suitable for the formal language implicitly defined by the abstract model and its concrete mapping.

A diagram summarizing the traditional language design process is shown in Figure 1, whereas the corresponding diagram for the model-based approach is shown in Figure 2. It should be noted that ASMs represent non-tree structures whenever language elements can refer to other language elements, hence the use of the 'abstract syntax graph' term.

The ASM is built on top of basic language elements, which can be viewed as the tokens in the model-driven specification of a language. ModelCC provides the necessary mechanisms to combine those basic elements into more complex language constructs, which correspond to the use of concatenation, selection, and repetition in the syntax-driven specification of languages.

When the ASM represents a tree-like structure, a model-based parser generator is equivalent to a traditional grammar-based parser generator in terms of expression power. When the ASM represents non-tree structures, reference resolution techniques can be employed to make model-based parser generators more powerful than grammar-based ones, as we will see in the next Section.

In ModelCC, the constraints imposed over ASMs to define a particular ASM-CSM mapping can be declared as metadata annotations on the model itself. Now supported by

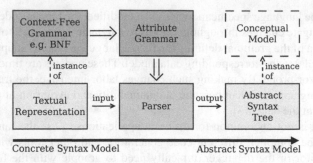

Fig. 1. Traditional language processing

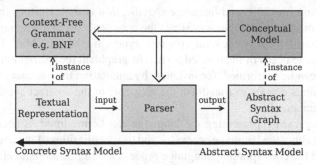

Fig. 2. Model-based language processing

all the major programming platforms, metadata annotations are often used in reflective programming and code generation. Table 1 summarizes the set of constraints supported by ModelCC for establishing ASM-CSM mappings between ASMs and their concrete representation in textual CSMs.

It should be noted that model-based language specification techniques allow lexical and syntactic ambiguities: each language element is defined as a separate and independent entity, even when their pattern specification or syntactic specification are in conflict. Therefore, model-based language specification techniques require a lexical analysis algorithm with ambiguity support and a corresponding parsing algorithm with lexical and syntactic ambiguity support.

2.2 Lexical Analysis Algorithms with Ambiguity Support

Given a language specification describing the tokens listed in Figure 3, the string "&5.2& /25.20/" can correspond to the four different lexical analysis alternatives shown in Figure 4, depending on whether the sequences of digits separated by points are considered real numbers or integer numbers separated by points.

The productions shown in Figure 5 illustrate a scenario of lexical ambiguity sensitivity. Sequences of digits separated by points should be considered either *Real* tokens or *Integer Point Integer* token sequences depending on the surrounding tokens, which

Table 1. Summary of the basic metadata annotations supported by ModelCC

Constraints on...	Annotation	Function
Patterns	@Pattern	Pattern definition of basic language elements.
	@Value	Field where the matched input will be stored.
Delimiters	@Prefix	Element prefix(es).
	@Suffix	Element suffix(es).
	@Separator	Element separator(s).
Cardinality	@Optional	Optional elements.
	@Minimum	Minimum element multiplicity.
	@Maximum	Maximum element multiplicity.
Evaluation order	@Associativity	Element associativity (e.g. left-to-right).
	@Composition	Eager or lazy policy for nested composites.
	@Priority	Element precedence.
References	@ID	Identifier of a language element.
	@Reference	Reference to a language element.

may be either *Ampersand* tokens or *Slash* tokens. The desired result of analyzing the input string "&5.2& /25.20/" is shown in Figure 6.

The further application of a parser supporting lexical ambiguities would produce the only possible valid sentence, which, in turn, would be based on the only valid lexical analysis for our example. The intended results are shown in Figure 8.

The Lamb lexical analyzer [22] captures all possible sequences of tokens within a given input string and it generates a lexical analysis graph that describes them all, as shown in Figure 7. In these graphs, each token is linked to its preceding and following tokens. There may also be several starting tokens. Each path in these graphs describes a possible sequence of tokens that can be found within the input string.

To the best of our knowledge, the only way to process lexical analysis graphs consists of extracting the different paths from the graph and parse each of them. This process is inefficient, as partial parsing trees that are shared among different token sequences have to be created several times.

2.3 Syntactic Analysis Algorithms

Traditional efficient parsers for restricted context-free grammars, such as the LL [20], LR [16], LALR [5,7], and SLR [6] parsers, do not consider ambiguities in syntactic analysis, so they cannot be used to parse ambiguous languages. The efficiency of these parsers is $O(n)$, being n the token sequence length.

```
(-|\+)?[0-9]+              Integer
(-|\+)?[0-9]+\.[0-9]+      Real
\.                         Point
\/                         Slash
\&                         Ampersand
```

Fig. 3. Specification of token types as regular expressions for a lexically-ambiguous language

- `Ampersand Integer Point Integer Ampersand Slash Integer Point Integer Slash`
- `Ampersand Integer Point Integer Ampersand Slash Real Slash`
- `Ampersand Real Ampersand Slash Integer Point Integer Slash`
- `Ampersand Real Ampersand Slash Real Slash`

Fig. 4. Different possible token sequences in the input string "&5.2& /25.20/" due to the lexically-ambiguous language specification shown in Figure 3

```
E ::= A B
A ::= Ampersand Real Ampersand
B ::= Slash Integer Point Integer Slash
```

Fig. 5. Context-sensitive productions that resolve the ambiguities in Figure 4

Generalized LR (GLR) parsers [17] parse in linear to cubic time, depending on how closely the grammar conforms to the underlying LR strategy. The time required to run the algorithm is proportional to the degree of nondeterminism in the grammar. The Universal parser [28] is a GLR parser used for natural language processing. However, it fails for grammars with epsilon productions and infinitely recursive production sets.

Existing chart parsers for unrestricted context-free grammar parsing, as the CYK parser [30,12] and the Earley parser [8], can consider syntactic ambiguities but not lexical ambiguities. The efficiency of these general context-free grammar parsers is $O(n^3)$, being n the token sequence length.

3 Fence

In this section, we introduce Fence, an efficient bottom-up chart parser that produces a parse graph that contains as many root nodes as different parse trees exist for a given ambiguous input string.

In contrast to the parsing techniques mentioned in the previous section, Fence is able to process lexical analysis graphs and, therefore, it efficiently considers lexical ambiguities.

Fence also considers syntactic ambiguities, allows the specification of constraints, and supports every possible context-free language construction, particularly epsilon productions and infinitely recursive production sets.

The Fence parsing algorithm consists of three consecutive phases: the extended lexical analysis graph construction phase, the chart parsing phase, and the constraint enforcement phase.

Subsection 3.1 introduces the terminology used in this section. Subsection 3.2 describes the extended lexical analysis graph construction phase. Subsection 3.3 describes the chart parsing phase. Subsection 3.4 describes the constraint enforcement phase.

3.1 Terminology

A context-free grammar is formally defined [3] as the tuple (N, Σ, P, S), where:

- N is the finite set of nonterminal symbols of the language, sometimes called syntactic variables, none of which appear in the language strings.

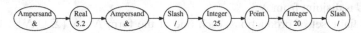

Fig. 6. Desired lexical analysis of the lexically ambiguous "&5.2& /25.20/" input string

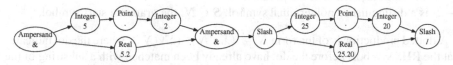

Fig. 7. Lexical analysis graph, as produced by the Lamb lexer

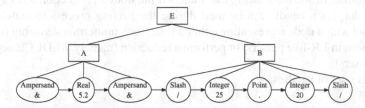

Fig. 8. Syntactic analysis graph, as produced by applying a parser that supports lexical ambiguities to the lexical analysis graph shown in Figure 7. Squares represent nonterminal symbols found during the parsing process.

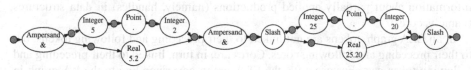

Fig. 9. Extended lexical analysis graph corresponding to the lexical analysis graph shown in Figure 7. Gray nodes represent cores.

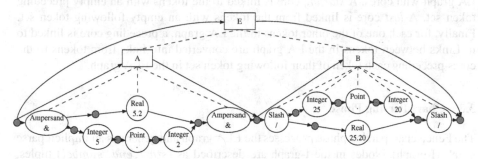

Fig. 10. Parse graph corresponding to the extended lexical analysis graph shown in Figure 9. Squares represent nonterminal symbols found during the parsing process. Dotted lines represent the explicit parse graph node.

- Σ is the finite set of terminal symbols of the language, also called tokens, which constitute the language alphabet (i.e. they appear in the language strings). Therefore, Σ is disjoint from N.
- P is a finite set of productions, each one of the form $N \rightarrow (\Sigma \cup N)^*$, where $*$ is the Kleene star operator, $\cup$ denotes set union, the part before the arrow is called the left-hand side (LHS) of the production, and the part after the arrow is called the right-hand side (RHS) of the production.
- S is a distinguished nonterminal symbol, $S \in N$: the grammar start symbol.

A dotted production is of the form $N \rightarrow (\Sigma \cup N)^* . (\Sigma \cup N)^*$, where the dot indicates that the RHS symbols before the dot have already been matched with a substring of the input string.

A handle is a tuple $(dottedproduction, [start, end])$, where $start$ and end identify the substring of the input string that matched the dotted production RHS symbols before the dot. Each handle can be used during the parsing process to match a rule RHS symbol with a node representing either a token or a nonterminal symbol (namely, SHIFT actions in LR-like parsers) or perform a reduction (namely, REDUCE actions in LR-like parsers).

A core is a set of handles.

3.2   Extended Lexical Analysis Graph Construction Phase

In order to efficiently perform the parsing process, Fence converts the input lexical analysis graph (LA graph) into an extended lexical analysis graph (ELA graph) that stores information about partially applied productions (namely, handles) in data structures (namely, cores).

In an ELA graph, tokens are not linked to their preceding and following tokens, but to their preceding and following cores. Cores are, in turn, linked to their preceding and following token sets. For example, the ELA graph corresponding to the LA graph in Figure 7 is shown in Figure 9.

The conversion from the LA graph to the ELA graph is performed by completing the LA graph with cores. A *starting* core is linked to the tokens with an empty preceding token set. A *last* core is linked from the tokens with an empty following token set. Finally, for each one of the other tokens in the LA graph, a preceding core is linked to it. Links between tokens in the LA graph are converted into links from tokens to the cores preceding each token of their following token set in the ELA graph.

3.3   Chart Parsing Phase

The Fence chart parsing phase processes the ELA graph and generates an implicit parse graph (I-graph). Nodes in the I-graph are described as $(start, end, symbol)$ tuples, where $start$ and end identify the substring of the input string, and $symbol$ identifies the production LHS. It should be noted that ambiguities, both lexical and syntactic, are implicit in the I-graph nodes, as they contain no information about their contents. The I-graph contains a set of starting nodes, each of which may represent several parse tree roots. The parsing itself is performed by progressively applying productions and storing handles in cores.

The grammar productions with an empty RHS (i.e. epsilon productions) are removed from the grammar and their LHS symbol is stored in the *epsilonSymbols* set. This set allows these parse symbols being skipped when found in a production, as if a reduction using the epsilon production were applied.

```
procedure addHandle(Production p, int matched,
                    ImplicitNode first, ImplicitNode n,
                    Stack<[Handle,ImplicitNode]> agenda):
  offset = 0
  do:
    next = matched+offset
    nextSymbol = p.right[next].symbol
    h = new Handle(p,next,first,first.startIndex)
    if !n.core.contains(h):
      n.core.add(h)
    if n.symbol == nextSymbol:
      if !alreadyGenerated.contains([h,n]):
        agenda.push([h,n])
        alreadyGenerated.add(]h,n])
    offset++
  while epsilonSymbols.contains(nextSymbol) && next<r.right.size
```

Fig. 11. Pseudocode of the ancillary *addHandle* procedure

```
agenda = {}
for each Production p in productionSet:
  for each ImplicitNode n in nodeSet:
    addHandle(p,0,n,n,agenda)
```

Fig. 12. Pseudocode of the chart parser initialization

The agenda is a stack of (*handle*, *node*) in which the node can match the symbol after the dot in the dotted rule of the handle. It is initially empty.

The *alreadyGenerated* handle set contains all the agenda entries ever generated and inhibits the generation of duplicate entries.

The parser is initialized by generating a handle for each production and adding them to every core, as shown in Figure 12.

The *addHandle* procedure in Figure 11 is responsible for adding a handle to a core. It also adds the corresponding agenda entries for that handle with the nodes that follow the core and match the symbol after the dot in the dotted production of the handle. It should be noted that the *addHandle* procedure considers epsilon productions: if a production RHS symbol is in the *epsilonSymbols* set, both the possibilities of it being reduced or not by that production are considered; that is, a new handle that skips that element is added to the same core. It should also be noted that element are skipped iteratively, as many consecutive RHS symbols of a production could be in the *epsilonSymbols* set.

```
while !agenda.empty:
  [h,n] = agenda.pop()
  if h.dotposition == h.production.right.size-1:
    // Production matched all its elements. i.e. Reduction
    nn = new ImplicitNode(h.startIndex,n.endIndex,p.left.symbol)
    h.first.core.following.add(nn)
    nn.preceding.add(h.first.core)
    for each Core c in n.following:
      c.preceding.add(nn)
      nn.following.add(c)
    for each Handle hn in h.first.core.waitingFor(nn.symbol):
      hadd = new Handle(hn.production,hn.next,hn.first,hn.startIndex)
      agenda.push([hadd,n])
  else:
    // i.e. Shift
    for each Core c in n.following:
      for each ImplicitNode nnext in c.following:
        addHandle(h.production,h.next+1,h.first,h.startIndex,agenda)
```

Fig. 13. Pseudocode of the Fence parsing phase

The parsing process consists in iteratively extracting entries consisting of handles and nodes from the agenda and matching the next symbol of the RHS of the handle production with the node. The handles whose productions are successfully matched are added to the cores following the node and the agenda is updated with the entries that contain any of the newly generated handles. In case all the symbols of a production RHS match a sequence of nodes, a new node is generated by reducing them. The new *node* start index is obtained from the handle, its *end* position is obtained from the last node matched, and its *symbol* is the LHS symbol of the production. When a newly generated node only has the *starting* core in its preceding core set and the *final* core in its following core set, and its *symbol* corresponds to the initial symbol of the grammar, it is added to the parse graph starting node set, which means that that node represents a valid parse. The pseudocode for this process is shown in Figure 13.

The result of the chart parsing phase is an I-graph, which the constraint enforcement phase accepts as input.

The Fence chart parsing phase order of efficiency is theoretically equivalent to existing Earley chart parsers. That is, $O(n^3)$ in the general case, $O(n^2)$ for unambiguous grammars, and $O(n)$ for almost all LR(k) grammars, being n the length of the input string.

3.4   Constraint Enforcement Phase

The Fence constraint enforcement phase processes the I-graph and generates an explicit parse graph (E-graph, or just parse graph) by enforcing the constraints defined for the language. Nodes in the E-graph that represent tokens are still defined as $(start, end, symbol)$ tuples. Nodes in the E-graph that represent nonterminal symbols reference the list of nodes that matched the production used to generate those nodes. It should be noted that ambiguities, both lexical and syntactic, are explicit in the E-graph, as it represents several parse trees corresponding to all the possible interpretations of the

```
procedure expand(ImplicitNode n, Set<ImplicitNode> history,
                 Map<ImplicitNode,Set<Node>> alreadyExpanded)
                 returns Set<Symbol>:
  if alreadyExpanded.contains(n): // memoization
    return alreadyExpanded.get(n)
  else:
    // the history set avoids infinite loop in recursive production sets
    if !history.contains(n):
      history.add(n);
      // try to apply every production
      for each Production p with LHS symbol == n.symbol:
        for every ImplicitNode pn with startIndex == n.startIndex:
          if pn != n && pn.endIndex<=n.endIndex:
            if p.mayMatch(pn.symbol):
              // apply production p to each expanded symbol of pn
              pn.expandeds = expand(pn,history,alreadyExpanded)
              for each Node nn in pn.expandeds:
                out += apply(p,nn,0,{},alreadyExpanded,history)
    alreadyExpanded.put(n,out)
    return out
```

Fig. 14. Pseudocode of the *expand* procedure that obtains every possible derivation of a given node in the parse graph

input string. The E-graph contains a set of starting nodes, each of which represents a parse tree root. Constraint enforcement is performed by converting each implicit node into every possible explicit node sequence that can be derived from the implicit node and satisfies the specified constraints; that is, by expanding the each implicit node.

Only the nodes that conform valid parse trees are needed in the parse graph. In order to generate only these nodes, each one of the implicit nodes in the starting node set of the I-graph is recursively expanded using memoization. Each possible resulting explicit node is the root of a parse tree in the E-graph.

Algorithm Description. The expansion of an implicit node is performed by finding every possible reduction of a sequence of explicit nodes that generates that node. Each one of these reductions produces an explicit node. Whenever an implicit node is found and needed in order to make the reductions progress, it is expanded recursively. It should be noted that this procedure is different from parsing itself in that the actual bounds of the reductions for every node are known.

The *expand* procedure in Figure 14 expands an implicit node by applying every possible production that could generate it and produces a set of explicit nodes. The use of the *history* set inhibits entering an infinite loop when processing infinitely recursive production sets, as it avoids the expansion of a node as an indirect requirement of expanding the same node.

The *apply* procedure in Figure 15 applies a production by matching the RHS symbol given by the $matched + 1$ index of it with the n node, expanding the nodes that follows it, and recursively applying the next RHS symbols of the production.

```
procedure apply(Production p, Node n, int matched, List<Node> content,
                Map<ImplicitNode,Set<Node>> alreadyExpanded,
                Set<ImplicitNode> history) returns Set<Node>:
  if matched == p.right.size:
    n = new Node(p.symbol,p,content)
    if checkConstraints(n):
      return {n}
  else:
    offset = 0
    next = matched+offset
    do:
      if p.right[next].symbol == n.symbol:
        for each ImplicitNode pn in n.followingNodes():
          if pn is the next symbol to match in the production:
            // keep applying production to each expanded symbol of pn
            expandeds = expand(pn,history,alreadyExpanded)
            for each Node nn in expandeds:
                out += apply(p,nn,next+1,content+n,alreadyExpanded,history)
      offset++
      next = matched+offset
    while epsilonSymbols.contains(nextSymbol) && next<r.right.size &&
          p.right[next].symbol == n.symbol
    return out
```

Fig. 15. Pseudocode of the ancillary *apply* procedure that applies a production

The *checkConstraints* procedure is the responsible for the enforcement of the constraints specified by the developer.

Supported Constraints. Fence supports associativity constraints, selection precedence constraints, composition precedence constraints, and custom-designed constraints.

The fact that the constraint check is performed during the graph expansion improves the parser performance, as the sooner constraints are applied, the more interpretations are discarded. For example, in the case of a binary expression with left-to-right associative operators, the string "2+5+3+5+6+2+1+5+6+3" can be expanded in 10! possible ways when not considering the associativity constraint, and in just 1 possible way when considering it.

- **Associativity constraints** allow the specification of the associative property for binary operators. The application of a production is inhibited when any of the nodes that matches its RHS symbols has an associativity constraint and is followed (for left-to-right associativity constraints), preceded (for right-to-left associativity constraints), or either followed or preceded (for non-associative associativity constraints) by a node that was derived using the same production.
- **Selection precedence constraints** allow the resolution of syntactic ambiguities caused by different explicit nodes (i.e. interpretations) resulting from a single implicit node. For example, a *Statement* can be either an *OutputStatement* or a *FunctionCall*. Both *OutputStatement* and *FunctionCall* can match the input string

"output(var);", therefore *OutputStatement* can be set to precede *FunctionCall*, which will inhibit that string from being considered a function call. The application of a production is inhibited when it is preceded by a different production and both of them match the same node sequence.

- **Composition precedence constraints** allow the resolution of syntactic ambiguities when a node derived using a production cannot be derived using another production. For example, one of the productions *ConditionalStatement ::= "if" Expression Sentence* and *ConditionalStatement ::= "if" Expression Sentence "else" Sentence* can be set to precede the other one in order to resolve the ambiguity in "if expr1 if expr2 sent1 else sent2", in which "else sent2" could be assigned to either the inside or outside conditional sentence. The application of a production is inhibited when it precedes any of the productions used to derive the nodes that matched its RHS symbols.

- **Custom-designed constraints** allow the specification of any other constraints (e.g. semantic constraints). In order to enforce custom-designed constraints, an evaluator can be assigned to any production. Whenever a node is generated, the evaluator of the production used to derive it gets executed and determines whether the node satisfies the constraint or not. In the later case, its generation is inhibited. Custom-designed constraints provide a very extensible framework which allows developers to design complex syntactic or semantic constraints (e.g. probabilistic constraints, corpus-based constraints) that effectively limit the possible interpretations of an input string and, as a side effect, improve the performance of the parser, as pruned partial interpretations are discarded as soon as they do not fulfill the constraints.

The result of the constraint enforcement step is an E-graph or parse graph, such as the one shown in Figure 10.

The Fence constraint enforcement phase improves the performance of traditional techniques phases in practice, as all constraints are applied at the earliest possible time, thus discarding possibilities that would otherwise be processed later.

4   Conclusions and Future Work

We have presented Fence, an efficient bottom-up chart parsing algorithm with lexical and syntactic ambiguity support. Its constraint-based ambiguity resolution mechanism enables the use of model-based language specification in practice. In fact, the ModelCC model-based language specification tool [24,25,21] generates Fence parsers.

Fence accepts a lexical analysis graph as input, performs syntactic analysis conforming to a formal context-free grammar specification and a set of constraints, and produces as output a compact representation of the set of parse trees accepted by the language.

Fence applies constraints while expanding the parse graph. Thus, it improves the performance of traditional techniques in practice, as the sooner constraints are applied, the less processing time and memory the parser will require.

In the future, we plan to apply ModelCC, Lamb, and Fence to natural language processing.

Acknowledgements. Work partially supported by research project TIN2012-36951, "NOESIS: Network-Oriented Exploration, Simulation, and Induction System", co-funded by the Spanish Ministry of Economy and the European Regional Development Fund (FEDER).

References

1. Aho, A.V., Lam, M.S., Sethi, R., Ullman, J.D.: Compilers: Principles, Techniques, and Tools, 2nd edn. Addison Wesley (2006)
2. Aho, A.V., Ullman, J.D.: The Theory of Parsing, Translation, and Compiling, Volume I: Parsing & Volume II: Compiling. Prentice Hall, Englewood Cliffs (1972)
3. Chomsky, N.: Three models for the description of language. IRE Transactions on Information Theory 2, 113–123 (1956)
4. Crescenzi, V., Mecca, G.: Automatic information extraction from large websites. Journal of the ACM 51, 731–779 (2004)
5. DeRemer, F.L.: Practical translators for LR(k) languages. Technical report, Cambridge, MA, USA (1969)
6. DeRemer, F.L.: Simple LR(k) grammars. Communications of the ACM 14(7), 453–460 (1971)
7. DeRemer, F.L., Pennello, T.: Efficient computation of LALR(1) look-ahead sets. ACM Transactions on Programming Languages and Systems 4(4), 615–649 (1982)
8. Earley, J.: An efficient context-free parsing algorithm. Communications of the ACM 26, 57–61 (1983)
9. Fowler, M.: Domain-Specific Languages. Addison-Wesley (2010)
10. Hudak, P.: Building domain-specific embedded languages. ACM Computing Surveys 28(4es), art. 196 (1996)
11. Jurafsky, D., Martin, J.H.: Speech and Language Processing: An Introduction to Natural Language Processing, Computational Linguistics and Speech Recognition, 2nd edn. Prentice Hall (2009)
12. Kasami, T., Torii, K.: A syntax-analysis procedure for unambiguous context-free grammars. Journal of the ACM 16, 423–431 (1969)
13. Kats, L.C.L., Visser, E., Wachsmuth, G.: Pure and declarative syntax definition: paradise lost and regained. In: Proceedings of the ACM International Conference on Object Oriented Programming Systems Languages and Applications (OOPSLA 2010), pp. 918–932 (2010)
14. Klein, D.: Christopher d. manning. In: Proceedings of the 42nd Annual Meeting on Association for Computational Linguistics (ACL 2004), pp. 478–485 (2004)
15. Kleppe, A.: Towards the generation of a text-based IDE from a language metamodel. In: Akehurst, D.H., Vogel, R., Paige, R.F. (eds.) ECMDA-FA. LNCS, vol. 4530, pp. 114–129. Springer, Heidelberg (2007)
16. Knuth, D.E.: On the translation of languages from left to right. Information and Control 8, 607–639 (1965)
17. Lang, B.: Deterministic techniques for efficient non-deterministic parsers. In: Loeckx, J. (ed.) ICALP 1974. LNCS, vol. 14, pp. 255–269. Springer, Heidelberg (1974)
18. Mernik, M., Heering, J., Sloane, A.M.: When and how to develop domain-specific languages. ACM Computing Surveys 37, 316–344 (2005)
19. Nawrocki, J.R.: Conflict detection and resolution in a lexical analyzer generator. Information Processing Letters 38, 323–328 (1991)
20. Oettinger, A.: Automatic syntactic analysis and the pushdown store. In: Proc. of the Symposia in Applied Math, vol. 12, pp. 104–129 (1961)

21. Quesada, L.: A model-driven parser generator with reference resolution support. In: Proceedings of the 27th IEEE/ACM International Conference on Automated Software Engineering, pp. 394–397 (2012)
22. Quesada, L., Berzal, F., Cortijo, F.J.: Lamb — a lexical analyzer with ambiguity support. In: Proceedings of the 6th International Conference on Software and Data Technologies, vol. 1, pp. 297–300 (2011)
23. Quesada, L., Berzal, F., Cortijo, F.J.: Fence — a context-free grammar parser with constraints for model-driven language specification. In: Proceedings of the 7th International Conference on Software Paradigm Trends, pp. 5–13 (2012)
24. Quesada, L., Berzal, F., Cubero, J.-C.: A language specification tool for model-based parsing. In: Yin, H., Wang, W., Rayward-Smith, V. (eds.) IDEAL 2011. LNCS, vol. 6936, pp. 50–57. Springer, Heidelberg (2011)
25. Quesada, L., Berzal, F., Cubero, J.-C.: A tool for model-based language specification. ArXiv e-prints (2011), http://arxiv.org/abs/1111.3970
26. Schmidt, D.C.: Model-driven engineering. IEEE Computer 39, 25–31 (2006)
27. Tan, P.-N., Steinbach, M., Kumar, V.: Introduction to Data Mining. Addison Wesley (2006)
28. Tomita, M., Carbonell, J.G.: The universal parser architecture for knowledge-based machine translation. In: Proceedings of the 10th International Joint Conference on Artificial Intelligence, vol. 2, pp. 718–721 (1987)
29. Turmo, J., Ageno, A., Cataà, N.: Adaptive information extraction. ACM Computing Surveys 38(2), art. 4 (2006)
30. Younger, D.H.: Recognition and parsing of context-free languages in time n^3. Information and Control 10, 189–208 (1967)

Cross-Platform Application Development
Using AXIOM as an Agile Model-Driven Approach

Xiaoping Jia and Chris Jones

School of Computing, DePaul University, 243 S. Wabash Ave., Chicago, IL, U.S.A.
{xjia,cjones}@cdm.depaul.edu

Abstract. The development and maintenance of cross-platform mobile applications is expensive. Two approaches for reducing this cost are model-driven engineering (MDE) and Agile development. In this paper, we present AXIOM, a model-driven approach for developing cross-platform mobile applications in ways that also support Agile principles. Our approach uses a domain specific language (DSL) for defining platform-independent models (PIM) of mobile applications. AXIOM defines a multi-phase, customizable transformation process to convert platform-independent models into native applications for target mobile platforms. Our approach could significantly reduce development time and cost while increasing the quality of mobile applications. A prototype tool has been developed to demonstrate the feasibility of the approach. The preliminary findings are promising and show significant gains in development productivity.

1 Introduction

In recent years, there has been tremendous growth in the popularity of mobile applications targeting smart phones and tablets. With the ever-improving capabilities of these devices, mobile applications are becoming increasingly sophisticated and complicated, while also having to address challenging constraints and requirements, such as responsiveness, limited memory and low energy consumption. Furthermore, there are currently several competing mobile platforms on the market, including Google's Android and Apple's iOS. For mobile application developers, it is highly desirable for their applications to run on all major mobile platforms. Although these competing platforms are similar in capability, they differ significantly in programming languages and APIs, making it expensive to port a mobile application to different platforms.

An appealing approach to cross-platform development is model-driven engineering (MDE). In MDE, software systems are built by first defining platform-independent models (PIMs), which capture the compositions and core functionalities of the system in a way that is independent of implementation concerns. The PIMs are then transformed into platform-specific models (PSMs), from which the native application code for each platform can be generated. MDE shifts the development focus away from writing code [1] and toward the development of models, such as those in UML and its profiles.

Despite its potential benefits and proven success in large-scale industrial applications [2], MDE faces significant challenges to its widespread adoption including: limitations of UML [3, 4]; inadequate tool support; model transformation complexity; and

J. Cordeiro, S. Hammoudi, and M. van Sinderen (Eds.): ICSOFT 2012, CCIS 411, pp. 36–51, 2013.

apparent incompatibility with popular Agile software development methodologies such as eXtreme Programming (XP) and Scrum.

The Agile and MDE approaches to software development are each oriented toward different kinds of software. For example, MDE often targets mature middleware platforms with widely adopted common standards such as JEE, .NET, and SOA. In contrast, applications developed using Agile techniques often fit certain well-understood patterns, such as being web-based and database-driven, and using an n-tier MVC architecture. It would be beneficial if the strengths of these two approaches could be combined and their shortcomings mitigated.

In this paper, we present a novel model-driven approach to cross-platform mobile application development using a domain specific language (DSL), called *AXIOM* (Agile eXecutable and Incremental Object-oriented Modeling). Our approach defines a framework for describing the PIMs, design decisions, and implementation details of applications. We also provide tools to carry out the transformation of PIMs into native implementations across multiple platforms. A prototype tool has been developed to demonstrate the feasibility of the approach. The prototype currently targets mobile applications in general with an emphasis on the Android and iOS platforms in particular.

2 Approaches to Platform-Independence

Platform-independence is not a new goal and the cost savings that can be realized through such independence have long been recognized. The advent of high-level languages signified an early means of providing such platform-independence through the use of greater abstractions. Languages such as C and C++ were only partially successful in achieving platform-independence because of the decision to leave some runtime aspects of the language, such as integral datatype sizing [5, 6], up to compiler providers. This allowed the same source code to be compiled for many different target platforms, but did not guarantee that all of the runtime semantics would be consistent across those platforms.

Languages based on virtual machines (VMs), like Java [7], provide true platform-independence by specifying a well defined, standardized runtime environment. Higher-level languages are converted into VM instructions, which are then executed on the target platform using the native instruction set. Because both the language and the VM are governed by specifications the behavior of the application across different platforms tends to be more consistent than when using languages without such comprehensive specifications.

The combination of high-level languages with a standardized runtime environment provides a powerful foundation on which platform-independent applications can be built. This approach can be further refined through the use of domain-specific languages (DSLs), which expose domain-specific concepts to developers, thus providing a high level of abstraction and expressiveness within that domain. DSLs are available for specific domains like mobile and web development.

DSLs can be external, meaning that their syntax is not the same as the host language, or internal, where they share the host language. This flexibility allows for DSLs that can be transformed into higher-level languages, directly into VM instructions, or even into native code for the target platform. DSLs based on languages like Ruby or Groovy are internal and ultimately generate high-level language code based on the host language. The benefit to this approach is that the DSL can take advantage of the power of its host language, including its compiler and associated optimizations.

A second approach is to provide a DSL that ultimately produces native VM instructions. This provides a mechanism that allows for the power of a DSL along with potential optimizations for a particular VM instruction set. However, the process of converting the DSL code into VM instructions involves the same effort as writing a compiler, potentially making it a more expensive approach than allowing the DSL to produce high-level language code for which a compiler already exists.

A third approach is to use a DSL that produces native code for the target platform. The same drawbacks exist for this approach that exist for the conversion to VM instructions. However, done well, the potential power and optimizations realized by converting directly to the native instruction set can prove valuable. This approach may also be used when few, if any, compilers exist for a target platform, such as might be the case with specialized hardware or chipsets.

3   UML as a Basis for MDE and Agile Approaches

DSLs have also been used in the form of modeling notations, the best-known of which is UML [8], which, along with OCL [9], seeks to provide a common language for describing software models. The Object Management Group's (OMG) approach to model-driven engineering, MDA [10], relies on UML models that are then consumed and transformed into executable code.

Unfortunately, MDE has not seen the same industry adoption rates as Agile [11] approaches like XP [12] and Scrum [13]. Some reasons for this may include:

- A lack of adequate tool support in creating, maintaining and understanding the complex models derived from UML and related OMG standards. Visual models make complex structures comprehensible, but are difficult and time consuming to create and maintain without strong tool support.
- The difficulty in the interchange of visual models across different tools using the XMI [14] standard for UML interchange. One study of some of the most commonly used UML tools showed that the success rate of attempted model interchanges amongst these tools was less than 5% [15].
- The lack of executability in UML models leads to long development cycles. UML models are thus ill-suited for Agile development processes and are generally used only for heavyweight processes.
- A lack of modeling resources comparable to the extensive frameworks and libraries available to Agile approaches. Most models must be developed from scratch rather than being built on known, proven, and previously adopted solutions.

There is evidence showing that Agile processes can deliver significantly improved productivity of software development efforts of small to medium sizes in companies with limited organizational complexity [16–18]. However, because MDE is often characterized as architecture-centric and design-first, it is perceived as antithetical to Agile approaches that are often code-centric with architecture as an emergent property resulting from iterative refactoring.

Despite these differences, there are also critical similarities between Agile and MDD practices. For instance, both practices focus on a single deliverable; code, in the case of Agile approaches, models, in the case of MDE. Hybrid approaches such as *Agile Model Driven Development (AMDD)* [19] and *Continuous Model Driven Engineering (CMDE)* [20] have been developed, but these approaches either de-emphasize the use of UML or abandon the idea of completely generative models altogether.

We propose an approach that emphasizes the similarities between MDE and Agile approaches while de-emphasizing their differences.

4   AXIOM: DSL-Based MDE

We propose to leverage the power of a DSL based on the dynamic language, Groovy, to provide a new approach to model-driven engineering called AXIOM [21, 22]. AXIOM retains the key elements of MDE such being model-centric and using using transformations to convert the models into executable code, but differs in the specifics. Whereas MDA relies on MOF [23] metamodels to facilitate the transformation of UML models into executable code, AXIOM instead provides a modeling DSL written in a dynamic language. AXIOM supports a limited subset of UML in the form of class diagrams and state charts as a means if visualizing the DSL models. This allows it to maintain some of the most powerful aspects of MDD such as model visualization, while also being easily accessible to existing designers and developers who are familiar with UML and its notation.

AXIOM defines a Groovy-based DSL specifically for modeling mobile applications. The DSL provides an abstraction of the features and capabilities supported by the Android and iOS platforms. The aim of the DSL is to provide an abstract way of accessing the complete native API of each platform, and not just a limited subset of the API (often known as the lowest common denominator). By using a DSL, AXIOM also allows platform-independent models to be executable. This shortens development time and allows for the early detection and remediation of errors and anomalies. Because AXIOM is Groovy-based, it has access to a rich set of modeling elements and frameworks that UML alone does not provide.

AXIOM supports customizable model transformations and code generation. It permits both kinds of MDE: *completely generative*, where all of the code comes from the model, and *partially generative*, where nearly complete code is generated with some parts to be completed manually. The model transformations can be customized through the use of annotations on the model as well as developer-customizable code templates for patterns and idioms. The aim is to allow the generated code to be optimized for performance and other quality requirements through techniques supported by native platforms including multi-threading, memory management, and application life-cycle management.

It should be noted that while we emphasize the development of mobile applications for our initial research and in this paper, AXIOM is by no means limited to such applications. As we will see, AXIOM's basic DSL-centric approach is suited to a variety of applications.

5   AXIOM Intent Models

Applications are first defined as platform-independent *intent models* using AXIOM's DSL. Intent models describe the core functions, user interfaces, and interactions of the application in a way that is completely devoid of references to implementation-specific aspects of any platform. The intent model is composed of two core perspectives: the *interaction perspective*, visualized using UML state diagrams, and the *domain perspective*, visualized using UML class diagrams.

Consider a simple application that associates users with roles, perhaps as part of a broader application security component. We want the ability to associate each user with multiple roles, from which they will ultimately derive their application privileges. To provide these capabilities we must be able to manage both user and role information as well as manage the associations of users to roles. In the next few sections we examine how AXIOM represents the key elements of this simple application.

5.1   Interaction Perspective

The interaction perspective describes the user interface and the application's behavior in response to user and system events. The basic state diagram representing the two screens is shown at the top of Fig. 1. This state diagram is realized into a graphical view of the interaction perspective represented by the associated wireframes shown in the middle of Fig. 1. A partial AXIOM DSL that encodes the state diagram and the associated graphical representation is shown at the bottom of Fig. 1.

The interaction perspective defines the composition of the two screens. The first screen is a list view with several sections. The names ListView, Section, and Item in the model (see A in Fig. 1) refer to the UI elements. The second screen is a view containing several types of *logical* UI controls including labels, buttons, a text field, and a selection. The logical UI controls in the intent model only define their intended functions and not the actual widgets that implement these functions. The names View, Panel, Label, Button, Text, and Selection in the model also refer to UI elements (see B). Each view in the UI corresponds to a state in the interaction model. Transitions are defined as the next attribute of the UI control that triggers the transition (see C, D, and E). Optional guard conditions and actions can also be defined on the transitions.

5.2   Domain Perspective

The domain perspective describes business entities. These are typically persistent and are transferred and referenced among different parts of the application. Figure 2 shows the domain perspective for our simple example including the class diagram and the corresponding AXIOM DSL.

AXIOM's domain perspective is defined using a notation based on the GORM [24] framework. GORM provides for persistence and relationship management between persistent objects. This makes it suitable for defining both standalone domain objects as well as for incorporating persistence when required.

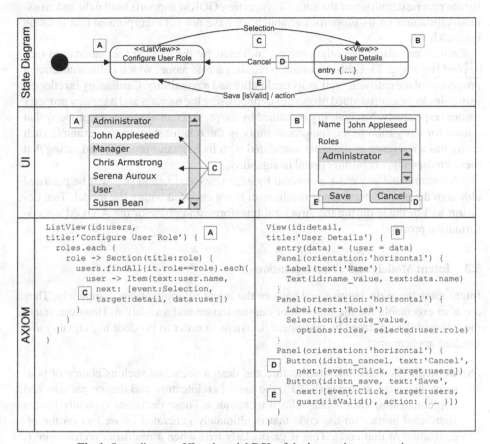

Fig. 1. State diagram, UI and partial DSL of the interaction perspective

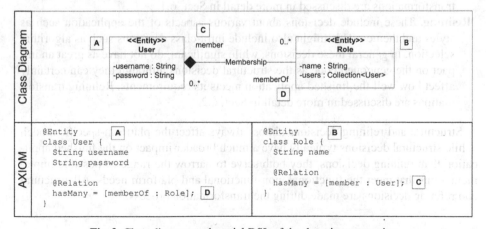

Fig. 2. Class diagram and partial DSL of the domain perspective

Each entity describes the properties and relationships of a domain object. This allows for the precise definition of the entity's properties. GORM supports both field and cross-field validations on its properties although we have not yet incorporated that notation into AXIOM.

Entities can also have relationships, indicated by the @Relation annotation (see [C] and [D] in Fig. 2). Each relationship requires a role name, which defines additional properties of the entity, as well as its cardinality and navigability. Cardinality is reflected using single- or multi-valued properties defined using the hasOne and hasMany property names respectively. Navigability is defined by the presence or absence of a property that allows for navigation to the reciprocal entity in the relationship. In this example each entity has a reference to the other associated with its hasMany property, indicating that these entities support bi-directional navigability.

We assume that any class annotated by @Entity (see [A] and [B]) will be persisted although the precise persistence mechanism is not encoded within the model. That decision will be made during the structural transformation phase of the AXIOM's transformation process.

5.3   Intent Models and Transformations

Intent models are declarative and capture the intent of applications completely. They are also executable for the purpose of demonstration and validation. However, intent models must be informed by additional decisions in order to produce high quality and finished applications:

Structural. These include architecture and design decisions such as choice of platform, language, framework, API; the use of architecture and design patterns and implementation idioms and related techniques. These decisions typically have a significant impact on the code that is ultimately generated as well as on the organization of that code. This is particularly true when a multi-tier architecture is desired or when specific non-functional requirements must be satisfied. Structural transformations are discussed in more detail in Sect. 6.1.

Refining. These include decisions about various aspects of the application such as styles and themes. This might also include intra-class decisions such as algorithm selection. In general these decisions, while significant, do not have as great an impact on the generated code as the structural decisions although they can certainly affect how well the finished application meets its requirements. Refining transformations are discussed in more detail in Sect. 6.2.

Structural and refining decisions almost always affect the platform-specific model. While structural decisions typically have a much broader impact on the finished application than refining decisions, they both serve to narrow the range of possible implementations that meet the functional, non-functional and platform needs. All structural and refining decisions are made during the transformation process.

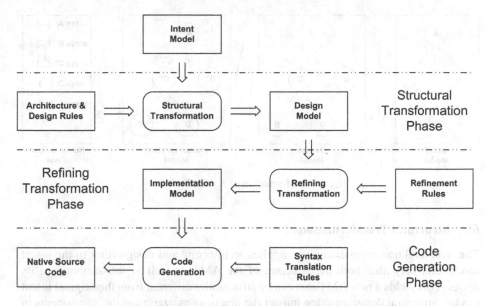

Fig. 3. AXIOM transformation process

6   AXIOM Transformation Process

A critical component of MDE is model transformation, which converts the abstract PIM of an application into executable code. The structural and refining decisions are introduced during AXIOM's three-phase transformation process that includes: *structural transformation*, *refining transformation*, and *code generation* as shown in Fig. 3.

All AXIOM models are represented as *abstract model trees* (AMTs) corresponding to the logical structure and elements of the models. For example, each UI view and logical UI control in the intent model is represented as a node in the AMT. The AMT is similar to an AST, but allows for cross-node relationships and references. Each node in the AMT supports attributes both in the form of simple name-value pairs as well as more complex types such as collections and closures.

Each node on an AMT has a set of attributes defined as name-value pairs, which makes it similar to an attribute grammar [25]. In addition to the simple types supported by traditional attribute grammars, AXIOM AMTs also support complex types such as collections and closures. This introduces the potential for AXIOM to perform model analysis based on both inherited and synthesized attributes thereby supporting the identification of mismatched requirements. These attributes can also be used by the model transformation process to further refine the generated code.

Each phase in an AXIOM model transformation reconfigures the AMT. Figure 4 illustrates the changes introduced by each phase of the transformation process.

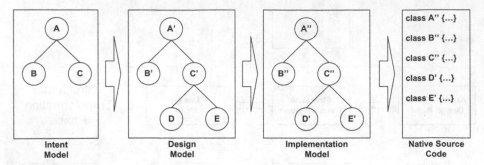

Fig. 4. Transformation of AXIOM AMTs

6.1   Structural Transformations

The structural transformation phase applies architecture and design rules to the intent model and may alter both the structure of the AMT as well as the attributes of its nodes. This yields a new AMT that can be structurally different from the original intent model. Structural decisions often impact the macro-organization of the components in the application and their interactions. The structural transformations are rule-based and generally reusable. The result of the structural transformation is a *design model* that is functionally isomorphic to the original intent model, but that also defines the macro-organization of the application driven by the platform-specific technology and API. The design model can be mapped to a design of the application with the modules, classes and their relations determined.

Common examples of structural decisions include target language and platform, framework selection, and code distribution. For instance, in the simple example of users and roles, we have seen that we can define simple entities. During the structural transformation phase, we might determine that these entities will be persisted to a remote database or conversely, we might decide that the data should be persisted to a local file store. These choices will yield very different designs when the intent model is transformed in support of an iOS-based mobile versus a JEE-based web application.

6.2   Refining Transformations

During the refining transformation phase, the structure of the design model AMT is preserved but the attributes of the nodes may be changed. This results in an output tree that is not only functionally isomorphic to the original intent model, but that is also structurally isomorphic to the design model. Refining transformations decorate the design model with additional platform-specific elements to address intra-class, micro-organizational decisions. The resulting *implementation model* maintains the macro-organization of the design model, but includes all the necessary details needed to generate high quality, efficient code. The decorations applied during the refining transformation phase are usually not application specific, and are highly reusable.

Examples of refining transformations include algorithm selection, visual layout and theme. In the case of our security example, these decisions might indicate whether or not we wish to use JPA, Hibernate or Spring JDBC for our persistence layer. Similarly, we might opt to generate DAOs as a means of enforcing a separation of concerns within the generated code.

By deferring these lower-level decisions until this phase of the transformation, we are able to make selections that are appropriate for the desired overall characteristics of the target runtime environment. For example, while it may be a functional requirement that a list of items be sortable within the UI, we can refine the approach to emphasize the characteristics of one sort algorithm over another depending on if we're running on a mobile platform or a JEE server. Such discrimination is critical given that we must make different time-space tradeoffs based on the target platform.

6.3 Code Generation

During the code generation phase, the implementation model is converted into native source code for the target platform. In our security example, this means that we will generate the appropriate annotations and code for each persistable entity based on the structural and refining decisions made earlier.

Code generation is based on a set of platform-specific templates that are application-independent and reusable. The code generation is completely automated and highly customizable.

7 Benefits

AXIOM has several notable benefits for software development. First, the DSL provides higher levels of abstraction that enable the construction of the platform-independent intent models while also permitting a high degree of expressiveness. Because the DSL is written in Groovy, modelers gain instant access to existing Java-based frameworks and libraries, which saves the effort that would otherwise be required to model them. The DSL also grants the AXIOM intent models a degree of executability that facilitates rapid development and verification, an approach that aligns perfectly with the principles of modern Agile approaches, which emphasize a rapid turnaround from concept to completion.

Second, the fact that AXIOM is encoded in a textual model rather than a graphical one ensures a degree of tool independence; all that is required is a text editor. Related problems such as concurrent model development, model versioning, and model merging can be addressed through existing source code control systems.

Third, even though the models look more like a programming language, AXIOM supports a limited subset of UML models, thus retaining some of the visual expressiveness of UML.

Finally, the AXIOM transformation rules and templates can be used across entire families of applications and technologies rather than being specific to a particular application domain as is often the case with many model compilers. In addition, while many model compilers are "black box" in the sense that a change to the generated code often requires a change to the compiler's code, AXIOM attempts to take a "white box" approach by externalizing the various transformation rules and templates. This approach allows for the reuse of the templates and transformation rules across different applications rather than binding them to only a single application.

AXIOM also has some limitations. First, AXIOM only honors a subset of the available UML diagrams, specifically class diagrams and state charts. Other UML diagrams may provide additional benefits, but are currently unrecognized. Second, AXIOM cannot easily make up for the limitations of a given platform, a challenge for any MDE approach. Finally, AXIOM deviates from the standard OMG definition of MDA by using a DSL for its representation rather than a MOF-based metamodel.

8   The Prototype and Preliminary Results

A proof-of-concept prototype tool has been developed to demonstrate the feasibility of AXIOM. The prototype targets two popular mobile platforms: Android and iOS. AXIOM models can be transformed into native implementations in Java for Android and Objective-C for iOS. The generated application source code is then compiled using the native SDKs on the target platform to produce executable applications. The design of the generated code follows the common MVC architecture.

Table 1. LOC of intent model vs. generated code

$(n = 29)$	AXIOM	iOS	Android	AXIOM as % of iOS	Android	ρ_L compared to iOS	Android
Median	19.5	168.0	279.0	10.3	7.0	8.6	14.3
Average	27.2	222.1	328.5	11.5	7.7	8.2	12.1
Minimum	8.0	126.0	77.0	5.8	3.2	15.8	9.6
Maximum	98.0	539.0	646.0	31.9	15.2	5.5	6.6

Using the prototype tool, we conducted preliminary analyses to assess the effectiveness of AXIOM. Using a small set of working examples ($n = 29$), we compared the sizes of the AXIOM intent models and the generated source code on both iOS and Android platforms. Our assumptions are that: a) developer productivity measured in *lines-of-code per person-hour* (LOC/PH) is roughly constant regardless of languages used; and b) the native applications produced by the prototype tool are comparable in size and complexity to the same applications developed manually. An admittedly subjective review of the code generated by AXIOM is that it is consistent with industry best-practices such as separation of concerns and the corresponding creation of appropriate abstraction layers.

Under these assumptions the reduction in the size of the AXIOM intent models compared to the size of the generated applications would translate into a significant reduction in development time, hence an increase in development productivity. Based on our preliminary studies, shown in Table 1, the median size (in LOC) of the AXIOM intent models is 7% of the size of the generated applications for Android and about 10% of the size of the generated applications for iOS.

Similarly, Kennedy's relative power metric [26], ρ_L, also based on LOC, measures the impact of AXIOM on developer productivity. Kennedy's relative power metric is given by:

$$\rho_L = \frac{I_N(P)}{I_A(P)} \tag{1}$$

where I_N and I_A are the lines of native and AXIOM code respectively that are required to implement application P.

These early results suggest a potentially significant increase in productivity when compared with manually developed applications using standard development tools on native mobile platforms.

9 Related Work

9.1 Model-Driven Engineering

There are different approaches to MDE. Some of these closely follow the MDA standard while others amend either the MDA process or its deliverables.

AndroMDA [27] is an open-source, UML-based, template-driven MDA framework. It accepts UML models in an XMI format and uses them for code generation. AndroMDA is not a modeling environment and is thus limited by the quality of the XMI output produced by other tools.

The Eclipse Foundation provides UML-based technologies that support MDD in terms of both model construction and model transformation. These projects include Generative Modeling Technologies (GMT) [28] and the ATL Transformation Language (ATL) [29].

Executable UML (xUML) is an approach to software development that uses UML models as the primary mechanism by which applications are built [30]. Like AXIOM, xUML advocates the benefits of UML executability. One significant challenge of xUML is that the process of writing a model compiler may require as much effort as producing the original models. There are examples of publicly available xUML compilers such as xUmlCompiler [31], but each compiler targets a specific set of technologies for its code generation processes.

There have also been attempts to introduce more formalism into MDE. Examples include Alloy [32], UML Specification Environment (USE) [33, 34], Z [35, 36] and its object-oriented extensions like MooZ [37], Object-Z [38], OOZE [39], Z++ [40], and ZEST [41].

The overall process of MDE has also been examined for ways to improve on its ability to deliver applications. Continuous Model Driven Engineering (CMDE) as defined by eXtreme model-driven design (XMDD) [20] uses process modeling as its means of eliciting the necessary requirements and behavior. Agile Model Driven Development (AMDD) [19] shares the notations and tools commonly used in MDD but retains code as the central focus of the development effort. AMDD has been executed in combination with the MIDAS framework [42, 43] as a means of implementing web-based applications.

Each of these approaches takes a slightly different approach to MDE and thus has its own challenges. Many of the approaches are deeply rooted in UML and thus suffer from

UML's shortcomings including the lack of first-class support for UI design. Approaches that rely on the creation of custom model compilers or transformations simply shift the development burden from the application and its models to the transformation framework. Most formal approaches were never designed for MDE and thus do not provide true model executability. Approaches that change the overall MDD process either lose model-centricity or are rooted in notations that deviate from mainstream UML.

AXIOM encourages the development of executable models using a DSL that supports interaction, UI and domain design while also retaining the widely adopted graphical notation associated with UML class and state diagrams.

9.2 DSL-Based Development

One approach for cross-platform mobile application development is to use languages and virtual machines that are common across different platforms, such as HTML and JavaScript [44, 45]. While this approach is adequate for certain types of applications, it has known shortcomings and limitations. Canappi [46] uses a DSL to define and generate cross-platform mobile applications as front-ends to web services. Unlike AXIOM, it allows neither access to native APIs nor customizable code generation.

WebDSL and Mobl [47, 48] are two DSLs that target web and mobile applications specifically. WebDSL is similar to Ruby's Rails and Groovy's Grails in that it allows for the rapid development of applications using a custom DSL. However, neither Mobl nor WebDSL addresses the model-driven aspect of the development process. Thus while the DSL code may indeed be ultimately transformed into executable code, the models themselves are not executable and are not considered major artifacts of the software development process.

AXIOM is partly based on the ZOOM [49–51] project as well as on OMG's MDA. AXIOM retains some key parts of UML, such as state and class diagrams, but unlike MDA, AXIOM defines a domain-specific modeling notation and a transformation framework that is not based on MOF.

10   Future Work

Our research into the AXIOM approach is in its early stages yet, but the preliminary results are promising. We intend to continue refining the approach so that it can work with even more complex models. One key area of work that remains is the further development of the rule-based transformations and the associated templates. In particular these transformations must be able to handle cases where given functionality is supported to different extents on different platforms. Some of those challenges have already been encountered and addressed in the user interface, but other such challenges remain such as the implementation of persistence.

Another area that remains to be addressed is the introduction of non-functional requirements into the models and the various decisions that advise the structural and refining transformations. Such architectural concerns are central to the ability to model and transform an application for a particular platform. For example, it would be desirable for the model transformations to choose algorithms that are appropriate for each target platform's memory and persistent storage characteristics.

These enhanced models will be used to drive comparative experiments to determine if the early benefits seen in the preliminary results continue to manifest as the scale and complexity of the applications increases, particularly in the areas of developer productivity, generated source code quality, and the runtime performance, efficiency and defect densities of the executable application.

11 Conclusions

AXIOM is a model-driven approach for developing high quality, cross-platform applications. We have successfully demonstrated its feasibility in developing cross-platform mobile applications for Android and iOS platforms. AXIOM uses a DSL to provide a high level abstraction of mobile platforms. Applications are represented as intent models using the DSL and are then augmented with structural decisions and refined with other platform-specific elements during a multi-phase transformation process to produce source code for native applications.

The potential benefits of AXIOM include significant cost savings in software development owing to dramatic increases in productivity. AXIOM supports executable models, which enable iterative and incremental development and allow early validation of the applications. Product quality can be significantly improved due to the reduced amount of hand-written code. The transformation process offers a high degree of control over code generation and enables transformation logic to be re-used across applications rather than building a single, monolithic model compiler for each individual application. This improves developer productivity and overall application quality.

AXIOM's approach to software development seeks to combine the best aspects of the Agile and MDE development. By defining a dynamic modeling language based on an existing dynamic language, AXIOM is immediately accessible to a large population of the Agile development community. By continuing to emphasize the use of completely generative models, AXIOM remains true to the intent of MDA, even though it differs in the underlying approach.

Our preliminary findings in terms of the potential gains in productivity are promising. We intend to further enhance the prototype tool to provide more comprehensive support of mobile platforms. This will enable us to conduct more extensive comparative studies and experiments using AXIOM. We plan to collect and analyze data in a number of different aspects, including developer productivity, the source code quality of generated applications, and the performance, efficiency and defect density of generated applications.

References

1. Selic, B.: The pragmatics of model-driven development. IEEE Software 20, 19–25 (2003)
2. Object Management Group: Success stories (2011),
   http://www.omg.org/mda/product_success.htm/
3. France, R.B., Ghosh, S., Dinh-Trong, T., Solberg, A.: Model-driven development using UML 2.0: Promises and pitfalls. Computer 39, 59–66 (2006)
4. Henderson-Sellers, B.: UML - the good, the bad or the ugly? perspectives from a panel of experts. Software and System Modeling 4, 4–13 (2005)

5. Kernighan, B., Ritchie, D.: The C Programming Language, 2nd edn. Prentice Hall (1988)
6. Ellis, M.A., Stroustrup, B.: The Annotated C++ Reference Manual. Addison Wesley (1990)
7. Gosling, J., Joy, B., et al.: The Java Language Specification, 2nd edn. Addison Wesley (2000)
8. Object Management Group: Unified Modeling Language (2010),
   http://www.omg.org/spec/UML/2.3/
9. Object Management Group: UML 2.0 OCL (2003),
   http://www.omg.org/docs/ad/linebreak03-01-07.pdf
10. Object Management Group: MDA guide (2003), http://www.omg.org/mda
11. Cockburn, A.: Agile software development. Addison-Wesley Longman Publishing Co., Inc.,
    Boston (2002)
12. Beck, K.: Extreme Programming Explained. Addison-Wesley, New York (2000)
13. Schwaber, K., Beedle, M.: Agile Software Development with SCRUM. Pearson Technology
    Group (2002)
14. Object Management Group: XML model interchange (XMI), version 2.11 (2007),
    http://www.omg.org/spec/XMI/2.1.1/
15. Lundell, B., Lings, B., Persson, A., Mattsson, A.: UML model interchange in heterogeneous
    tool environments: An analysis of adoptions of XMI 2. In: Wang, J., Whittle, J., Harel,
    D., Reggio, G. (eds.) MoDELS 2006. LNCS, vol. 4199, pp. 619–630. Springer, Heidelberg
    (2006)
16. Dyba, T., Dingsayr, T.: What do we know about agile software development? IEEE Software,
    6–9 (September/October 2009)
17. Layman, L., Williams, L., Cunningham, L.: Exploring extreme programming in context: An
    industrial case study. In: Agile Development Conference, pp. 32–41 (2004)
18. Lindvall, M., Basili, V., Boehm, B., Costa, P., Dangle, K., Shull, F., Tesoriero, R., Williams,
    L., Zelkowitz, M.: Empirical findings in agile methods. In: XP/Agile Universe 2002,
    Chicago, IL (2002)
19. Ambler, S.: Agile model driven development (AMDD): The key to scaling agile software
    development (2009), http://www.agilemodeling.com/essays/amdd.htm/
20. Margaria, T., Steffen, B.: Agile it: Thinking in user-centric models. In: Margaria, T., Steffen,
    B. (eds.) ISoLA. CCIS, vol. 17, pp. 490–502. Springer, Heidelberg (2008)
21. Jia, X., Jones, C.: Dynamic languages as modeling notations in model driven engineering.
    In: ICSOFT 2011, Seville, Spain, pp. 220–225 (2011)
22. Jia, X., Jones, C.: Axiom: A model-driven approach to cross-platform application develop-
    ment. In: ICSOFT 2012, Rome, Italy, pp. 24–33 (2012)
23. Object Management Group: OMG's MetaObject Facility (2006),
    http://www.omg.org/spec/MOF/2.0/PDF/
24. Rocher, G., Ledbrook, P., et al.: GORM - standalone GORM (2009),
    http://www.grails.org/GORM+-+StandAlone+Gorm
25. Knuth, D.E.: Semantics of context-free languages. Mathematical Systems Theory 2, 127–
    145 (1968)
26. Kennedy, K., Koelbel, C., et al.: Defining and measuring the productivity of programming
    languages. The International Journal of High Performance Computing Applications 18(4),
    441–448 (2004)
27. Bohlen, M., Brandon, C., et al.: AndroMDA (2003),
    http://www.andromda.org/docs/index.html
28. The GMT Team: GMT Project (2005), http://www.eclipse.org/gmt/
29. The ATL Team: ATL Transformation Language (2005), http://eclipse.org/atl/
30. Mellor, S.J., Balcer, M.J.: Executable UML: A Foundation for Model-Driven Architectures.
    Addison-Wesley Longman Publishing Co., Inc., Boston (2002); Foreword By-Ivar Jacoboson
31. xUML Compiler: xUML Compiler- Java Model compiler Based on "Executable UML" pro-
    file (2009), http://code.google.com/p/xuml-compiler/

32. Jackson, D.: Alloy: a lightweight object modelling notation. ACM Trans. Softw. Eng. Methodol. 11, 256–290 (2002)
33. Gogolla, M., Büttner, F., et al.: USE: A UML-Based Specification Environment for Validating UML and OCL. Science of Computer Programming 69, 27–34 (2007)
34. Kuhlmann, M., Gogolla, M.: Modeling and Validating Mondex Scenarios Described in UML and OCL with USE. Formal Aspects of Computing 20, 79–100 (2008)
35. Clarke, E.M., Wing, J.M., et al.: Formal methods: state of the art and future directions. ACM Computing Surveys 28, 626–643 (1996)
36. Hamilton, D., Covington, R., et al.: Experiences in applying formal methods to the analysis of software and system requirements. Workshop on Industrial-Strength Formal Specification Techniques, p. 30 (1995)
37. Meira, S.R.L., Cavalcanti, A.L.C.: Modular Object-Oriented Z Specifications. In: Nicholls, J. (ed.) Z User Workshop. Workshops in Computing, pp. 173–192. Springer, Oxford (1990)
38. Smith, G.: (Object-Z), http://itee.uq.edu.au/~smith/objectz.html
39. Alencar, A.J., Goguen, J.A.: OOZE: An object oriented Z environment. In: America, P. (ed.) ECOOP 1991. LNCS, vol. 512, pp. 180–199. Springer, Heidelberg (1991)
40. Lano, K.: Z++, an object-orientated extension to z. In: Proceedings of the Fifth Annual Z User Meeting on Z User Workshop, pp. 151–172. Springer, London (1991)
41. Cusack, E., Rafsanjani, G.H.B.: Zest. In: Object Orientation in Z. Workshops in Computing, pp. 113–126. Springer (1992)
42. Cáceres, P., Daz, F., et al.: Integrating an Agile Process in a Model Driven Architecture (2004)
43. Cáceres, P., Marcos, E., et al.: A mda-based approach for web information system development. In: Proceedings of Workshop in Software Model Engineering (2003)
44. Appcelerator, Inc.: Appcelerator (2011), http://www.appcelerator.com/
45. The JQuery Project: JQuery Mobile Framework (2011), http://www.jquerymobile.com/
46. Convergence Modelling LLC.: Canappi (2011), http://www.canappi.com/
47. Visser, E., et al.: WebDSL (2010), http://webdsl.org/home
48. Hammel, Z., Visser, E., et al.: mobl: the new language of the mobile web (2010), http://www.mobl-lang.org/
49. Liu, H., Jia, X.: Model transformation using a simplified metamodel. Journal of Software Engineering and Applications 3, 653–660 (2010)
50. Jia, X., et al.: Executable visual software modeling:the ZOOM approach. Software Quality Journal 15 (2007)
51. Jia, X., Liu, H., et al.: A model transformation framework for model driven engineering. In: MSVVEIS-2008, Barcelona, Spain (2008)

Rapidly Implementing EMF Applications
with EMF Components

Lorenzo Bettini*

Dipartimento di Informatica, Università di Torino, Italy
bettini@di.unito.it

Abstract. Most Eclipse projects which deal with modeling data are based on the Eclipse Modeling Framework (EMF) which provides code generation facilities for building tools and applications based on structured data models. However, from the user interface point of view, the development of applications based on EMF could be made simpler with more code reuse. For this reason, we propose EMF Components, a lightweight framework that allows easy and quick development of applications based on EMF. Besides providing a set of reusable components like trees, tables and detail forms that manage the model with the introspective EMF capabilities, EMF Components also comes with a DSL to make the configuration and customization of all the components much faster.

1 Introduction

The *Eclipse Modeling Framework* (EMF) [1] simplifies the development of complex software applications based on structured data models. Starting from the metamodel specification (which can be described in XMI, UML or annotated Java) EMF produces a set of Java classes for the model, along with a set of adapter classes for editing facilities. However, we think that from the user interface point of view, the development of applications based on EMF could be made simpler, with more code reuse, and without having to deal with too many internal details. For this reason, we propose the EMF Components framework.

EMF Components is a lightweight framework for easily and quickly developing applications based on EMF. It can be configured to use all kinds of EMF persistence implementations (e.g., XMI, Teneo, CDO). Our framework provides a set of reusable components like trees, tables and detail forms that manage the model with the introspective EMF capabilities. Using these components one can easily build more complex widgets, editors and applications. All the components are customizable with injection mechanisms (based on *Google Guice* [2], a *Dependency Injection* framework [3]). The EMF Components framework is available as an open source project at http://code.google.com/ a/eclipselabs.org/p/emf-components. The first version of EMF Components was presented in [4]; this paper describes the new version, in particular, it introduces the new DSL that has been recently implemented to make the configuration and customization of all the components much faster.

---

* The paper was partly supported by RCP Vision, www.rcp-vision.com

J. Cordeiro, S. Hammoudi, and M. van Sinderen (Eds.): ICSOFT 2012, CCIS 411, pp. 52–65, 2013.
© Springer-Verlag Berlin Heidelberg 2013

```
1  adapterFactory = new ComposedAdapterFactory(ComposedAdapterFactory.Descriptor.
       Registry.INSTANCE);
   adapterFactory.addAdapterFactory(new ResourceItemProviderAdapterFactory());
3  adapterFactory.addAdapterFactory(new MyModelItemProviderAdapterFactory());
   adapterFactory.addAdapterFactory(new ReflectiveItemProviderAdapterFactory());
5  BasicCommandStack commandStack = new BasicCommandStack();
   commandStack.addCommandStackListener(new CommandStackListener() {...});
7  editingDomain = new AdapterFactoryEditingDomain(adapterFactory, commandStack, ...);
   Tree tree = new Tree(composite, SWT.MULTI);
9  TreeViewer viewer = new TreeViewer(tree);
   viewer.setContentProvider(new AdapterFactoryContentProvider(adapterFactory));
11 viewer.setLabelProvider(new AdapterFactoryLabelProvider(adapterFactory));
   viewer.setInput(editingDomain.getResourceSet());
13 new AdapterFactoryTreeEditor(viewer.getTree(), adapterFactory);
```

Listing 1.1. An example of typical recurrent use of EMF functionalities to setup a tree viewer

1.1 Motivations

EMF provides some mechanisms for generating user interface code, in particular, it can also generate an editor (based on a tree viewer) for an EMF metamodel. Indeed, besides the classes for the model, EMF can generate an additional plugin (called *edit* plugin) with an editing framework, i.e., classes not directly dealing with UI functionalities, but that can be used for generic editing features (based on EMF.Edit [5,1]); then, it generates a plugin which directly deals with the UI part, in the shape of an editor and some wizards, which rely on the generated editing framework for the metamodel.

The main problem for the programmer is that all these mechanisms have to be setup and initialized correctly in order to achieve the desired functionalities; this initialization requires many lines of code, which are recurrent, require some deeper knowledge, and tend to fill the code with too many distracting details. For instance, in Listing 1.1 we show the typical Java code which is very recurrent in applications that use EMF models and UI functionalities to setup a tree viewer. Note that such code is full of many internal details. As we will show in the next sections, our goal is to factor out this recurrent code in such a way that UI components can be setup with only a few lines of code (Listing 1.4, Section 2.1).

EMF standard generation mechanisms are based on specific Javadoc comments, i.e., @generated, for fields, methods and classes: future generations will overwrite all the previously generated Java code elements unless the user removes that @generated from specific declarations (or replaces it with @generated NOT). An example of customization of labeling in a class generated by EMF into the edit plugin (related to the classic EMF Library example) is shown in Listing 1.2. We observe that even for specifying the image for instances of Book we need to go into the generated Item-Provider class, and specify the path of the image (note also other distracting details like overlayImage, ResourceLocator, etc.). If we need to customize the images for all the EClasses of our model, we need to modify every generated Item-Provider class. Instead, we would like to specify these customizations more directly,

```
public class BookItemProvider extends ... {
  /** @generated NOT */
  @Override public Object getImage(Object object) {
    return overlayImage(object, getResourceLocator().getImage("mypath/
        custom_book.png"));
  }

  /** @generated NOT */
  @Override public String getText(Object object) {
    return "Book: " + " " + ((Book)object).getTitle();
  }
```

Listing 1.2. An example of typical customization of EMF labeling

and possibly grouped in one place, which is easier to maintain. We will show our customization strategies in Section 3. Another problem with this @generated and @generated NOT mechanism is that it might easily get difficult to keep track of custom modifications to the generated code.

Moreover, the editor generated by EMF is not effectively designed to promote code reuse: the generated editor is a monolithic class consisting of more than two thousand lines of code, with many inner classes. Indeed, if one compares the editors generated for two different metamodels, the differences are really minimal, thus the classes generated by EMF for the UI components lead to a huge amount of duplicated code.

The paper is structured as follows: in Section 2 we describe some components of our framework, with some examples. Section 3 describes how the components of our framework can be customized. Section 4 introduces our new DSL for easily specifying customizations in a compact form (the DSL will then generate automatically the corresponding Java classes). Section 5 concludes the paper with related work and hints for future directions.

2 EMF Components

Our main design choice in developing EMF Components was to split responsibilities into small classes (following the *Single Responsibility Principle* [6]), so that customizing a single aspect of UI components does not require to subclass the components themselves, but only to specialize the class that deals with that specific aspect. Custom implementations of specific aspects will be injected using dependency injection; this way, all components relying on that aspect will be assured to use the custom version. The *Dependency Injection* pattern [3] is used to "inject" actual implementation classes into a class hierarchy in a consistent way. This is useful when classes delegate specific functionalities to other classes: messages are simply forwarded to the objects referenced in fields (which abstract the actual behavior). These fields will then be instantiated through injection mechanisms so that we do not have the implementation classes' names hardcoded in the code of the classes that will use them, and we are sure that, if we switch the implementation classes, we will do that consistently throughout the code. Typically the same goal can be achieved manually by implementing *factory*

```
public class MyEmfComponentsModule extends EmfComponentsGenericModule {
    public Class<? extends ResourceLoader> bindResourceLoader() {
        return MyResourceLoader.class;
    }
    public Class<? extends ViewerMouseAdapter> bindViewerMouseAdapter() {
        return ViewerMouseAdapter.class;
    }
    public Class<? extends PropertyDescriptionProvider>
            bindPropertyDescriptionProvider() {
        return PropertyDescriptionProvider.class;
    }
}
```

Listing 1.3. A module with bindings

method and *abstract factory* patterns [7], but with dependency injection frameworks it is easier to keep the desired consistency, and the programmer needs to write less code.

To this aim, we use Google Guice [2] which provides a framework for dependency injection that makes all the injection mechanisms really easy to use, and relieves the programmer from the most internal details of dependency injection. Guice relies on Java annotations [8], in particular, @Inject, for specifying the fields that will be injected, and on a *module* which configures the bindings for the actual implementation classes; from the module we can build an *injector* which will be used to create the actual instances of classes, where the fields will be actually injected according to the bindings.

The user of EMF Components has to declare a subclass of EmfComponents-GenericModule with custom bindings. Indeed, the programmer does not have to perform all the initial setup operations: we provide a wizard that creates a new plugin project with all these classes, and the programmer will only have to provide the custom injection bindings. Furthermore, EMF Components relies on the enhancements that Xtext [9,10][1] added to Guice's Module API: Xtext provides an abstract base class, which reflectively looks for certain methods in order to find declared bindings. The most common kind of method that we rely on is of the shape bindXXX where XXX is the name of the class for which we need to specify a binding. An example of custom bindings relying on this reflective mechanisms is shown in Listing 1.3.

In the following we present the most important UI components provided by the EMF Components framework; more components will be provided in the future.

2.1 Viewers

Eclipse JFace UI components often rely on viewers (e.g., tree viewers, table viewers, etc.) which are not intended to be subclassed: indeed, they are parametrized over the content provider, which takes care of providing the contents based on the input, and other providers for the layout, for instance the label provider, which provides a textual representation and an image for the elements to be shown by the viewer.

---

[1] An Eclipse framework for the development of programming languages.

```
1  public class MyView extends ViewPart {
       @Inject ViewerInitializer initializer;
3
       @Override public void createPartControl(Composite parent) {
5          ...
           viewer = new TreeViewer(parent, ...);
7          // initialize with an EMF Resource
           initializer.initialize(viewer, resource);
9          // or alternatively, if you have an EObject
           initializer.initialize(viewer, eObject);
11     }
```

Listing 1.4. Initialization of a viewer with EMF Components

We provide a `ViewerInitializer`, with many overloaded methods, which can be used to initialize the viewer with all the EMF mechanisms, but hiding the details from the programmer. In Listing 1.4 we show an example of a view with a viewer. It uses the injected `ViewerInitializer` to initialize the tree viewer (it can initialize it based on an EMF Resource, or an EObject).

We invite the reader to compare the initialization code in Listing 1.4 with the one which is typically used without using EMF Components, in Listing 1.1. All the initialization details are carried on transparently by EMF Components classes. As we said, there are several initialization methods available, and if the programmer needs it, he can also specify all the providers for the viewers. In particular, if the programmer needs access to the EMF `EditingDomain`, he can create it and pass it to the initialization; but also in this case, we provide utility mechanisms for creating (and initializing) an `EditingDomain` without having to worry about initializing the adapter factories for the editing domain itself (see the manual initialization in Listing 1.1).

2.2 Composites

The smallest components that EMF Components provides as reusable units are Eclipse `Composites`. We provide composites to be reused in views and editors based on several viewers. Also in this case, the setup instructions for these components is minimal.

The problem with SWT Composites is that they do not expose a default constructor; this is crucial for dependency injection to work. Thus, we provide factories to be used to actually create these composites; the idea is that one passes to the factory the arguments for the constructor, and, internally, the factory will also setup all the injection mechanisms.

We will not describe here all the composites provided by the EMF Components framework; we concentrate on the *form* composite `FormDetailComposite` which shows the details of an EObject in a SWT form, and allows to edit such details. This is something that was currently missing in the EMF framework itself: the EMF framework only provides mechanisms to edit details of an EObject in the Eclipse standard *Properties* view, which might be limited in its functionalities. The SWT form toolkit instead provides richer UI features.

```
 1  public class MyView extends ViewPart implements ISelectionChangedListener {
        @Inject FormFactory factory;
 3      Composite detail;
        FormDetailComposite detailForm;
 5
        @Override
 7      public void createPartControl(Composite parent) {
            detail = new Composite(this, SWT.BORDER);
 9      }
 
11      @Override
        public void selectionChanged(SelectionChangedEvent event) {
13          EObject selectedObject = getFirstSelectedEObject(event.getSelection());
            if (selectedObject != null) {
15              // relevant lines
                detailForm = factory.createFormDetailComposite(detail, SWT.BORDER);
17              detailForm.init(selectedObject);
            }
19      }
        ...
21  }
```

Listing 1.5. Using the `FormDetailComposite`

In Listing 1.5 we show a possible use of `FormDetailComposite`: we create a view which reacts on selections from other elements of the workbench, and if the selected element is an EObject it shows its details in the form. We highlighted the two relevant lines in the Listing which show how easy is to create this composite and set it up: we create an instance of the form using the injected factory and we initialize it with selected object. All the other code in Listing 1.5 has to do with Eclipse and SWT, not with EMF Components itself. Indeed, we showed the code in Listing 1.5 as an example of use of EMF Components; however, this view class is already part of EMF Components framework, and it can already be reused in applications (as in the Mail example in Section 4).

In Figure 1 we show a reusable editor provided by EMF Components and the form view implemented in Listing 1.5 (which shows the currently selected object fields for editing). Note that the "dirty" state (the * in the tab) is handled by the EMF Components framework automatically. Moreover, any change to the model in any view or editor which is connected to the same resource will soon be reflected in all the components using that resource: this takes place transparently, since the EMF Components widgets rely on EMF Databinding [11], which connects the model and the user interface.

3 Customizations

If one has used the EMF standard generation mechanisms to generate the edit plugin, and possibly customized some behavior in the edit plugin, all these customizations will be honored by EMF Components UI widgets.

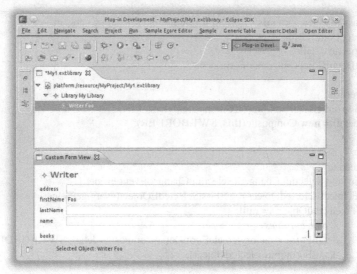

Fig. 1. A tree editor and a form view

However, in EMF Components, we provide the customization mechanisms (based on injection) which aim at making the customization of editing functionalities easier than the standard EMF.Edit framework.

The Xtext framework (on which we rely to implement some internal mechanisms of EMF Components) provides a mechanism, through the class `PolymorphicDispatcher`, for performing (overloaded) method dispatching according to the runtime type of arguments, a mechanism known as *dynamic overloading* [12,13][2]. This dispatching mechanism does not require a visitor structure [7] since it inspects the available methods in a class and selects the method using reflection. By relying on this, we can provide a declarative way of specifying custom behaviors according to the class of objects of an EMF model (though the internal details about the use of `PolymorphicDispatcher` are hidden to the programmer).

For instance, by implementing a derived `ViewerLabelProvider` (the label provider of our framework), the programmer can specify the text and image for labels of the objects of the model by simply defining several methods `text` and `image`, respectively, using the classes of the model to be customized as parameters. An example is shown in Listing 1.6 (applied to the classic EMF Library example). These methods will be used internally by our label provider to implement the `LabelProvider`'s methods `getText` and `getImage`. Compare this code, which allows to customize in only one place the representation of the elements of a model, with the code in Listing 1.2, which refers to one single customization. With respect to Listing 1.2 we would also like to observe the absence of inner details (especially for the images). Injecting this customization in the framework is just a matter of defining the binding in the Guice module, as shown in Listing 1.7.

---

[2] While most compiled or statically-typed languages (such as Java) determine which implementation to call at compile-time.

```
public class CustomLabelProvider extends ViewerLabelProvider {
    public String text(Book book) { return "Book:   " + book.getTitle(); }
    public String image(Book book) { return "book.png"; }
    public String text(Borrower b) { return "Borrower:   " + b.getFirstName(); }
    // other customizations
}
```

Listing 1.6. An example of customization of labeling in EMF Components

```
public class MyCustomModule extends EmfComponentsGenericModule {
    public Class<? extends ViewerLabelProvider> bindViewerLabelProvider() {
        return CustomLabelProvider.class;
    }
    ...
}
```

Listing 1.7. An example of bindings of customization of labeling

Another thing that the programmer might want to customize is the representation of the `EStructuralFeatures` of the model, i.e., the descriptions of the fields of the elements of the model. Again, we provide a declarative way to do this, through a `PropertyDescriptionProvider`, as illustrated in Listing 1.8; note that this time, the name of the method for customizing the text of the feature must contain the name of the EClass and the name of the specific feature of such EClass. For instance, `text_Person_firstName` will be called to get the description of the feature `firstName` of a `Person`.

```
public class CustomPropertyDescriptionProvider extends PropertyDescriptionProvider {
    public String text_Person_firstName() { return "First name"; }
    public String text_Person_lastName() { return "Surname"; }
}
```

Listing 1.8. An example of customization of EStructuralFeatures label representations in EMF Components

Similarly, we might want to specify only a subset of features to be shown in the UI components of a model; for this task, the EMF Components framework relies on `FeaturesProvider`; the programmer can customize it and specify the features to be shown for some of the classes of the model; the customization shown in Listing 1.9 should be self-explanatory[3]: for an object of class `Library` we want to show only its features `name` and `address`, etc.

Note that the customizations are not limited to classes belonging to a single EMF metamodel package: in one single place we can provide customization for every EMF classes that we intend to use with EMF Components widgets.

All these classes are used internally by the EMF Framework to represent models in the widgets; thus a custom injected implementation will be used consistently throughout

---

[3] Due to lack of space, we do not show here the corresponding mechanism dealing with the customization of EMF generated code; the interested reader can compare our solution with the typical example of EMF: the Library example.

```
import static org.eclipse.emf.examples.extlibrary.EXTLibraryPackage.Literals.*;

public class CustomFeaturesProvider extends FeaturesProvider {
    @Override protected void buildMap(EClassToEStructuralFeatureMap map) {
        super.buildMap(map);
        map.mapTo(LIBRARY,
                LIBRARY_NAME, ADDRESSABLE_ADDRESS);
        map.mapTo(PERSON,
                PERSON_FIRST_NAME, PERSON_LAST_NAME,
                ADDRESSABLE_ADDRESS);
        map.mapTo(WRITER,
                PERSON_FIRST_NAME, PERSON_LAST_NAME,
                WRITER_BOOKS);
    }
}
```

Listing 1.9. An example of customization of EStructuralFeatures to be represented in EMF Components

the application for all the UI components created with the same injector. For instance, the custom implementations shown in Listing 1.8 and 1.9 will be used when building the forms (described in Section 2.2) and the column headers for table viewers (as shown in Figure 2).

In Figure 2 we show the same components of Figure 1, after applying the customizations of Listing 1.8 and 1.9. The customizations of Listing 1.8 can be seen in the form where the labels for the features firstName and lastName have been changed; the customizations of Listing 1.9 can be seen again in the form: only the features first-Name, lastName and books are represented (see the last mapping in Listing 1.9). In Figure 2 we also show a tabular view (another example of use of EMF Components framework which we did not illustrate in this paper); note that since the same customized FeaturesProvider was used, the headers of the columns in the table for the selected writer respect the customizations of Listing 1.8 and 1.9.

4   A DSL for Customization

To make EMF Components easier to use we recently developed a DSL with Xtext [9,10]. Xtext is a framework for the development of programming languages: it provides high-level mechanisms that generate all the typical and recurrent artifacts necessary for a fully-fledged IDE on top of Eclipse. With our DSL we can easily specify and customize the components without writing Java classes and custom Guice module bindings (that we illustrated in Section 3). From such a specification the DSL will then generate all the Java classes to implement the customized aspects and also the Guice module with the correct bindings.

This DSL relies on Xbase [14], a reusable expression language, completely integrated with Java, and shipped with Xtext. From Xbase the DSL "inherits" a rich Java-like syntax for expressions (notably, *closures* and type inference, so that the programmer is not requested to write types in declarations explicitly) and the complete

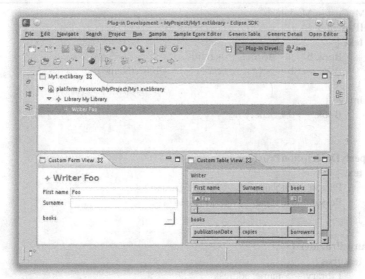

Fig. 2. A tree editor, a form view and a tabular view with customizations

Java type system. Xbase also provides some syntactic sugar, like extension methods and a concise getter/setter syntax (e.g., foo(a, b) can be written as a.foo(b), and a.getFirstName() as a.firstName). In particular, the expression parts of the DSL will be handled directly by Xbase, relieving the programmer from the big burden of having to reimplement repetitive type checks. Xbase also allows to debug Xbase expressions, thus it is also possible to directly debug the code of our DSL from the Eclipse JDT debugger.

With the EMF Components DSL one defines a **module** which will correspond to a Guice module in the generated Java code; inside this **module** definition the programmer can specify customizations for the aspects we described in Section 3; the DSL will then generate the corresponding Java classes, and the corresponding custom bindings in the generated Guice module. To give an idea of the compactness of this specification, we note that the specification in Listing 1.10 corresponds to all the Java code manually written in Listings from 1.6 to 1.9.

Most of all, the class names in Listing 1.10 actually refer to the corresponding Java classes, and from the DSL editor one can directly navigate to their sources; furthermore, the editor provides syntax highlighting and code completion for all Java types. Moreover, the feature names in **propertyDescriptionProvider** and **featuresProvider** are bound to the corresponding EMF features; again, one can navigate to those features and get code completion for the features of the corresponding EMF class (Figure 3). This also means that the DSL checks that the features specified actually belong to the corresponding EMF class (Figure 4). This additional static checking is not available when writing Java code manually. For instance, in Listing 1.8 one could easily mispell the method name, e.g., text_Person_fstName and get no static error (but at runtime the GUI widgets will not have the desired behavior); similarly, in Listing 1.9 one could map a feature to the wrong class (e.g., PERSON_FIRST_NAME to LIBRARY)

```
 1 module MyCustomModule {
       labelProvider {
 3         text {
               Book b -> "Book:  " + b.title
 5             Borrower b -> {"Borrower:  " + b.firstName}
           }
 7         image {
               Book -> "book.png"
 9         }
       }
11     propertyDescriptionProvider {
           text {
13             Person : firstName -> "First name"
               Person : lastName -> "Surname"
15         }
       }
17     featuresProvider {
           features {
19             Library -> name, address
               Person -> firstName, lastName, address
21             Writer -> firstName, lastName, books
           }
23     }
   }
```

Listing 1.10. An example of module definition in EMF Components DSL

without getting an immediate error. Instead, with the DSL, these checks are performed statically, as shown in Figure 4.

As a final example, in Figure 5, we show an RCP application implemented with EMF Components and its DSL. This is similar to the classic Mail RCP application example which comes with Eclipse. It is not intended to be an actual email client, but it concentrates on the user interface part.

We refer to http://code.google.com/a/eclipselabs.org/p/emf-components for the complete source code of the example. Here, we only want to stress that for implementing this user interface we had to write only about 15 lines of Java code for each view, and an average of 15 lines of EMF Components code for the customization.

Since our DSL relies on Xbase, we can specify, for instance, the **labelProvider** with a Java-like syntax, as shown in Listing 1.11. Thus, using the DSL instead of Java does not prevent from writing involved customizations.

5   Related Work and Conclusions

Most of the projects that deal with customization in the context of EMF are based on the generative approach. Indeed, EMF itself relies on JET (a template system) for code generation. Thus, the programmer could also provide custom templates to drive the generation of Java code performed by EMF. Other similar technologies (like EEF and EGF),

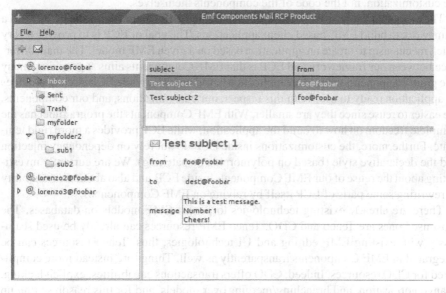

```
featuresProvider {
    features {
        Writer -> books, firstName, lastName, name
        Library -> b|
    }
}

labelProvider {
    text {
        Library -> "
    }
}
```

Fig. 3. Code completion for EMF features

```
🖿 module.emfcomponent ⊠
    module my.custom.mymodule {
        featuresProvider {
            features {
                Writer -> books, firstName, lastName, name
                Library -> address, firstName
            }
        }

        propertyDescriptionProvider {
            text {
                Person : fstName -> ""
            }
        }
    }
```

Fig. 4. Validation in the DSL editor

Fig. 5. An RCP application implemented with EMF Components

which are available from Eclipse Modeling Framework Technology (EMFT) [15] are also based on the generative approach. The EMF Components framework can be seen as complementary to the generative approaches. Our framework is also orthogonal to

```
...
2    labelProvider {
        image {
4           Account -> "account.gif"
            Folder -> {
6              switch (name) {
                  case "Inbox" : "inbox.gif"
8                 case "Sent" : "sent.png"
                  case "Trash" : "trash.png"
10                default: "folder.gif"
               }
12          }
        }
14  ...
```

Listing 1.11. Customization of the label provider for accounts view

GUI builders, since EMF Components is more related to bridging the models to the abstract editing parts, and not to the actual GUI framework.

Thus EMF Components does not generate code for the components and does not require the programmer to modify that generated code: the programmer uses the provided components and injects the customized code. The only point where we use code generation is in the DSL (Section 4); but also in this case we only generate the code for the customization, not the code of the components themselves.

The work that is closest to our framework is the EMF Client Platform (ECP) [16], a framework to build EMF-based client applications. The goal of ECP is to provide a very quick mechanism to create an application based on a given EMF model. The main difference between our framework and ECP is that EMF Components aims at providing many fine grain components to build an application based on EMF, while ECP already provides an application ready to use. With this respect, our customizations, and our components, are easier to reuse since they are smaller. With EMF Components the programmer has the complete freedom on how to build the application, while ECP provides a more rigid template. Furthermore, the customizations inside ECP do not rely on dependency injection and the declarative style (based on polymorphic dispatching). We are currently investigating about the reuse of our EMF Components inside ECP, and also about the possibility of rewriting some parts of ECP itself by relying on EMF Components.

There are already existing technologies to persist EMF models on databases. The most used ones are Teneo and CDO. Teneo EMF resources can already be used seamlessly with existing EMF editing and UI technologies, thus, Teneo resources can be integrated in EMF Components transparently as well. Things are instead more complicated for CDO resources. Indeed, CDO offers transactions capabilities, explicit locking, change notification, and branching/merging over models, and for this reason setting up a CDO resource requires more work. EMF Components internally recognizes CDO resource URIs and uses a dedicated resource loader which automatically creates a transaction (or a view, in case we use read-only widgets) and returns the associated CDO resource. Thus, also CDO resources can be used transparently inside EMF Components, relieving the programmer from all the internal details.

Simply by using a CDO URI format for a resource, all existing code implemented using EMF Components can already be reused for models stored using CDO. Indeed EMF Components was designed with test driven development [17] and agile programming [6] in mind; thus, it must be easy to switch from a development/testing environment to a production one. With the mechanism described above to hide the details of the actual storage of a model, it is straightforward to use, for instance, an in memory model during development stage, and an actual CDO model for the production.

We are planning to integrate other EMF technologies in the EMF Components framework, like queries, transactions and advanced validation mechanisms (though the standard EMF validation mechanisms are already handled inside EMF Components).

Acknowledgements. The author is grateful to all the people from RCP Vision for their help, support and contribution to the development of EMF Components.

References

1. Steinberg, D., Budinsky, F., Paternostro, M., Merks, E.: EMF: Eclipse Modeling Framework, 2nd edn. Addison-Wesley (2008)
2. Google: Google Guice (2012), http://code.google.com/p/google-guice
3. Fowler, M.: Inversion of Control Containers and the Dependency Injection pattern (2004), http://www.martinfowler.com/articles/injection.html
4. Bettini, L.: EMF Components - Filling the Gap between Models and UI. In: ICSOFT, pp. 34–43. SciTePress (2012)
5. EMF.Edit: EMF.Edit (2004), http://help.eclipse.org/galileo/index.jsp?topic=/org.eclipse.emf.doc/references/overview/EMF.Edit.html.
6. Martin, R.: Agile Software Development: Principles, Patterns, and Practices. Prentice Hall (2003)
7. Gamma, E., Helm, R., Johnson, R., Vlissides, J.: Design Patterns: Elements of Reusable Object-Oriented Software. Addison-Wesley (1995)
8. Sun Microsystems, Inc.: JSR 308: Annotations on java types (2007), http://jcp.org/en/jsr/detail?id=308
9. Itemis: Xtext (2012), http://www.eclipse.org/Xtext
10. Eysholdt, M., Behrens, H.: Xtext: implement your language faster than the quick and dirty way. In: SPLASH/OOPSLA Companion, pp. 307–309. ACM (2010)
11. Schindl, T.: EMF Databinding (2009), http://www.eclipse.org/resources/resource.php?id=511
12. Castagna, G.: Object-Oriented Programming: A Unified Foundation. Progress in Theoretical Computer Science. Birkhauser (1997)
13. Bettini, L., Capecchi, S., Venneri, B.: Featherweight Java with Dynamic and Static Overloading. Science of Computer Programming 74, 261–278 (2009)
14. Efftinge, S., Eysholdt, M., Köhnlein, J., Zarnekow, S., von Massow, R., Hasselbring, W., Hanus, M.: Xbase: implementing domain-specific languages for Java. In: GPCE, pp. 112–121. ACM (2012)
15. Eclipse Modeling Framework Technology: Eclipse Modeling Framework Technology (EMFT) (2012), http://www.eclipse.org/modeling/emft/
16. EMF Client Platform: EMF Client Platform (2012) http://www.eclipse.org/emfclient.
17. Beck, K.: Test Driven Development: By Example. Addison-Wesley (2003)

Generic Programming in Pharo

Alexandre Bergel[1,*] and Lorenzo Bettini[2]

[1] Pleiad Lab, Computer Science Department (DCC), University of Chile, Santiago, Chile
[2] Dipartimento di Informatica, Università di Torino, Italy
abergel@dcc.uchile.cl, bettini@di.unito.it

Abstract. Dynamically typed object-oriented languages have been left out of the scope of generic programming: in a dynamically typed setting, the need for generic programming has been less prominent since no restriction applies over the kind of elements a collection may contain. However, when creating an object, the class name is hardcoded in the program, and this makes the object instantiation process hard to abstract from.

In this paper, we describe our implementation of generic programming in Pharo, a Smalltalk dialect, showing how programmers can benefit from generic programming even in a dynamically typed language. Furthermore, we enhance the expressiveness of generic programming with *reverse generics*, a mechanism for automatically deriving new generic code starting from existing non-generic one.

As a case study, we show how we used generics and reverse generics in Pharo to reuse unit test cases and to identify a number of bugs and anomalies in the stream class hierarchy.

1 Introduction

Generic programming [1, 2], a mechanism for abstracting specific types used in classes and programs, has a widespread use in statically typed programming languages (e.g., Java [3], C++ [4], C#[5], Scala [6]). Generics in Java and C# were introduced to statically check code validity as a safer alternative to down-casts. Generics are also a useful mechanism to promote code reuse [7]. In the context of C++ and its STL (Standard Template Library) [1, 8], generic programming mainly deals with *generic algorithms*, i.e., implementations of standard algorithms which are independent of the underlying data structure representations; then, in the STL, generic programming is extended also to standard data structures such as lists, stacks, etc.

On the contrary, in a dynamically typed language like Smalltalk, where types are absent in declarations of linguistic entities (like methods, fields, local variables), the need for generic programming has been less prominent since no restriction applies over the kind of elements a collection may contain. However, there is still a crucial context where types (i.e., class names) appear statically in a dynamically typed language: class references. In particular, when creating an object, the class name is hardcoded in the program, and this makes the object instantiation process hard to abstract from. There

---

* This author has been partially supported by Program U-INICIA 11/06 VID 2011, grant U-INICIA 11/06, University of Chile, and by FONDECYT number 1120094.

J. Cordeiro, S. Hammoudi, and M. van Sinderen (Eds.): ICSOFT 2012, CCIS 411, pp. 66–79, 2013.

are some patterns to deal with this problem, such as *Factory Method* [9], *Dependency Injection* [10], *Virtual classes* [11] and ad-hoc linguistic constructs [12]. However, these mechanisms are effective when future extensions are foreseen: they provide little help in a scenario of unanticipated code evolution in which the programming language does provide dedicated evolutionary construct.

In [13] we first introduced *Reverse generics*, the dual generic programming mechanism that enables the definition of a generic class from a non generic one. We call this mechanism *generalization*. It allows obtaining a brand new generic class from an existing class by "removing" hardwired class references, and by replacing them with parametrized types. For instance, G<T> = C>C'< generates the new generic class G<T> starting from the class C by replacing each reference of a class C' contained in C with the type parameter T in G. It is the dual operation of the *instantiation* operation offered by generics. The generic class G can then be instantiated into G<U> for a provided class U. Note that, the reverse generics mechanism satisfies the property C = (C>T<) <T>.

An important point is that the original class C remains unmodified. For this reason, reverse generics are useful under the basic assumptions that (i) the code to be reused has to be left intact (it cannot be the subject of refactoring) and (ii) the host programming language does not implicitly support for looking up classes dynamically (as this is the case in most dynamically languages, except for NewSpeak that supports virtual classes [11]). Thus, the main aim of reverse generics is to provide a *generative* approach, where new generic code is (automatically) generated starting from existing one, and the latter will not be modified at all; for this reason, reverse generics are not, and they do not aim at, a refactoring technique (we also refer to Section 7).

In this paper we present our implementation of *generics* and *reverse generics* in the Pharo Smalltalk programming language with. We adapted the reverse generics to cope with the lack of static type information (in [13] reverse generics were studied in the context of statically typed languages such as Java and C++). We also provide mechanisms for structural and nominal requirements both for generics and reverse generics in Pharo: these requirements on type parameters can be a safety net for a sound instantiation.

Although our implementation has been realized in a dialect of Smalltalk, nothing prevents from using this mechanism in other dynamically typed languages, like, e.g., Ruby and Python. Even though similar mechanisms have been proposed in Groovy [14], to the best of our knowledge, this is the first attempt to add a generic-like construct to Smalltalk. (The Groovy case is discussed in the related work section).

We employed reverse generics to face a classical code reuse problem. Unit tests in Pharo are inherited from Squeak, a Smalltalk dialect that served as a base for Pharo. Those tests have been written in a rather disorganized and ad-hoc fashion. This situation serves as the running example of this paper and was encountered when evolving the Pharo runtime. This helped us identify a number of bugs and anomalies in the stream class hierarchy.

The paper is structured as follows: in Section 2 we define our mechanism for generics in Pharo and in Section 3 we describe the reverse generics model in Pharo; the implementation of both mechanisms is presented in Section 4. In Section 5 we use the described mechanisms to a non trivial case study. In Section 6 we describe the integration of our generic programming mechanism in the Pharo programming environment. Section 7 summarizes the related work and Section 8 concludes the paper and gives some perspectives on future work. This paper is the revised and extended version of [15].

2   Generics in Pharo

This section presents a mechanism for generic programming for the Pharo/Smalltalk programming language[1].

As popularized by mainstream statically typed programming languages, generic programming provides a mechanism for defining *template* classes where some types are variables/parameters and then for providing arguments for those type variables, thus *instantiating* template classes into concrete and complete classes. In the following, we then use the term *template class* to refer to a class where some types are parametrized; accordingly, we refer to a *concrete/complete class* when all the arguments for parametrized types are provided.

The presentation of the mechanism is driven by a test-reuse scenario. We will first define a test called GCollectionTest. This test will be free from a particular class of the collection framework. GCollectionTest will be instantiated twice, for two different fixtures based on OrderedCollection and SortedCollection.

Consider the following code snippet containing a test that verifies elements addition.

```
"Creation of the class T"
GenericParameter subclass: #T
```

```
"Creation of the class GCollectionTest with a variable"
TestCase subclass: #GCollectionTest
   instanceVariableNames: 'collection'
```

```
"Definition of the setUp method"
"It instantiates T and add 3 numbers in it"
GCollectionTest>> setUp
   collection := T new.
   collection add: 4; add: 5; add: 10.
```

```
"Definition of the test method testAddition"
"It adds an element in the collection defined in setUp"
GCollectionTest>> testAddition
   | initialSize |
   initialSize := collection size.
   collection add: 20.
   self assert: (collection includes: 20).
   self assert: (collection size = (initialSize + 1)).
```

GCollectionTest is a standard unit test in the spirit of the xUnit framework (most of the 115 classes that test the Pharo collection library follow a very similar structure). No reference to a collection class is made by GCollectionTest. The method setUp refers to

---

[1] http://www.pharo-project.org

the empty class T. GCollectionTest may be instantiated into OrderedCollectionTest and SortedCollectionTest as follows:

"Instantiate GCollectionTest and replace
occurrences of T by OrderedCollection"
(GCollectionTest @ T-> OrderedCollection)
        as: #OrderedCollectionTest

"Replace T by SortedCollection"
(GCollectionTest @ T -> SortedCollection)
        as: #SortedCollectionTest

The generic class GCollectionTest has been instantiated twice, each time assigning a different class to the parameter T. We adopted the convention of defining generic parameter as subclasses of GenericParameter. This convention has a number of advantages, as discussed in Section 4. Since GCollectionTest contains references to T, it is a generic class. There is therefore no syntactic distinction between a class and a generic class. GCollectionTest is a generic class only because T is a generic parameter and T is referenced in setUp.

Pharo has been extended to support the (... @ ... -> ...) as: ... construct. These three operators defines the life cycle of a generic in Pharo.

2.1   Requirements for Generic Parameters

In order for a generic class to be instantiated, a class needs to be provided for each generic parameter. To prevent generic instantiation to be ill-founded, requirements for a generic parameter may be declared. These requirements are enforced when a generic class is instantiated. Requirements are formulated along nominal and structural definitions of the base code.

Nominal Requirements. Static relationship between types may be verified when instantiating a generic class. In the example above, T must be a subtype of Collection[2]. This is specified by defining a method requirements that returns myself inheritsFrom: Collection:

T>> requirements
   ^(myself inheritsFrom: Collection)

In that case, instantiation of GCollectionTest raises an error if a class that is not a subclass of Collection is provided as parameter.

Note that we introduced the myself pseudo variable. This variable will be bound to the class provided as the generic parameter when being instantiated. The variable self, which references the receiver object, cannot be used within requirements.

---

[2] We use the following convention: a class is a type when considered at compile time, and it is an object factory at runtime.

Structural Requirements. In addition to nominal requirements, a generic parameter may be also structurally constrained. A constraint is satisfied based on the presence of some particular methods. In the example above, a method check may return

myself includesSelectors: {#add: . #includes: . #size}

In that case, only a class that implements the method add:, includes:, and size can be provided in place of T.

We express a requirement as a boolean expression. The keyword inheritsFrom: and includesSelectors: are predicates. They may therefore be combined using boolean logic operators. For instance, we can express all the above requirements as follows:

```
T>> requirements
  ^(myself inheritsFrom: Collection)
        and: [myself includesSelectors:
                {#add: . #includes: . #size}]
```

Dynamically typed languages favor sophisticated debugging and testing sessions over static source code verification. The lack of static type annotation makes any isolated check on a generic not feasible. Completeness of T's requirements cannot be verified by the compiler, thus, it is up to the programmers to provide a set of satisfactory requirements when defining generic parameters. In practice, this has not been a source of difficulties.

3   Reverse Generics in Pharo

This section presents the reverse generics mechanism in Pharo; we will use a scenario that consists of reusing unit tests. Consider the following class WriteStreamTest taken from an earlier version of Pharo:

ClassTestCase subclass: #WriteStreamTest

```
WriteStreamTest >> testIsEmpty
  | stream |
  stream := WriteStream on: String new.
  self assert: stream isEmpty.
  stream nextPut: $a.
  self deny: stream isEmpty.
  stream reset.
  self deny: stream isEmpty.
```

The class WriteStreamTest is defined as a subclass of ClassTestCase, itself a subclass of SUnit's TestCase. WriteStreamTest defines the method testIsEmpty, which checks that a new instance of WriteStream is empty (i.e., answers true when isEmpty is sent). When the character $a is added into the stream, it is not empty anymore. And resetting a stream moves the stream pointer at the beginning of the stream, without removing its contents. WriteStreamTest has 5 other similar methods that verify the protocol of WriteStream.

We consider that most of the important features of WriteStream are well tested. However, WriteStream has 27 subclasses, which did not receive the same attention in terms of testing. Only 3 of these 27 classes have dedicated tests (FileStream, Read-WriteStream and MultiByteFileStream). Manually scrutinizing these 3 classes reveals that the features tested are different than the one tested in WriteStreamTest[3].

The remaining 24 subclasses of WriteStream are either not tested, or indirectly tested. An example of an indirect testing: CompressedSourceStream is a subclass of WriteStream for which the feature of WriteStream are not tested. CompressedSourceS-tream is essentially used by the file system with FileDirectory, which is tested in FileDirectoryTest.

The situation may be summarized as follows: WriteStream is properly tested and has 22 subclasses, but none of these subclasses have the features defined in WriteStream tested for their particular class.

This situation has been addressed by refactoring the collection framework using TraitTest [16]. We make a different assumption here: the base system must be pre-served, which implies that a refactoring is not desirable. Refactoring may have some implications on the overall behavior, especially in terms of robustness and efficiency. It has been shown that inheritance is not that helpful in this situation [17, 18].

With our implementation of reverse generics in Pharo, a generic class GStreamTest can be obtained from the class WriteStreamTest by turning all references of WriteStream into a parameter that we name T.

```
Generic
   named: #GStreamTest
   for: WriteStream -> T @ WriteStreamTest
```

Following a Java-like syntax [13], the above code corresponds to the following re-verse generic definition:

```
class GStreamTest<T> = WriteStreamTest>WriteStream<
```

The generic GStreamTest is defined as a copy of WriteStreamTest for which all ref-erences to WriteStream have been replaced by the type T introduced in the previous section (Section 2). GStreamTest may now be instantiated by replacing all references of WriteStream with untested subclasses of WriteStream as illustrated in Section 2:

```
"Instantiate GStreamTest and replace occurrences of T
by ZipWriteStream"
(GStreamTest @ T-> ZipWriteStream)
        as: #ZipWriteStreamTest


"Replace T by HtmlFileStream"
(GStreamTest @ T -> HtmlFileStream)
        as: #HtmlFileStreamTest
```

---

[3] According to our experience, this is a general pattern. Often programmers focus essentially on testing added methods and variable when subclassing.

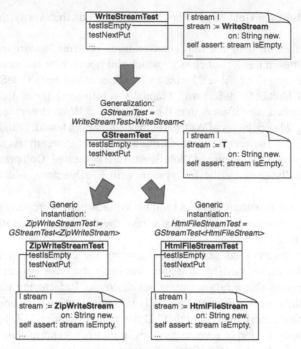

Fig. 1. Reusing WriteStreamTest.

Figure 1 summarizes the generalization and instantiation of the WriteStreamTest example. Reverse generic targets class instantiation and sending messages to a class.

The above scenario could be solved by having a super abstract class in which the class to be tested is returned by a method. This method could then be overridden in subclasses (*factory method* design pattern [9]). However, this solution is not always the best approach: First, tests of the collection libraries cannot be optimally organized using single inheritance [16]. Second, the code to be reused may not always be editable and modifiable. This is often a desired property to minimize ripple effects across packages versions.

3.1   Requirements when Generalizing

We have previously seen that requirements may be defined on generic parameters (Section 2.1). These requirements equally apply when generalizing a class. Turning references of WriteStream into a parameter T may be constrained with the following requirements:

```
T>> requirements
   ^(myself inheritsFrom: Stream)
        and: [ myself includesSelectors: {#isEmpty . #reset} ]
```

Further requirements could be that the parameter T understands the class-side message on:, and the instance-side message nextPut:. However, this will be redundant with the requirement myself inheritsFrom: Stream, since Stream defines the method nextPut: and on:.

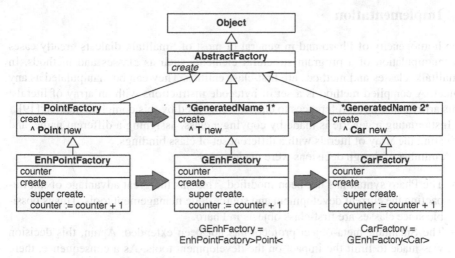

Fig. 2. Copying superclasses, illustrated with a generic class factory

Requirements may also be set for class methods, e.g.,myself class includesSelector: {#new: } makes the presence of the class method new: mandatory.

3.2 Capturing Inherited Methods

Instantiating a generic G, which is obtained from generalizing a class C, makes copies of C with connections to different classes. This process may also copy superclasses of C when methods defined in superclasses need to have new references of classes. This situation is illustrated in Figure 2.

A different example is adopted in this figure. The class AbstractFactory has an abstract method create. PointFactory is a subclass of it that creates instances of Point (not represented on the figure). This class is subclassed into EnhPointFactory that overrides create to count the number of instances that have been created.

Consider the generic

GEnhFactory<T> = EnhPointFactory>Point<.

This generic may be instantiated with a class Car to produce cars instead of points:

CarFactory = GEnhFactory<Car>.

The class Point is referenced by the superclass of EnhPointFactory. Generalizing and instantiating EnhPointFactory has to turn the Point reference contained in PointFactory into Car. This is realized in reverse generics by automatically copying also the superclass into a new generic class with a generated name.

The class inheritance is copied until the point in the hierarchy where no superclass references a generic parameter.

4   Implementation

The homogeneity of Pharo and in general of most of Smalltalk dialects greatly eases the manipulation of a program structural elements such as classes and methods. In Smalltalk, classes and methods are first-class entities. They can be manipulated as any object. A compiled method is a set of bytecode instructions with an array of literals. This array contains all references to classes being used by this compiled method [19].

Instantiating a generic is made by copying a class, assigning a different name, and adjusting the array of literals with a different set of class bindings.

A number of design decisions were made:

– The Pharo syntax has not been modified. This has the great advantage of not impacting the current development and source code management tools. This is possible since classes are first-class objects in Pharo.
– The Smalltalk meta-object protocol has not been extended. Again, this decision was made to limit the impact on the development tools. As a consequence, there is no distinction between a generic and a class, thus the generic mechanism can be implemented as a simple library to load.

Indeed these design choices are based also on past experience in Smalltalk extensions: the last significant change of the language was realized in 2004 [20], when traits have been introduced in Squeak, the predecessor of Pharo. In the current version of Pharo, the support of traits is fragile at best (bugs are remaining and many tools are not traits aware). This experience gained with traits suggests that realizing a major change in the programming language is challenging and extremely resource consuming.

Note that, by using our reverse generics, one can modify the original existing code (i.e., the classes that are not generic), and then, automatically, spread the modifications to the one obtained by reverse generics.

The implementation presented in this paper is freely available (under the MIT license) at http://www.squeaksource.com/ReverseGeneric.html.

5   Case Study: Application to the Pharo Stream Hierarchy

The situation described in Section 3 is an excerpt of the case study we realized. For each of the 24 subclasses of WriteStream, we instantiated GStreamTest. This way, about 24 new unit tests were generated. The WriteStreamTest class defines 6 test methods. We therefore generated 24 * 6 = 144 test methods. Each of the generated test is a subclass of ClassTestCase, which itself defines 3 test methods. Running these 24 unit tests executes 144 + 27 * 3 = 225 test methods.

Running these 225 test methods results in: 225 runs, 192 passed, 21 failures, 12 errors. Since the 6 tests in WriteStreamTest pass, this result essentially says that there are some functionalities that are verified for WriteStream, but they are not verified for some of its subclasses. An example of the culprit test methods for the failures are CrLfFileStreamTest>> testNew and LimitedWriteStreamTest>> testSetToEnd. The fact that these two tests fail uncovers some bugs in the classes CrLfFileStream and Limited-WriteStream.

The body of CrLfFileStreamTest>> testNew is

self should: [CrLfFileStream new] raise: Error

meaning that a CrLfFileStream should not be instantiated with new. However, the class can actually be instantiated with new, resulting in a meaningless and unusable object.

Another example of a bug was found in LimitedWriteStream. This class is used to limit the amount of data to be written in a stream. The body of LimitedWriteStreamTest>> testSetToEnd is:

```
LimitedWriteStreamTest>> testSetToEnd
  | string stream |
  string := 'hello'.
  stream := LimitedWriteStream with: ''.
  stream nextPutAll: string.
  self assert: stream position = string size.
  stream setToEnd.
  self assert: stream position = string size.
  self assert: stream contents = string
```

It essentially verifies the behavior of the stream index cursor. This test signals an error in the expression stream nextPutAll: string. By inspecting what triggered the error, we discovered that when a LimitedWriteStream is instantiated with with: '', the object is initialized with a nil value as the limit, resulting in a meaningless comparison (newEnd > limit in the method LimitedWriteStream>> nextPutAll:).

Not all the test methods that fail and raise an error are due to some bugs in the stream class hierarchy. We roughly estimate that only 11 test methods of these 33 methods have uncovered tangible bugs. The remaining failures and errors are due to some differences on how class should be initialized. For example, the test StandardFileStreamTest>>test-SetToEnd raises an error because a StandardFileStream cannot be instantiated with the message with: (it is instantiated with fileNamed:, which requires a file name as argument). Although no bug have been located, this erroneous test method suggests that the method write: should be canceled (i.e., raise an explicit error saying it should be not invoked).

This experiment has a number of contributions:

- it demonstrates the applicability of our generics and reverse generics to a non-trivial scenario,
- it helped us identify a number of bugs and anomalies in the Pharo stream hierarchy.

6   Integration in the Programming Environment

When put in practice, our generic mechanism raises a number of concerns, including creation and instantiation of generics and navigation within generic code. In the previous section we have presented the approach from a programmatic point of view. However, comfortably programming with generics involves a support from the programming environment. We have extended the Pharo programming environment to cover basic needs.

Figure 3 lists the actions that should be supported by the programming environment to cover elementary programming scenarios, such as creating and instantiating generics and running unit tests. Each thick gray line represents a navigation command actionable via a key shortcut.

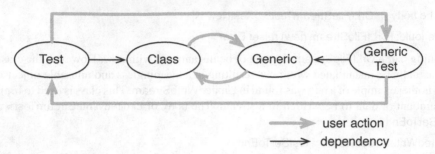

Fig. 3. Actions supported by the programming environment

A practitioner may jump from the definition of a class to the generics that have been created from. From a generic, one can jump to the classes instantiated and originating. Use of test case is prominent in Pharo and our extension of the Pharo programming environment covers the need to turn a unit test into a generic test.

Since highly parametrized software can be hard to understand [9], we may think of a programming methodology where a specific class is developed and tested in a non-generic way, and then it is available to the users via its "reversed" generic version (in this case, we really need the non generic version for testing purposes, so the code must not be refactored). Thus, reverse generics can be used as a development methodology, not only as a way to turn previous classes into generic: one can develop, debug and test a class with all the types instantiated, and then expose to the "external world" the generic version created through reverse generics.

7   Related Work

In dynamically typed languages, like Smalltalk, where types are not used in declarations, the context where generics are useful is in object instantiation; thus, with this respect, the generics presented in this paper are related to C++ templates, rather than to Java generics. (Indeed, due to the *type erasure* model [21, 3], generic types cannot be instantiated in Java; we refer to [22, 23, 13] for a broader comparison between Java generics and C++ templates.) The generics needed in the context of Smalltalk act at a meta-level, by generating new classes starting from existing ones, thus, they have similarities with *generative programming* mechanisms [24] and C++ meta programming [25]. This meta programming mechanism is evident also in our generics and reverse generics implementation in Pharo: new code is generated starting from existing one, without modifying the latter. This takes place in two steps: with reverse generics a brand new generic version is obtained starting from existing code; then, by instantiating generic classes, the generic code is adapted and reused in a new context.

In order for generic types to be used and type checked in a generic class, those types must be constrained with some type requirements. Constraints on generic types are often referred to as *concepts* [26, 8]. Java generics require explicit constraints, thus a concept is defined using a Java interface or a base class, and a type satisfies a concept if it implements that specific interface or it extends that specific base class. On the contrary, the C++ compiler itself infers type constraints on templates and automatically checks whether they are satisfied when such generic type is instantiated. In our implementation, generic parameters can be assigned constraints using nominal (similarly to Java) and structural requirements (similarly to concepts), as illustrated in Section 2.1.

There are similarities among reverse generics and some refactoring approaches: however, the intent of reverse generics is not to perform reverse engineering or refactoring of existing code, (see, e.g., [27–29]) but to extrapolate possible generic "template" code from existing one, and reuse it for generating new code. Note that this programming methodology will permit modifying the original existing code, and then, automatically, spread the modifications to the one obtained by reverse generics.

A first attempt to automatically extract generic class definitions from an existing library has been conveyed by Duggan [27], well before the introduction of generics into Java. Besides the reverse engineering aspect, Duggan's work diverges from reverse generics regarding downcast insertion and parameter instantiation. Duggan makes use of *dynamic subtype constraint* that inserts runtime downcasts. A parametrized type may be instantiated, which requires some type-checking rules for the creation of an object: the actual type arguments must satisfy the upper bounds of the formal type parameters in the class type. Kiezun et al. propose a type-constraints-based algorithm for converting non-generic libraries to add type parameters [29]. It handles the full Java language and preserves backward compatibility.

A limitation of first-order parametric polymorphism is that it is not possible to abstract over a type constructor. Therefore, one cannot pass a type constructor as a type argument to another type constructor. Template template parameters[4] [30] in C++ provide a means to abstract over type constructors. Moors, Piessens and Odersky [31] extended the Scala language [32] with type construction polymorphism to allow type constructors as type parameters. Therefore, it is possible not only to abstract over a type, but also over a type constructor; for instance, a class can be parametrized over Container[T][5], where Container is a type constructor which is itself abstracted and can be instantiated with the actual collection, e.g., List or Stack, which are type constructors themselves. The generics mechanism presented in this paper acts at the same level of first-order parametric polymorphism, thus, it shares the same limitations. An interesting extension would be to be able to switch to the higher level of type constructor polymorphism, but this is an issue that still needs to be investigated.

The *Dependency Injection* pattern [10] is used to "inject" actual implementation classes into a class hierarchy in a consistent way. This is useful when classes delegate specific functionalities to other classes. The reverse generics mechanism is not related to object composition and delegation, i.e., the typical context of the *inversion of control* philosophy that dependency injection deals with. With reverse generics the programmer does not have to design classes according the pattern of abstracting the actual behavior and then delegate it to factory methods; on the contrary the reverse generics mechanism allows generating new code (i.e., new classes) from existing one, without modifying the original code.

Package Template [33] is a mechanism for reusing and adapting packages by rebinding class references (including class renaming and merging). A version has been

---

[4] The repetition of "template" is not a mistake.
[5] Scala uses [] instead of <>.

proposed for Groovy [14]. The reverse generics mechanism is able to turn a non generic class into a generic one, while Package Template is not designed for this purpose.

Traits [34] were introduced in language Squeak/Smalltalk to counter the problems of class-based inheritance with respect to code reuse: they provide reuse by sharing methods across classes. Instead, generic programming (and also our generics) provides a mechanism to abstract from the type implementing specific behavior. Combining our generic mechanism with traits looks promising in that respect, also for the meta-programming features of traits themselves [35].

8   Conclusions

The mechanisms presented in this paper provide features both to write generic code in a dynamically typed language and to extrapolate possible generic "template" code from existing one, and reuse it for generating new code. In our approach, class generalization and generic instantiation is based on class copying, similarly to C++ templates. Although this implies some code duplication in the generated code, this is consistent with the meta-level which is typical of *generative programming* mechanisms [24].

A limitation of the implementation presented in this paper is that the generic parameters (like T in Section 2 and Section 3) are global subclasses, thus there can be only one such generic parameter (together with its requirements). However, in this first prototype implementation of generics and reverse generics in Pharo, this did not prevent us from using these mechanisms effectively (like the case study of Section 5) and to study their applicability. In future versions, we will deal with this issue, and remove the "globality" of generic parameters.

At the best of our knowledge, no generic (and reverse generic) programming language construct is available in Smalltalk, Ruby and Python that achieve the same capabilities as we presented in this paper. It is subject of future work to further investigate whether our proposal can be applied to other dynamically typed languages.

References

1. Musser, D.R., Stepanov, A.A.: Generic programming. In: Gianni, P. (ed.) ISSAC 1988. LNCS, vol. 358, pp. 13–25. Springer, Heidelberg (1989)
2. Dos Reis, G., Järvi, J.: What is generic programming? In: Proc. of LCSD (2005)
3. Bracha, G., Odersky, M., Stoutamire, D., Wadler, P.: Making the future safe for the past: adding genericity to the Java programming language. In: OOPSLA, pp. 183–200. ACM (1998)
4. Stroustrup, B.: The C++ Programming Language, 3rd edn. Addison Wesley (1997)
5. Microsoft: Generics (C# Programming Guide) (2005), http://msdn.microsoft.com/en-us/library/512aeb7t(VS.80).aspx
6. Oliveira, B.C., Gibbons, J.: Scala for generic programmers. In: WGP, pp. 25–36. ACM (2008)
7. Meyer, B.: Genericity versus Inheritance. In: OOPSLA, pp. 391–405. ACM (1986)
8. Austern, M.H.: Generic Programming and the STL: using and extending the C++ Standard Template Library. Addison-Wesley (1998)
9. Gamma, E., Helm, R., Johnson, R., Vlissides, J.: Design Patterns: Elements of Reusable Object-Oriented Software. Addison-Wesley (1995)

10. Fowler, M.: Inversion of Control Containers and the Dependency Injection pattern (2004),
    http://www.martinfowler.com/articles/injection.html
11. Bracha, G., von der Ahé, P., Bykov, V., Kashai, Y., Maddox, W., Miranda, E.: Modules as
    Objects in Newspeak. In: D'Hondt, T. (ed.) ECOOP 2010. LNCS, vol. 6183, pp. 405–428.
    Springer, Heidelberg (2010)
12. Cohen, T., Gil, J.: Better Construction with Factories. JOT 6, 103–123 (2007)
13. Bergel, A., Bettini, L.: Reverse Generics: Parametrization after the Fact. In: Software and
    Data Technologies. CCIS, vol. 50, pp. 107–123. Springer, Heidelberg (2011)
14. Axelsen, E.W., Krogdahl, S.: Groovy package templates: supporting reuse and runtime adap-
    tion of class hierarchies. In: DLS, pp. 15–26. ACM (2009)
15. Bergel, A., Bettini, L.: Generics and Reverse Generics for Pharo. In: ICSOFT, pp. 363–372.
    SciTePress (2012)
16. Ducasse, S., Pollet, D., Bergel, A., Cassou, D.: Reusing and Composing Tests with Traits. In:
    Oriol, M., Meyer, B. (eds.) TOOLS EUROPE 2009. LNCS, vol. 33, pp. 252–271. Springer,
    Heidelberg (1975)
17. Flatt, M., Felleisen, M.: Units: Cool Modules for HOT Languages. In: PLDI, pp. 236–248.
    ACM (1998)
18. Bergel, A., Ducasse, S., Nierstrasz, O.: Classbox/J: Controlling the Scope of Change in Java.
    In: OOPSLA, pp. 177–189. ACM (2005)
19. Goldberg, A., Robson, D.: Smalltalk 80: the Language and its Implementation. Addison-
    Wesley (1983)
20. Lienhard, A.: Bootstrapping Traits. Master's thesis, University of Bern (2004)
21. Odersky, M., Wadler, P.: Pizza into Java: Translating theory into practice. In: POPL, pp.
    146–159. ACM (1997)
22. Ghosh, D.: Generics in Java and C++: a comparative model. ACM SIGPLAN Notices 39,
    40–47 (2004)
23. Batov, V.: Java generics and C++ templates. C/C++ Users Journal 22, 16–21 (2004)
24. Eisenecker, U.W., Czarnecki, K.: Generative Programming: Methods, Tools, and Applica-
    tions. Addison-Wesley (2000)
25. Abrahams, D., Gurtovoy, A.: C++ Template Metaprogramming: Concepts, Tools and Tech-
    niques from Boost and Beyond. Addison-Wesley (2004)
26. Kapur, D., Musser, D.R., Stepanov, A.A.: Tecton: A Language for Manipulating Generic
    Objects. In: Staunstrup, J. (ed.) Program Specification 1981. LNCS, vol. 134, pp. 402–414.
    Springer, Heidelberg (1982)
27. Duggan, D.: Modular type-based reverse engineering of parameterized types in Java code.
    In: OOPSLA, pp. 97–113. ACM (1999)
28. von Dincklage, D., Diwan, A.: Converting Java classes to use generics. In: OOPSLA, pp.
    1–14. ACM (2004)
29. Kiezun, A., Ernst, M.D., Tip, F., Fuhrer, R.M.: Refactoring for Parameterizing Java Classes.
    In: ICSE, pp. 437–446. IEEE (2007)
30. Weiss, R., Simonis, V.: Exploring template template parameters. In: Bjørner, D., Broy, M.,
    Zamulin, A.V. (eds.) PSI 2001. LNCS, vol. 2244, pp. 500–510. Springer, Heidelberg (2001)
31. Moors, A., Piessens, F., Odersky, M.: Generics of a higher kind. In: OOPSLA, pp. 423–438.
    ACM (2008)
32. Odersky, M., Spoon, L., Venners, B.: Programming in Scala. Artima (2008)
33. Sørensen, F., Axelsen, E.W., Krogdahl, S.: Reuse and combination with package templates.
    In: MASPEGHI, pp. 1–5. ACM (2010)
34. Ducasse, S., Nierstrasz, O., Schärli, N., Wuyts, R., Black, A.P.: Traits: A Mechanism for
    fine-grained Reuse. ACM TOPLAS 28, 331–388 (2006)
35. Reppy, J., Turon, A.: Metaprogramming with Traits. In: Ernst, E. (ed.) ECOOP 2007. LNCS,
    vol. 4609, pp. 373–398. Springer, Heidelberg (2007)

Peer-to-Peer Remote Service Discovery
in Pervasive Computing*

Stefan D. Bruda[1], Farzad Salehi[1], Yasir Malik[2], and Bessam Abdulrazak[2]

[1] Bishop's University, Sherbrooke, QC J1M 1Z7, Canada
[2] Université de Sherbrooke, Sherbrooke, QC J1K 2R1, Canada
stefan@bruda.ca, salehi@cs.ubishops.ca,
{yasir.malik,bessam.abdulrazak}@usherbrooke.ca

Abstract. Service discovery is important in realizing the concept of pervasive computing; consequently, service discovery protocols must be able to work in the heterogeneous environment offered by this computing paradigm. Remote service discovery in particular has not been properly achieved so far. In an attempt to remedy this we propose a new architecture for enabling local service discovery mechanisms to discover services remotely. We first base our architecture on Universal Plug and Play (UPnP) as an example of local service discovery protocols, and Gnutella as an example of peer-to-peer distributed search protocols. We introduce a module called *service mirror builder* to the UPnP protocol, and a remote communication protocol over a Gnutella network. We then note that our architecture is actually independent on any locally deployed discovery protocol and thus supports full interoperability.

1 Introduction

Mark Weiser gave birth to the vision of "ubiquitous computing" or "pervasive computing" (as named throughout this paper). He defined it as follows: *Ubiquitous computing is the method of enhancing computer use by making many computers available throughout the physical environment, but making them effectively invisible to the user* [1]. Computing anytime, anywhere, and in any device means a massive presence of computing devices in the physical world. At the same time, people should be able to access information and computation in a user-centric way i.e., user interaction with such a system must be natural and comfortable.

Pervasive computing offers an environment saturated with sensors, actuators, cameras, and other sorts of computing devices; all these devices should work together and satisfy users' needs with minimal user intervention. Service discovery protocols are one tool that accomplished this. Many service discovery protocols have been designed. The dominant protocols (at least for home appliances) include Microsoft Universal Plug and Play or UPnP [2], Bluetooth Service Discovery Protocol [3], Apple's Bonjour, and Sun's Jini technology [4].

Current service discovery protocols are designed for home or enterprise environments [5]; the pervasive computing environment is however far more heterogeneous

---

* This research was supported by the Natural Sciences and Engineering Research Council of Canada. Part of this work was also supported by Bishop's University.

J. Cordeiro, S. Hammoudi, and M. van Sinderen (Eds.): ICSOFT 2012, CCIS 411, pp. 80–95, 2013.
© Springer-Verlag Berlin Heidelberg 2013

and sophisticated. Furthermore, most service discovery protocols are designed to work only in a local area network (LAN) [6], which is justified for the many services that are physically-oriented (such as video projectors or coffee machines). Still, many other services are not physically-oriented and are accessed by users physically far away from them (such as the digital data in someone's home, or sensors, actuators, and cameras present in a place for security or health care purposes). Computing anywhere is also the very definition of the concept of pervasive computing. While it is not possible to provide all services anywhere, remote access to any services (from anywhere) makes sense. For this purpose service discovery protocols must be able to discover services remotely in order to be able to work in a pervasive computing environment. A combination of existing technologies and services enables some level of remote access, but seamless discovery and control of remote services is currently not possible [6–8].

The objective of this work is to enable local service discovery protocols (such as UPnP) to discover remote services which are not available locally. We lay the basis of such remote service discovery by proposing a suitable architecture. We use UPnP as an example of service discovery protocols. In our architecture each local UPnP network is enhanced by a function called service mirror builder. A service mirror builder presents local services as remote services to other UPnP networks, and also builds mirrors of remote services in its local network. The process of finding a remote service uses the distributed peer-to-peer search protocol Gnutella (though other implementations are also possible).

A service mirror builder is seen as an UPnP enabled device in the local UPnP network. It is worth emphasizing that UPnP is just an example; the service mirror builder can be generally defined as a service discovery enabled device with respect to any service discovery protocol.

1.1 Motivation

Between other things pervasive computing means spatial heterogeneity: some places offer all the needed services and others only have a few services to offer. Therefore a combination of remote and local services is sometimes needed. The following scenarios motivate our quest for remote service discovery.

One example of pervasive computing environment is a *connected (smart) home*, which is a dwelling incorporating a communications network that connects key devices (sensors and actuators, electrical appliances) and allows them to be remotely controlled, monitored or accessed [7]. To realize a smart home we thus need to have a mechanism to access its services remotely. In addition, most of us desire seamless storage, access and consumption of digital content from and to any compatible digital device in a home or smart home; ideally, users should be able to access their residential services from anywhere using any type of terminal [8]. Overall use cases for remote service discovery therefore include lighting, residential climate control, home theater, audio entertainment systems, domestic security, domestic health care systems, etc.

Vendors need to connect to their devices for various purposes such as to update their software or perform routine checks (*remote support*). Security and health care companies in particular need to be in contact with their customers and their products continuously. The information from sensors, actuators and cameras can be monitored by such companies, which can then take action in case of any threat, but also control devices to be more efficient and usable. The vendors can also advertise features and offer upgrades to their devices (*continuing close presence*).

Massively Multiplayer Games (MMGs) are traditionally supported by a client-server architecture, but such a centralized architecture lacks flexibility and can put communication and computation stress on the servers [9]. To overcome these problems inherent to centralized solutions, peer-to-peer networks are emerging as a promising architecture for MMGs [9]. Running MMGs with the help of remote service discovery and without any centralized coordinator is arguably the best use cases to motivate our research contribution.

2 Preliminaries

2.1 UPnP

The role of Universal Plug and Play (UPnP) [2] is the automatic discovery and configuration of any new devices that connect to a computer network. UPnP supports zero configuration networking or Zeroconf, meaning that UPnP creates an IP network without any need of manual configuration or configuration servers.

UPnP uses the Internet protocol suite. Special features include the following [2]: *media and device independence* (any network media or device which supports IP can be a basis for the establishment of UPnP), *user Interface (UI) control* (devices can have a UI written by XML which is readable by a browser), and *operating system and programming language independence*.

UPnP has three major components: *device* (contains one or more services), *service* (performs actions and shows its state; consists of a state table, control server and event server), and *control point* (a system that discovers and then controls services and devices). The functioning of UPnP then involves six steps:

Addressing. Each device must have a Dynamic Host Configuration Protocol (DHCP) client. When the device connects to the network for the first time it must search for a DHCP server. If a DHCP server exists, then the device receives an IP address this way. Otherwise the device must assign an IP address to itself (Auto-IP [10]).

Discovery. Discovery is the process of discovering the capabilities of the devices on the network. It can take place in two ways.

First, when a new device gets an IP address and so is connected to the network, the device must multicast discovery messages, advertising its embedded devices and services. This process is called *discovery-advertisement*. Any interested control point in the network can listen to these advertisements and then connect and control the originating devices or only some of their services.

Secondly, when a new control point is established in the network. Such a new control point multicasts a Simple Service Discovery Protocol (SSDP) message [11], searching for available devices and services. All devices in the network must listen to this kind of messages and respond to them whenever any of their services or embedded devices matches the criteria from the SSDP messages. This process is called *discovery-search* [2].

Description. Once discovery is complete and the control point knows about the existence of one device or service, it must also find out how to invoke that device or service. The respective control point retrieves the device description from the URL provided by the device in the discovery message. The UPnP description for a device is expressed in XML and includes vendor-specific information, manufacturer information, a list of any embedded devices or services, as well as URLs for control, eventing, and presentation [2].

Control. Now that the control point has a clear overview of the service and knows how to control it, it can send an action request. The control point sends a control message to the device according to the respective service control description. Control messages are expressed in XML. In response, the service will return action specific values or fault codes [2].

Eventing. Services keep control points informed by sending them event messages. Event messages contain the last update of changed state variables in the service. This process is called eventing [2].

Presentation. Some devices have URLs for presentation. Such an URL can be fetched and then presented in a browser by the control point. According to the device capabilities and URL presentation definition, a user can then see the status of the service and even control it [2].

2.2 Gnutella

A distributed network architecture may be called peer-to-peer (P2P) whenever the participants share a part of their own hardware resources (processing power, storage capacity, network link capacity, printers, etc.) with each other in order to provide the service and content offered by the network (e.g., file sharing or shared workspace for collaboration). Furthermore these resources are accessible by other peers directly, without passing through intermediate entities. The participants in such a network are thus resource providers and at the same time resource requesters (the "servent" concept) [12]. Peer-to-peer file sharing is a particular example of peer-to-peer network. Each peer in a peer-to-peer file sharing network is implemented by a client which uses some distributed search protocol to find other peers as well as the files that are being shared by them. Different protocols for distributed search are being used by peer-to-peer file sharing programs, the most prominent being BitTorrent [13] and Gnutella [14].

Because of the distributed nature of Gnutella and its independency from any central servers, a Gnutella network is highly fault-tolerant. Indeed, a network can work continuously despite the fact that different servents go off-line and back on-line [14]. We describe in what follows the Gnutella protocol [14–16]. The first time a servent wants to join a Gnutella network, its client software must *bootstrap* [17] and thus find at least one other servent (node, peer) in the network. The bootstrap can happen automatically or manually, either out of band or using Gnutella Web caches (caches that include a pre-existing list of addresses of possibly working hosts may be shipped with the Gnutella client software or made available over the Web).

A node connected to a Gnutella network keeps in touch periodically with its (directly connected) neighbours through ping messages. These messages are not only replied to (by pong messages) but they are also propagated to the other interconnected servents.

When a servent receives a ping message, it sends it to the nodes to which it is connected. Once the servent finds at least one active peer in the Gnutella network, it can create an updated list of active servents by observing the ping and the corresponding pong messages.

When a client wants to search for a file (or as we will see in Sect. 4 for a service), it sends a query to all its directly connected neighbour servents (except the one which delivered this query message), which forward the query to their neighbours, and so on. This process repeats throughout the network. A *query message* is the primary mechanism for searching the distributed network. If a servent receives a query and finds a match in its directory, it will respond to it with a *query-hit message*. A query-hit contains enough information for the retrieval of the data matching the corresponding query.

To avoid flooding the network the query messages contain a TTL (Time To Live) field. It is possible that one query reaches a servent more than one time. To avoid serving a query more than once, each query is identified by a unique identification (muid). Before processing a query a servent checks the query's muid against a table of previous muids; a hit causes the query to be dropped.

The query-hit can go back along the reverse path of the query to reach the servent which requested it, or it can be sent directly to the requester.

3 Related Work

Along with summarizing previous work on remote service discovery we also anticipate a bit and take the opportunity to compare the previous research with our solution (which will actually be introduced later in Sect. 4).

3.1 Remote Access to UPnP Devices Using the Atom Publishing Protocol

The network topology of one architecture for remote service discovery in UPnP [6] consists of at least two network segments: the home network and the remote network. The architecture assumes that there is an IP tunnelling mechanism such as a Virtual Private Network (VPN) between the two network segments. The architecture introduces a new element called *UPnP Device Aggregator* which is acting as a proxy for the existing standard UPnP devices. *Enhanced UPnP Devices* or *Control Points* are then UPnP devices or control points which are compatible with this remote service discovery architecture. The UPnP Device Aggregator aggregates information about the services and devices in the local network as an Atom feed, which can then be retrieved (using GET commands) by the enhanced UPnP control points in the remote network. Additionally, a UPnP Device Aggregator can receive information from remote Enhanced UPnP Devices and present them to the local control points. This information can be received by the UPnP Device Aggregator via HTTP POST.

The main shortcoming of this architecture is the need for VPN. Indeed, VPN does not scale well, requiring careful administration of IP addresses and subnetworks [8]. VPN also limits the architecture to the domains within the VPN network (limiting heterogeneity). No such limiting factors are present in our architecture, which is substantially more scalable. In addition, all remote service discovery requests are addressed to the home network, so this architecture can be considered centralized or partially centralized: service coordinators (the UPnP Device Aggregators) register and cache services [7]. By contrast, our architecture is fully distributed: no centralized coordinator is necessary. We note that Gnutella has switched to a hybrid architecture using Ultrapeers [16] for efficiency purposes, but even in this case we obtain a more distributed architecture.

3.2 Presence-Based Remote Service Discovery

An architecture for remote service discovery and control based on presence service (as used in instant messaging and VOIP) was also proposed [8]. A presentity can be anything that can have a presence state (be present or absent); presence information is sent to a presence service, which is a network service that records and distributes presence information. In the remote service discovery architecture based on presence service [8] there are two new functions called *service discovery gateway* and *service virtualizer*. The gateways register local services as presentities in a presence server. They can also retrieve other presentities from the presence server and present them to the service virtualizer. The service virtualizer uses this presence information to virtualize a local service in the local network. That is, a service virtualizer presents a remote service as a local one.

This architecture is partially centralized, as remote service providers and remote service requesters must first find a presence server to register or request a service. Although presence servers (as service coordinators) provide service visibility, the benefit does not come without cost and complexity [7, 18]. By contrast, our architecture is fully distributed.

3.3 Transparent UPnP Interaction between UPnP Gateways

Dynamic Overlay Topology Optimizing Content Search (DOTOCS) [19] enables flexible content searches among UPnP gateways. DOTOCS aims to establish an optimized peer-to-peer overlay network among UPnP gateways. DOTOCS uses a communication protocol between UPnP local networks called transparent interaction solution and described elsewhere [20]: The communication between two connected UPnP local networks across the Internet is accomplished using the Web service technology. A local gateway encapsulates Simple Service Discovery Protocol (SSDP) messages into Simple Object Access Protocol (SOAP) messages and transmit them to another gateway over the global network. A Web service at the destination UPnP gateway extracts the SSDP message and replaces the original IP address (which is not valid in this local network) with the IP address of the gateway itself. The gateway then multicasts this discovery search message in the local UPnP network. If any device responds to that message (meaning that the device has the service demanded by the SSDP message), then the gateway encapsulates that message into another SOAP message and sends it back to the first network. This way one local UPnP network can discover remote services from a different UPnP network.

Scalability between local networks is manageable when this solution is used. However, each gateway multicasts in its local UPnP network any received discovery message (regardless whether the demanded service in that discovery message is locally available or not). This creates substantial traffic in the local network, most of it useless, which reduces scalability. Our protocol does not multicast remote requests to the local network (for indeed the service mirror builder has already discovered the locally available services), so the local UPnP network will not be loaded with spurious messages. Scalability therefore only depends on the Gnutella network (which is scalable to a high degree).

3.4 Peer-to-Peer Caching of Classes of Services

Chakraborty et. al. [21] propose a distributed service discovery protocol based on the concepts of peer-to-peer caching of service advertisements and group-based intelligent forwarding of service requests. Services are described using the Web Ontology Language (OWL). The semantic class/sub-class hierarchy of OWL is used to describe service groups and then this semantic information is used to selectively forward service requests. OWL-based service description also enables increased flexibility in service matching.

While the hierarchical structure of service classes improves efficiency, the protocol is mainly proactive rather than reactive: services need to advertise actively before becoming accessible to the remote devices. We believe that this can easily cause either increased traffic (when the time delay between successive advertisements is low) or increased response time (when the mentioned delays are large). This is all mitigated by the class/sub-class mechanism, but cannot be eliminated altogether. By contrast our architecture is completely reactive, thus minimizing network traffic.

4 A New Distributed Architecture for Remote Service Discovery

Recall that remote services are not present in the current physical location of the controller but are available to the controller upon request. A control point may also reside in a pervasive computing environment with heterogeneous protocols and networks. Even if some otherwise available services in the local domain could not be accessed because of heterogeneity in protocols (networks, ontologies, etc.), the controller may still be able to remotely access services within its capabilities but far from its physical location. In other words, sometimes service discovery protocols could not see all the available services in their domain, but if they could just bridge to neighbour networks (with the same protocols and ontologies) they could accomplish their tasks.

We propose a new architecture that accomplishes remote service discovery in a fully distributed manner i.e., without the need of any centralized, coordinating entity. Our architecture allows the discovery of services in local and remote domains, and offers a solution for automatic discovery and control of remote services. We use UPnP as an example in our architecture, but in fact we try not to depend on any particular service discovery protocol.

Fig. 1 shows our architecture. There are 5 local networks in the figure, labelled from 1 to 5. Each of these local networks offers local services, devices, and control points. These devices, services, and control points are connected with each other locally through UPnP. In each local network there is one special function called *service*

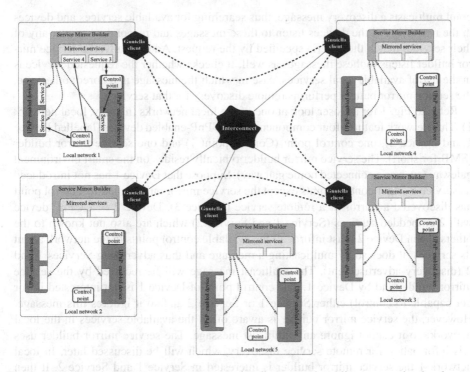

Fig. 1. A distributed architecture for remote service discovery (doted lines connecting local networks show the Gnutella network overlay)

mirror builder. This special function performs the actual remote service discovery and is seen by the local network as just another UPnP-enabled device.

In addition, each local network runs a Gnutella client software. These clients are specialized clients that share local services to the outside world and find services requested by their service mirror builder. The local networks establish a Gnutella network between them. Dotted lines connecting local networks in the figure show the overlay of the Gnutella network.

4.1 Changes to the Local Networks

Our architecture introduces a *service mirror builder* in every local network. The network is an IP based network with all of these devices connected through UPnP (the UPnP protocol with its six steps is described in Sect. 2). *Addressing* is accomplished using the normal UPnP protocol.

Discovery-advertising and *discovery-search* are then performed in the local network as prescribed by the local UPnP protocol. The service mirror builder must be aware of all the available services in the local network, so it never ignores any multicast message. It will also advertise its services (that are all remotely discovered as we will see later) as they become available. During any kind of discovery-search process (that is, whenever a control point becomes interested in a new service) the respective control point multicasts a discovery message, thus searching for available services and devices in the network. All the devices listen to these messages and respond whenever any of their services match the criteria specified by the request. Additionally, the service mirror builder listens to these messages as well. It checks whether the requested service is in the list of available local services, case in which the message is ignored; otherwise, the service mirror builder performs remote discovery for that service.

Refer to Fig. 1 for a closer look at one of the local networks (namely, local network 1). This network features four components: two UPnP-enabled devices (labelled Device 1 and Device 2), one control point (Control point 1) and one service mirror builder (SMB for short). The service mirror builder typically resides on the smart environment gateway (such as a connected home gateway). Suppose that Device 1 has not introduced its service to other control points except the service mirror builder, and its control point has discovered a mirror of a remote service (Service 3). Device 2 is a UPnP device with 2 embedded services (Service 1 and Service 2) which are also not known to the others. Then Device 2 must inform all the available control points in the network about its services; it does so by multicasting a message and thus advertising Services 1 and 2 (discovery-advertisement). The multicast message will be received by the service mirror builder and by Device 1. The control point of Device 1 is not interested in (or not capable to control) either Service 1 or Service 2 and so it ignores this message. However, the service mirror builder is aware of all the available services in the local network, so it cannot ignore any multicast message. The service mirror builder uses this information for remote service discovery, which will be discussed later. In local network 1 the service mirror builder is interested in Service 1 and Service 2. It then sends a message to device 1 to retrieve the description of the two services as per the description UPnP step.

Suppose now that Device 1, Device 2, and the service mirror builder have all discovered each other. Control point 1 then joins the network and obtains an IP address, but has not discovered any services to control yet. In such a case the newly added control point multicasts a Simple Service Discovery Protocol (SSDP) discovery message, thus searching for available services and devices in the network (discovery-search). The devices in the network listen to these messages and respond whenever any of their services match the criteria specified therein. The service mirror builder listens to all these messages and proceeds to remote discovery for the respective service whenever the requested service is not provided locally. In our example, Service 1 is matched with the request of Control point 1. Therefore Device 2 unicasts a response message to Control point 1. Now that Control point 1 has discovered the service, it asks for a description. Once the description is received, Control point 1 can control Service 1 in Device 2.

Consider now that Control point 1 multicasts a discovery-search message requesting a service which is not locally available (Service 4). The service mirror builder will recognize that this service is not locally available, and so it sends a query for that service to the local Gnutella client. The Gnutella client will then pass that query to the Gnutella network (see Sect. 4.2). Once such a service is found, a mirror of that service is made available in the local network. In local network 1 from Fig. 1 the mirrors of the remote services are shown in the service mirror builder box (Services 3 and 4).

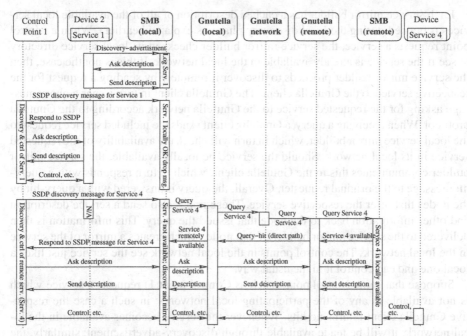

Fig. 2. A sequence diagram detailing the behaviour of our distributed architecture for remote service discovery

After the discovery step (which makes the control points aware of the available services), the control points must find out how to use these available services (*description*). Advertising messages circulated during discovery contain URLs from which the control points can retrieve the description of the respective devices. Once a control point has the device or service description it can invoke actions on that service and get result values in return. Invoking an action in UPnP is a particular instance of Remote Procedure Call [2]. The major focus of this research contribution however is service discovery so we will not discuss service control, eventing and presentation any further.

4.2 Remote Service Discovery

Two major characteristics of pervasive computing are distributedness and mobility. In such an environment we want to connect nodes in a distributed manner and without any dependency to a central server (such as the presence server used in Sect. 3.2). We therefore connect the local networks using Gnutella, a strongly decentralized peer-to-peer system [15].

Gnutella servents can share any type of resources [15]. In our design they are sharing the services available in their local networks. The overlaying Gnutella network (dotted lines in Fig. 1) is established according to the protocol.

Now that both the local networks and the Gnutella network are established, remote service discovery can begin. Such an event happens whenever a control point requests a service which is not locally available. The service mirror builder then activates and tries to remotely discover it.

Each service mirror builder has a cached description of all of the available local services (obtained during the local discovery phase as explained earlier). When a control point requests a service, the service mirror builder checks in its local service directory to see if the service is already available in the local network. If this is not the case, then the service mirror builder proceeds to discover it remotely by sending a request for the respective service to the Gnutella client. The Gnutella client in turn issues a query message asking for the requested service to the Gnutella network according to the Gnutella protocol. When receiving a query, a Gnutella client sends the included service request to the local service mirror builder, which in turn will check the availability of the requested service in its local network. Should the service be locally available, the service mirror builder communicates this to the Gnutella client, which in turn responds with a query-hit message to the original requester. Overall, the query is answered with a query-hit by the nodes that offer the respective service. These nodes also send a service description and other information back to the node that issued the query. This information is then delivered to the service mirror builder of that node, which creates a mirror of the service in the local network. The control points in the local network see the service just likes a local one and can control it in the usual way.

Suppose that some control point (such as Control point 1) requests a service which is not available in any of the participating local networks; in such a case the respective Gnutella client returns no hits. Whenever the service becomes available in the local network, it will be made available through discovery-advertisement; similarly, the Gnutella client will re-issue the corresponding query periodically until either (a) the service becomes available in the local network, (b) the service is discovered remotely, or (c) the control point that requested the service disappears. This mechanism extends the discovery-search mechanism almost transparently (but with some delay).

The functioning of the whole protocol is summarized in Fig. 2.

4.3   Gnutella and UPnP Messages in the New Architecture

We show the possibility of using the Gnutella distributed search protocol to search for services in remote networks (remote services). We do this by discussing the Gnutella and UPnP message structure and the modifications that are needed in our architecture.

In our architecture all local network components communicate and work with each other under UPnP protocol standards. All six steps in UPnP (addressing, discovery, description, control, eventing and presentation) are being done as per the UPnP protocol.

As far as the remote connections are concerned, all servents are working under the Gnutella standards and specification. All Gnutella connect, Gnutella OK, ping and pong messages are exactly according to the available Gnutella protocol. The only differences happen in the Gnutella query and Gnutella query-hit messages (since the original messages are used for requesting for and responding with shared files). We show the structure of these messages in more detail along with recommendations for changing them to work in the new architecture for the purpose of service discovery instead of file sharing.

All of the Gnutella protocol messages, including query and query-hit, include a header with the byte structure described in Table 1(a) [22]. The payload type indicates the type of the message. Other payload types can also be used as long as all the participating servents support them [22]. Payload length shows the size of the payload.

Table 1. Gnutella message header (a) and query message structure (b)

(a)

Bytes	Description
0-15	Message ID/GUID (Globally Unique ID)
16	Payload Type
	0x00 = Ping 0x01 = Pong
	0x02 = Bye 0x40 = Push
	0x80 = Query 0x81 = Query-Hit
17	TTL (Time To Live)
18	Hops
19-22	Payload Length

(b)

Bytes	Description
0-1	Minimum speed
2	Search criteria
Rest	Optional extension block

Table 2. Gnutella query-hit message structure

Bytes	Description	Result set structure:	
0	Number of Hits	Bytes	Description:
1-2	Port	0-3	File Index
3-6	IP Address	4-7	File Size
7-10	Speed	8-	File Name (null-terminated)
11-	Result Set	x	Extensions Block (null-terminated)

The whole Gnutella message should be no more than 4 kB in size. Immediately following the message header is a payload which can be one of the following messages: ping, pong, query, query-hit and push [22]. This message header structure will remain unchanged in our architecture.

The Query Message. Since queries are broadcast to many nodes, servents normally send query messages that are smaller than 256 bytes; however, query messages can be as large as 4 kB. A query message has the structure shown in Table 1(b) [22]. The rest field of a query message is used for the original query which in our case is a query for a remote service. The allowed extension types in the rest field can be specified using the Gnutella Generic Extension Protocol (GGEP), Hash/URN Gnutella Extensions (HUGE), and XML [22]. The Gnutella Generic Extension Protocol (GGEP) allows arbitrary extensions in a Gnutella message; a GGEP block is a framework for other extensions [22].

In a UPnP network service discovery is accomplished using Simple Service Discovery Protocol (SSDP). All SSDP messages are sent using the HTTP protocol. The HTTP and Gnutella protocols are both application layer protocols. The fundamental data in a SSDP discovery search or discovery-advertisement message (in a UPnP network) contains a few essential specifics about the device or one of its services (its type, universally unique identifier, etc.) [11]. All this information can be readily encoded in a GGEP extension by the service mirror builders and then sent to the Gnutella network agent. Then the Gnutella network agent can put this GGEP-formatted information in the Rest part of a Gnutella query message and send it to the Gnutella network.

The Query-hit Message. The structure of a query-hit message is shown in Table 2 [22]. The result set is used for the response to the query; its structure is also shown in the table.

The first three fields of the result set are defined specifically to hold information about a requested file or file portion, as Gnutella is mainly used for file sharing. In our case it is possible to redefine these fields; to prevent increased complexity and extra work to define a new specification, we recommend that these fields be filled with some default labels. In other words these fields of the result set are simply ignored.

GGEP, HUGE, and plain text metadata are all allowed in the extension block. We recommend that the response messages from service mirror builders be formatted in a GGEP extension and sent back to the network in the extensions field of the query-hit message.

5   Protocol Independence and Performance Considerations

The use of particular protocols (UPnP and Gnutella) are in fact necessary only for illustration purposes. The architecture described here can be in particular adapted in a trivial manner to handle any local service discovery protocol.

Through the use of UPnP we have included in our discussion a comprehensive set of features for the local service discovery protocol, but this is done without loss of generality: those protocols that lack some of the features can still function in our framework, which is agnostic with respect to which of the described services are actually used. Conversely, to our knowledge no protocol provides more features than the ones discussed here.

The peer-to-peer architecture is clearly immaterial to the discussion, as long as the architecture is capable of maintaining an ad-hoc network, propagating requests for distributed search throughout the network, and handling responses to such requests (all peer-to-peer protocols do). The implementer can in effect choose any other peer-to-peer protocol.

The only somehow substantial changes that are necessary to switch protocols are related to the form of the messages passed along between the peer-to-peer servents. The message structure outlined in Sect. 4.3 is specific to Gnutella; should another peer-to-peer network be chosen, this structure will likely change. Further encapsulation might be needed to pass along messages generated by different local service discovery protocol, though this is unlikely.

The performance of our architecture is the same as the performance of the underlying Gnutella (or more generally peer-to-peer) network. All the advantages (and also disadvantages) of Gnutella are thus maintained. This is actually one reason for our choice of peer-to-peer protocol. Indeed, Gnutella is one of the most studied such a protocol. Many changes and refinements have been added to it throughout the years to make it more efficient. Such refinements and techniques include Ultrapeers and Leaves, Distributed Hash Table, Query Routing Protocol (QRP), and so on. This all helps to reduce the traffic in the Gnutella network and generally increase the efficiency of the protocol. These refinements can be trivially added to our architecture. Future refinements of the protocol can also be readily integrated. It can be argued that Gnutella is not fully distributed, since the bootstrapping process is centralized. However, such a centralized mechanism is used for empirical reasons (works well in most cases), but different bootstrapping techniques exist, including random address probing and network layer probing with anycast or multicast messages [23]. These techniques can be readily used should a fully distributed architecture be necessary.

We already mentioned the advantages of our approach compared to the only other peer-to-peer approach known to us [21]. Indeed, our approach is reactive and so we believe that it minimizes the network traffic in the general case. True, a "sweet spot" can probably be achieved in the ontology-based approach [21] by changing the time delay between advertisements. Such a "sweet spot" has the potential of offering a better performance; however, it is also likely that different circumstances may require different values, making a global solution unlikely. By contrast Gnutella is designed to offer consistent performance in many circumstances; indeed, optimization adjustments are already implemented! We thus believe that overall our solution offers more consistent performance, in addition to being able to benefit from any future improvement of the Gnutella protocol (as mentioned above).

Classifying services based on an ontology [21] does reduce network traffic and has the potential of improving the overall efficiency. We believe that such a technique is orthogonal to the service discovery mechanism. We thus believe that the ontology-based approach can be used equally effectively in out setting. Doing this however is a subject of future research.

6 Conclusions

Service discovery plays an important role in pervasive computing. At the same time pervasive computing creates many challenges for service discovery protocols, one of them being remote service discovery. We introduced a new approach to remote service discovery that is flexible, decentralized, and fully distributed.

The core part of the new architecture is the new function in a UPnP network called service mirror builder and its cooperation with a specialized Gnutella client software to discover remote services and then present these remote services as local ones. Conversely, a service mirror builder can also control local services to serve them as remote services for other, remote service mirror builders. The service mirror builder communicates with the specialized Gnutella client software (from the point of view of the local network however the service mirror builder is just a UPnP-enabled device). We used UPnP for illustration purposes, but the service mirror builder can be defined based on *any* service discovery protocol (Bluetooth, Apple Bonjour, etc.). Our solution is in fact general and not dependent on any particular service discovery protocol.

We propose Gnutella as a distributed search protocol for discovering remote services. The very design of a Gnutella network as a decentralized and distributed protocol moves this remote service discovery architecture one step ahead toward truly distributed computing. Our architecture is also readily amenable to improvements in either the underlying peer-to-peer protocol or the ontology-based classification of services (or indeed both). We therefore believe that our approach offers better compatibility with pervasive computing.

References

1. Weiser, M.: Some computer science issues in ubiquitous computing. Communications of the ACM 36, 75–84 (1993)
2. Understanding Universal Plug and Play (2000), White paper: http://www.upnp.org/download/UPNP_understandingUPNP.doc
3. Bluetooth Special Interest Group (SIG): Specification of the Bluetooth System Version 1.1 (2001), http://www.tscm.com/BluetoothSpec.pdf
4. Sun Microsystems: Jini Technology Core Platform Specification Version 1.2 (2001), http://www-csag.ucsd.edu/teaching/cse291s03/Readings/core1_2.pdf
5. Zhu, F., Mutka, M., Ni, L.: Service discovery in pervasive computing environments. Pervasive Computing 4, 81–90 (2005)
6. Belimpasakis, P., Stirbu, V.: Remote access to universal plug and play (UPnP) devices utilizing the Atom publishing protocol. In: International Conference on Networking and Services, p. 59. IEEE Computer Society (2007)
7. Feng, W.: Remote Service Provision for Connected Homes. PhD thesis, De Montfort University (2010)
8. Häber, A.: Remote Service Discovery and Control for Ubiquitous Service Environments in Next-Generation Networks. PhD thesis, University of Agder (2010)
9. Buyukkaya, E., Abdallah, M., Cavagna, R.: VoroGame: A hybrid P2P architecture for massively multiplayer games. In: 6th IEEE Consumer Communications and Networking Conference (CCNC), pp. 1–5. IEEE (2009)
10. Cheshire, S., Aboba, B., Guttman, E.: Dynamic Configuration of IPv4 Link-Local Addresses. Internet Engineering Task Force, RFC 3927 (2005)
11. UPnP forum: UPnP Device Architecture 1.1 (2008), http://www.upnp.org/specs/arch/UPnP-arch-DeviceArchitecture-v1.1.pdf
12. Schollmeier, R.: A definition of peer-to-peer networking for the classification of peer-to-peer architectures and applications. In: 1st International Conference on Peer-to-Peer Computing, pp. 101–102 (2001)
13. Cohen, B.: The BitTorrent Protocol Specification (2008), http://www.bittorrent.org/beps/bep_0003.html
14. Clip2 Distributed Search Services: The Gnutella Protocol Specification Version 0.4 (2003), http://www.stanford.edu/class/cs244b/gnutella_protocol_0.4.pdf
15. Ilie, D.: Gnutella Network Traffic-Measurements and Characteristics. Master's thesis, Blekinge Tekniska Högskola (2006)
16. Oram, A.: Peer-to-Peer: Harnessing the Benefits of a Disruptive Technology. O'Reilly Media (2001)
17. Gtk-Gnutella: Gnutella Bootstrapping (2011), http://gtk-gnutella.sourceforge.net/en/?page=bootstrap
18. Engelstad, P., Zheng, Y., Tore, J.: Service discovery and name resolution architectures for on-demand MANETs. In: 23rd International Conference on Distributed Computing Systems, pp. 736–742. IEEE Computer Society (2003)
19. Kawamoto, E., Kadowaki, K., Koita, T., Sato, K.: Content sharing among UPnP gateways on unstructured P2P network using dynamic overlay topology optimization. In: 6th IEEE Consumer Communications and Networking Conference (CCNC), pp. 1–5. IEEE (2009)

20. Ogawa, M., Hayakawa, H., Koita, T., Sato, K.: Transparent UPnP interactions over global network. In: Proceedings of SPIE, vol. 6794 pp. 67944P (2007)
21. Chakraborty, D., Joshi, A., Yesha, Y., Finin, T.: Toward distributed service discovery in pervasive computing environments. IEEE Transactions on Mobile Computing 5, 97–112 (2006)
22. Klingberg, T., Manfredi, R.: Gnutella 0.6. Network Working Group (2002)
23. Conrad, M., Hof, H.-J.: A generic, self-organizing, and distributed bootstrap service for peer-to-peer networks. In: Hutchison, D., Katz, R.H. (eds.) IWSOS 2007. LNCS, vol. 4725, pp. 59–72. Springer, Heidelberg (2007)

Model Checking Combined Fragments
of Sequence Diagrams

Hui Shen, Mark Robinson, and Jianwei Niu

Department of Computer Science,
University of Texas at San Antonio, San Antonio, Texas, U.S.A.
{hshen,mrobinso,niu}cs.utsa.edu

Abstract. Graphical representations of scenarios using the Combined Fragments of UML Sequence Diagrams, serve as a well-accepted means for expressing an aggregation of multiple traces encompassing complex and concurrent behaviors. However, Combined Fragments increase the difficulty of analysis of scenarios. This paper introduces an approach to formally verify all the Combined Fragments, and nested Combined Fragments using model checking.

Keywords: Modeling, Model Checking, Sequence Diagram, Concurrency & Communication.

1 Introduction

In software development process, models enable software engineers to detect errors during early stage so as to improve the system quality. Scenario-based models have been widely employed for the description of interactions among environmental actors (*e.g.*, human beings) and the components (aka Lifeline) of the software systems through the exchange of messages. UML Sequence Diagrams, which graphically depict scenarios, serve as well-accepted and intuitive media among software engineers and tool builders. UML 2 provides many major structural control constructs, including Combined Fragments and Interaction Use, to allow multiple, complex scenarios to be aggregated in a single Sequence Diagram. However, Combined Fragments introduce concurrent behaviors, making analysis of the Sequence Diagrams difficult for the following reasons.

Combined Fragments permit different types of control flow, such as interleaving and branching, increasing a Sequence Diagram's expressiveness. Further, the Combined Fragments can also be nested to provide more complex control flows. These make it difficult to predict what behavior are represented. For example, if a Combined Fragment presenting branching behavior is nested within a Combined Fragment presenting iteration behavior, different choices may be made in different iterations. The semantics of Sequence Diagram with Combined Fragments is not formally defined compared to their precise syntax descriptions [1], making it is hard to derive the traces from Sequence Diagrams. Thus, subtle errors from concurrency can easily be introduced to Sequence Diagrams to evade discovery via manual inspection.

To address these problems, we introduce an automated technique to facilitate the verification of Sequence Diagrams by leveraging the analytical powers of model checking.

J. Cordeiro, S. Hammoudi, and M. van Sinderen (Eds.): ICSOFT 2012, CCIS 411, pp. 96–111, 2013.

Working towards similar goals, many researchers have verified different scenario-based models, including Sequence Diagram, Message Sequence Chart (MSC), and Live Sequence Chart (LSC). However, the previous work does not consider all the aspects of Combined Fragments. Our approach supports all the features of Combined Fragments, including all 12 Interaction Operators, nested Combined Fragments, both asynchronous and synchronous Messages, and Interaction Constraints.

We devise an approach to codify the semantics of Sequence Diagrams and Combined Fragments in the input language of NuSMV by deconstructing Sequence Diagrams and Combined Fragments to obtain fine-grained syntactic constructs (see section 2 and 3). We formally describe each Combined Fragment in terms of NuSMV [2] modules (see section 4). The model checking mechanism can explore all possible traces specified in the Sequence Diagram, verifying if the desired properties are satisfied. We have developed a tool suite to implement all of the techniques and have validated our technique by analyzing and discovering violations in two design examples taken from an insurance industry software application (see section 5). We have also created an Occurrence Specification Trace Diagram generator that automatically produces Sequence Diagram visualizations from NuSMV-produced counterexamples. This automation will increase the accessibility of our approach by allowing software engineers to remain focused in the realm of Sequence Diagrams.

2   UML 2 Sequence Diagram

In this section, we outline the syntax and semantics of a Sequence Diagram with Combined Fragments provided by OMG [1]. As the first step of defining a Sequence Diagram using NuSMV modules, we precisely define the semantics of Sequence Diagram with Combined Fragments, forming the basis of expressing the semantics in term of NuSMV models. We begin with the basic Sequence Diagram, then discuss the structured control constructs, including Combined Fragments and Interaction Use.

2.1   Basic Sequence Diagram

We refer to a Sequence Diagram without Combined Fragments as a basic Sequence Diagram (see figure 1a for an example with annotated syntactic constructs). A **Lifeline** is a vertical line representing a participating object. A horizontal line between Lifelines is a **Message**. A Message is the specification of an occurrence of a message type within the Sequence Diagram, while a message type is the signature of the form ⟨*message name, source Lifeline, target Lifeline*⟩. Within a Sequence Diagram, a message type can occur multiple times, which are associated with multiple Messages. Each Message is sent from its source Lifeline to its target Lifeline and has two endpoints. Each endpoint is an intersection with a Lifeline and is called an **Occurrence Specification (OS)**, denoting the specification of an occurrence of an event within a certain context, *i.e.*, a Sequence Diagram. Accordingly, multiple OSs within a Sequence Diagram can be associated with an event. Each Message is defined by its sending OS and receiving OS. We associate each OS with a location of a Lifeline. As each location is uniquely defined, each OS is uniquely defined. Thus, each Message is uniquely defined by its sending OS and receiving OS. OSs can also be the beginning or end of an **Execution Specification**, indicating

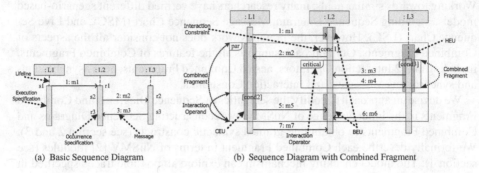

(a) Basic Sequence Diagram   (b) Sequence Diagram with Combined Fragment

Fig. 1. Sequence Diagram Syntax

the period during which a participant performs a behavior within a Lifeline, which is represented as a thin rectangle on the Lifeline.

The semantics of a basic Sequence Diagram is defined by a set of traces. A trace is a sequence of OSs expressing Message exchange among multiple Lifelines. We identify four orthogonal semantic aspects that must be considered for the basic Sequence Diagram [3,1,4]

1. Each OS can execute only once, *i.e.*, each OS is unique within a Sequence Diagram.
2. On each Lifeline, OSs execute in their graphical order from top to bottom.
3. For a single Message, the sending OS must take place before the receiving OS does.
4. In a Sequence Diagram, only one object can execute an OS at a time, *i.e.*, OSs on different Lifelines are interleaved.

Messages are of two types: asynchronous and synchronous. The source Lifeline can continue to send or receive other Messages after an asynchronous Message is sent. If a synchronous Message is sent, the source Lifeline blocks until it receives the target Lifeline's response [1].

2.2 Combined Fragment

Both Combined Fragments and Interaction Use are structured control constructs introduced in UML 2. A **Combined Fragment** (CF) is a solid-outline rectangle, which consists of an **Interaction Operator** and one or more **Interaction Operands**. Figure 1b shows example CFs with annotated syntactic constructs. A CF can enclose all, or part of, Lifelines in a Sequence Diagram. The Interaction Operands are separated by dashed horizontal lines. The Interaction Operator is shown in a pentagon in the upper left corner of the rectangle. OSs, CFs, and Interaction Operands are collectively called **Interaction Fragments**. An Interaction Operand may contain a boolean expression which is called an **Interaction Constraint** or Constraint. An Interaction Constraint is shown in a square bracket covering the Lifeline where the first OS will happen. BEU, HEU and CEU are defined in Section 3. An **Interaction Use** construct allows one Sequence Diagram to refer to another Sequence Diagram. The referring Sequence Diagram copies the contents of the referenced Sequence Diagram.

We identify three independent semantic rules general to all CFs, in the sense that these rules do not constrain each other.

1. OSs and CFs, are combined using Weak Sequencing (defined below). On a single Lifeline, a CF's preceding Interaction Fragment must complete the execution prior to the CF's execution, and the CF's succeeding Interaction Fragment must execute subsequently.
2. Within a CF, the order of the OSs and CFs within each Operand is maintained if the Constraint of the Operand evaluates to $True$; otherwise, the Operand is excluded.
3. The CF does not execute when the Constraints of all the Operands evaluate to $False$. Thus, the CF's preceding Interaction Fragment and succeeding Interaction Fragment are ordered by Weak Sequencing.

2.3 Interaction Operator

The semantics of each CF Operator determines the execution order of all the Operands. Each Operator has its specific semantic implications regarding the execution of the OSs enclosed by the CF on the covered Lifelines. The Operators are summarized as follows: **Alternatives**: one of the Operands whose Interaction Constraints evaluate to $True$ is nondeterministically chosen to execute. **Option**: its sole Operand executes if the Interaction Constraint is $True$. **Break**: its sole Operand executes if the Interaction Constraint evaluates to $True$. Otherwise, the remainder of the enclosing Interaction Fragment executes. **Parallel**: the OSs on a Lifeline within different Operands may be interleaved, but the ordering imposed by each Operand must be maintained separately. **Critical Region**: the OSs on a Lifeline within its sole Operand must not be interleaved with any other OSs on the same Lifeline. **Loop**: its sole Operand will execute for at least the minimum count (lower bound) and no more than the maximum count (upper bound) as long as the Interaction Constraint is $True$. **Assertion**: the OSs on a Lifeline within its sole Operand must occur immediately after the preceding OSs. **Negative**: its Operand represents forbidden traces. **Strict Sequencing**: in any Operand except the first one, OSs cannot execute until the previous Operand completes. **Weak Sequencing**: *on a Lifeline*, the OSs within an Operand cannot execute until the OSs in the previous Operand complete, the OSs from *different Operands on different Lifelines* may take place in any order (cf. Strict Sequencing). **Consider**: any message types other than what is specified within the CF is ignored. **Ignore**: the specified messages types are ignored within the CF.

The semantics of the seq Sequence Diagram is defined by two sets of traces, one containing a set of valid traces, denoted as $Val(seq)$, and the other containing a set of invalid traces, denoted as $Inval(seq)$. The intersection of these two sets is empty, *i.e.*, $Val(seq) \cap Inval(seq) = \emptyset$.

3 Sequence Diagram Deconstruction

To facilitate codifying the semantics of Sequence Diagrams and nested CFs in NuSMV models, we show how to deconstruct a Sequence Diagram and CFs to obtain fine-grained syntactic constructs. Eichner *et al.* have defined the Maximal Independent Set in [5] to deconstruct a Sequence Diagram into fragments, each of which covers multiple Lifelines. Their proposed semantics defines that entering a CF has to be done synchronously by all the Lifelines, *i.e.*, each CF is connected with adjacent OSs and CFs using Strict Sequencing. Recall that CFs can be nested within other CFs. OSs and CFs directly enclosed in the same CF or Sequence Diagram are combined using Weak Sequencing, constraining their orders with respect to each individual Lifeline only [1]. To express the semantics of Weak Sequencing, we further deconstruct a Sequence Diagram into syntactic constructs on each Lifeline, which also helps us to define the semantics of nested CFs.

We project every CF cf_m onto each of its covered Lifelines l_i to obtain a **compositional execution unit** (CEU), which is denoted by $cf_m \uparrow_{l_i}$. (The shaded rectangle on Lifeline *L1* in figure 1b shows an example).

Definition 1. A CEU is given by a three tuple $\langle l_i, oper, setEU \rangle$, where l_i is the Lifeline, onto which we project the CF, *oper* is the Interaction Operator of the CF, and *setEU* is the set of execution units, one for each Operand op_n enclosed in the CF on Lifeline l_i.

Every Operand op_n of CF cf_m is projected onto each of its covered Lifelines l_i to obtain an **execution unit** (EU) while projecting cf_m onto l_i, denoted by $op_n \uparrow_{l_i}$. If the projected Interaction Operand contains a nested CF, a **hierarchical execution unit** (HEU) is obtained; otherwise a **basic execution unit** (BEU) is obtained, *i.e.*, an EU is a BEU if it does not contain any other EUs. (The lower shaded rectangle on Lifeline *L2* in figure 1b shows an example of a BEU and the shaded rectangle on Lifeline *L3* shows an example of an HEU).

Definition 2. A BEU u is given by a pair, $\langle E_u, cond \rangle$, in which E_u is a finite set of OSs on Lifeline l_i enclosed in Operand op_n, which are ordered by the locations associated with them, and *cond* is the Interaction Constraint of the Operand. *cond* is *True* when there is no Interaction Constraint.

Definition 3. An HEU is given by $\langle setCEU, setBEU, cond \rangle$, where *setCEU* is the set of CEUs directly enclosed in the HEU, *i.e.*, the CEUs nested within any element of *setCEU* are not considered. *setBEU* is the set of BEUs that are directly enclosed in the HEU.

Projecting a Sequence Diagram onto each enclosing Lifeline also obtains an EU whose Constraint is *True*. The EU is an HEU if the Sequence Diagram contains CFs, otherwise, it is a BEU. In an HEU, we also group the OSs between two adjacent CEUs or prior to the first CEU or after the last CEU on the same level into BEUs, which inherit the parent HEU's Constraint, *cond*. (The upper shaded rectangle on Lifeline *L2* in figure 1b shows an example). The constituent BEU(s) and CEU(s) within an HEU execute sequentially, complying with their graphical order, as do the OSs in the BEU.

4   Verifying Sequence Diagrams via NuSMV

In this section, we develop techniques to translate Sequence Diagrams into the input language of NuSMV. The NuSMV model preserves the structure of the Sequence Diagrams (*e.g.*, Lifelines and CFs), which makes it easier to demonstrate that the semantics of the original notation is maintained.

4.1 NuSMV Overview

NuSMV is a model checking tool, which exhaustively explores all executions of a finite model to determine if a temporal logic property holds. For a property that does not hold, a counterexample is produced showing an error trace. A NuSMV model consists of one main module and may include other modules with formal parameters. An instance of a module can be created using the **VAR** declaration within main module or other module to create a modular hierarchy. To access variables of instance modules, the instance name with **. (DOT)** can be used to follow by the variable name. The composition of multiple modules can be parallel or interleaving.

NuSMV variables must be of finite types, declared inside each module. The initial states are defined by using an **init** statement of the form *init(x) := EXP*, which defines the value or set of values x can assume initially. Transitions are defined by using the **next** statements of the form *next(x) := EXP*, which defines the value or set of values that x can assume in the following state. All the transitions in a module execute concurrently in each step. Derived variables (*i.e.*, macros) are defined by using **DEFINE** statements of the form *x := EXP* and they are replaced by *EXP* in each state. The system's invariant is represented with the **INVAR** statement, which is a boolean expression satisfied by each state.

4.2 Mapping Overview

We base the mapping of a Sequence Diagram to the input language of NuSMV on syntactic deconstruction. A Sequence Diagram is represented as the main module. We map the Lifelines into respective NuSMV modules, which are instantiated and declared in the main module. Recall that a CF is projected onto each of its covered Lifelines to obtain a CEU. Accordingly, its Operand on each of the covered Lifelines forms an EU. Both CEUs and EUs are represented as NuSMV modules.

Each CEU is declared as a module instance, which we call a submodule in its Lifeline module. To enforce that multiple CEUs at the same level on each Lifeline adhere to their graphical order, we define a derived variable, *flag_final*, for each CEU module, to indicate whether the CEU completes its execution (the CF semantic rule 1). A CEU is composed of one or more EUs, each of which is instantiated as a submodule inside the CEU module. The execution order of multiple EUs (*i.e.*, the transfer of control among them) is determined by the Interaction Operator that composes them into the CEU (the translation of each Operator is discussed later in this section). In the case that a Sequence Diagram contains nested CFs (*i.e.*, a CEU consisting of an EU that encloses other CEUs), we map each enclosed CEU as a submodule of the containing EU's module. This procedure is recursively applied until all CEUs and EUs are mapped accordingly.

The semantic rules for a basic Sequence Diagram defined in section 2.1 are codified using NuSMV modules for Lifelines or EUs, and an INVAR statement. Within Lifeline or EU modules, a directly enclosed OS is represented as a boolean variable, which initializes to *False* (note that a CEU module does not contain OS variables). Once an OS occurs, its value is set to *True* and then to *False* in all the following states. This value transition expresses the fact that an OS can occur only once in the Sequence Diagram (the semantic rule 1). To record the execution history of OSs, we introduce an enumerated variable, *state*, for each Lifeline and EU module, expressing that respective OSs have taken place (the semantic rule 2). A CEU module contains one boolean variable, *cond*, for each of its EUs to represent the Interaction Constraint of the EU.

To express the interleaving semantics among Lifelines, we introduce an INVAR statement in the main module to assert that at most one OS on one of the Lifelines can take place in each step (the semantic rule 4). A boolean variable *chosen* is used for each Lifeline to restrict that: (1) a Lifeline is chosen only if it is enabled, *i.e.*, there is an OS that is ready to take place on the Lifeline, represented by the derived variable *enabled*; (2) either only one Lifeline can be chosen to execute an OS in each step if Lifelines are enabled (*i.e.*, before all OSs on the Lifelines have occurred); or no Lifeline can be chosen when all Lifelines are not enabled and all *chosen* variables remain *False* thereafter. A sending OS is enabled to execute if and only if the OSs prior to it on the same Lifeline have already occurred. A receiving OS is enabled to execute if and only if the OSs prior to it on the same Lifeline and the sending OS of the same Message have already occurred (the semantic rules 2 and 3). To execute the OSs enclosed in CFs, the variable *chosen* for each Lifeline is passed to the CEU and EU modules on that Lifeline as a parameter.

4.3   Basic Sequence Diagram with Asynchronous Messages

In this subsection, we illustrate our mapping strategy with an example basic Sequence Diagram as shown in figure 1a. Figure 2 shows the NuSMV description of the example, which contains a main module for the Sequence Diagram. We map the three Lifelines to three modules, which are instantiated as submodules l_L1, l_L2, and l_L3 in the main module. We show the implementation of module $L2$ here. Module $L2$ takes modules $L1$, $L3$ as parameters. Three OSs on Lifeline $L2$ are defined as boolean variables OS_r1, OS_s2, and OS_r3 in the VAR section. We define each OS as OS_sx or OS_rx, where s and r denote they are sending or receiving OSs, and x is the corresponding Message name. The enumerated variable *state* has four values, including an initial value *sinit* and three values to record the execution of the three respective OSs. A derived variable *enabled* for each OS represents the enabling condition of the OS by using the variable *state* in the DEFINE section. For instance, $r3\_enabled$ for OS $r3$ is *True* if and only if the sending OS of Message $m3$ and the preceding OS, OS_s2, on Lifeline $L2$ have occurred, *i.e.*, *state* on Lifelines $L2$ and $L3$ set to $s2$ and $s3$ respectively. The Lifeline $L2$ can be enabled if and only if one of $r1$, $s2$, and $r3$ is enabled. The variable *flag_final* checks whether the last OS, $r3$, on $L2$ takes place (*i.e.*, *state* sets to $r3$). If so, all OSs in module $L2$ have occurred. The ASSIGN section defines the transition relation of module $L2$. For example, OS_r3 is set to *False* initially. When it is chosen and enabled, it is set to *True*. It is set to *False* in the subsequent states to represent that an OS can execute exactly once. OS_r1 and OS_s2 take the same transition as OS_r3. Variable *state* is set to $r1$ in the same state where OS_r1 occurs.

```
MODULE main                          DEFINE
 VAR                                  r1_enabled := state=sinit&L1.state=s1;
  1_L1 : L1(1_L2, 1_L3);             s2_enabled := state=r1;
  1_L2 : L2(1_L1, 1_L3);             r3_enabled := state=s2&L3.state=s3;
  1_L3 : L3(1_L1, 1_L2);             enabled := r1_enabled|s2_enabled|r3_enabled;
 INVAR                                flag_final := state=r3;
  ((1_L1.chosen -> 1_L1.enabled)     ASSIGN
  &(1_L2.chosen -> 1_L2.enabled)     init(state) := sinit;
  &(1_L3.chosen -> 1_L3.enabled)     next(state) := case
  &((1_L1.chosen&!1_L2.chosen&!1_L3.chosen)    state=sinit & next(OS_r1)  :r1;
   |(!1_L1.chosen&1_L2.chosen&!1_L3.chosen)    state=r1 & next(OS_s2)     :s2;
   |(!1_L1.chosen&!1_L2.chosen&1_L3.chosen)    state=s2 & next(OS_r3)     :r3;
   |(!1_L1.enabled&!1_L2.enabled&!1_L3.enabled)))  1                       :state;
                                       esac;
MODULE L2(L1, L3)                      ...
 VAR                                  init(OS_r3) := FALSE;
  OS_r1 : boolean;                    next(OS_r3) := case
  OS_s2 : boolean;                     chosen & r3_enabled    :TRUE;
  OS_r3 : boolean;                     OS_r3                  :FALSE;
  state : {sinit, r1, s2, r3};         1                      :OS_r3;
  chosen : boolean;                   esac;
```

Fig. 2. Basic Sequence Diagram to NuSMV

4.4 Basic Sequence Diagram with Synchronous Messages

Sequence Diagram with synchronous Messages restricts that the sending Lifeline blocks until a reply Message is received. We introduce a boolean variable, *isBlock*, for each Lifeline to capture this semantic aspect. All OSs on a Lifeline include *isBlock* as an enabling condition, thus preventing the OSs from occurring while *isBlock* is *True*.

4.5 Combined Fragments

A CF enclosing multiple Lifelines is projected onto all the Lifelines to obtain a collection of CEUs, one for each Lifeline. A CEU contains a collection of EUs, one for each Operand on the same Lifeline. To preserve the structure of the Sequence Diagram during translation, we map a CF to NuSMV submodules, one for each Lifeline module, while the EUs are mapped to NuSMV sub-submodules of their parent CEU submodule separately. We implement the Interaction Constraint for each Operand with a boolean variable *cond*. We do not control the value of *cond* until the Operand is entered, representing the fact that a condition may change during the execution of the Sequence Diagram.

If *cond* evaluates to *True*, the Operand is entered, otherwise, the Operand is skipped (the CF semantic rule 2). Afterwards, the value of *cond* stays the same. While there is no Constraint in an Operand, *cond* is defined as constant *True*. An extra variable *op_eva* for each Operand indicates its respective execution status, including "not ready" (the OSs that may happen prior to the Operand on the Lifeline have taken place) by enumeration element *-1*, "ready but not enabled" (the Constraint evaluates to *False*) by enumeration element *0*, and "start" (Constraint evaluates to *True*) by enumeration element *1*.

```
MODULE main
VAR
 l_L1 : L1(l_L2, l_L3);
 l_L2 : L2(l_L1, l_L3);
 l_L3 : L3(l_L1, l_L2);
INVAR
 ( (l_L1.chosen -> l_L1.enabled)
 & (l_L2.chosen -> l_L2.enabled)
 & (l_L3.chosen -> l_L3.enabled)
 & ( (l_L1.chosen & !l_L2.chosen & !l_L3.chosen)
   | (!l_L1.chosen & l_L2.chosen & !l_L3.chosen)
   | (!l_L1.chosen & !l_L2.chosen & l_L3.chosen)
   | (!l_L1.enabled & !l_L2.enabled & !l_L3.enabled)))
INVAR
 ( (l_L1.CF1.op1.chosen -> l_L1.CF1.op1.enabled)
 & (l_L1.CF1.op2.chosen -> l_L1.CF1.op2.enabled)
 & ( (l_L1.CF1.op1.chosen & !l_L1.CF1.op2.chosen)
   | (!l_L1.CF1.op1.chosen & l_L1.CF1.op2.chosen)
   | (!l_L1.CF1.op1.enabled & !l_L1.CF1.op2.enabled)))
INVAR
 ( (l_L2.CF1.op1.chosen -> l_L2.CF1.op1.enabled)
 & (l_L2.CF1.op2.chosen -> l_L2.CF1.op2.enabled))
 & ( (l_L2.CF1.op1.chosen & !l_L2.CF1.op2.chosen)
   | (!l_L2.CF1.op1.chosen & l_L2.CF1.op2.chosen)
   | (!l_L2.CF1.op1.enabled & !l_L2.CF1.op2.enabled)))
INVAR
 ( (l_L3.CF1.op1.chosen -> l_L3.CF1.op1.enabled)
 & (l_L3.CF1.op2.chosen -> l_L3.CF1.op2.enabled))
 & ( (l_L3.CF1.op1.chosen & !l_L3.CF1.op2.chosen)
   | (!l_L3.CF1.op1.chosen & l_L3.CF1.op2.chosen)
   | (!l_L3.CF1.op1.enabled & !l_L3.CF1.op2.enabled)))

MODULE L2(L1, L3)
VAR
 CF1 : par_L2(state, chosen, L1.CF1, L3.CF1);
 ...
DEFINE
 r7_enabled := state=r1 & CF1.flag_final & L1.state=s7;
 enabled := r1_enabled | r7_enabled | CF1.enabled;
 ...

MODULE par_L2(state, L2_chosen, par_L1, par_L3)
VAR
 op1 : par_op1_L2(L2_chosen, par_L1.op1, par_L3.op1, op1_eva);
 op2 : par_op2_L2(L2_chosen, par_L1.op2, par_L3.op2, par_L1.op2_eva,
                              state, op1.CF2.op1.isCritical);
 cond1 : boolean;
 op1_eva : -1..1;
DEFINE
 enabled := op1.enabled | op2.enabled;
 flag_final := op1.flag_final & op2.flag_final;
ASSIGN
 init(op1_eva) := -1;
 next(op1_eva) := case
  op1_eva=-1 & next(state)=r1 & !next(cond1) :0;
  op1_eva=-1 & next(state)=r1 &  next(cond1) :1;
  1                                          :op1_eva;
 esac;
 init(cond1) := {TRUE, FALSE};
 next(cond1) := case
  op1_eva=-1                     :{TRUE, FALSE};
  op1_eva!=-1                    :cond1;
  1                             :cond1;
 esac;
```

Fig. 3. NuSMV module for Parallel

cond is evaluated when *op_eva* evaluates to either *0* or *1*. Both *cond* and *op_eva* for each Operand are instantiated and declared in the CEU module on the Lifeline where the Interaction Constraint of the Operand is located. The value of *op_eva* is passed to other CEUs of the same CF as parameters, which is further passed to all the EUs of the same Operand to coordinate multiple EUs. From the deconstruction of Sequence Diagrams and CFs (see section 3), we define the OSs as boolean variables in the respective EUs that directly enclose them, instead of the CEUs; OSs that are not enclosed in any CF are declared as boolean variables in their Lifeline module.

Concurrency. In a Parallel CF, the Operands are interleaved, which is captured using a strategy similar to the implementation of interleaved Lifelines modules. We introduce a boolean variable *chosen* for each EU module to indicate whether the EU is chosen to execute. We add an INVAR statement for each CEU to assert that (1) either only one EU module is chosen to execute or no EUs are enabled (*i.e.*, all EUs have completed execution or their Constraints evaluate to *False*), and (2) an EU module can be chosen only if it is enabled (*i.e.*, an OS within the EU is enabled to execute). All INVAR statements are combined using logical conjunctions to form a global invariant in the main module.

Figure 1b shows an example Sequence Diagram, in which a Parallel contains a Critical Region. The implementation of its main module and the modules of Lifeline *L2* and its CEU of the Parallel are shown in figure 3. In the module of Lifeline *L2*, the Parallel's CEU module is initialized as a module instance. Two EUs of the Parallel's Operands are initialized as two module instances within its CEU module.

In the Parallel, the Interaction Constraint of its Operand, *op1*, is located on *L2*. Thus, *cond1* for *op1* is initialized and declared in the Parallel's CEU module on *L2*. It is set to the value of the evaluation step and remains that value in the following steps. Variable *op1_eva* is initialized to *-1*, and then is set depending on the value of *cond1* when entering the CEU, *i.e.*, it is set to *1* if *cond1* evaluates to *True* or *0* otherwise. In each EU module of the Parallel, a variable *chosen* is used to denoted whether the EU is chosen to execute.

Atomic Execution. A Critical Region has a sole Operand while each CEU module having a single EU submodule. We use a boolean variable, *isCritical*, for each EU of the Critical Region's Operand, to restrict the OSs within the EU from interleaving with other OSs on the same Lifeline. Variable *isCritical* is initialized to *False* in each EU module of the Critical Region's Operand. It is set to *True* if the EU starts to execute OSs and stays *True* until the EU finishes execution. Once the EU completes, *isCritical* is set to *False*. The negation of *isCritical* of an EU is considered as an enabling condition for each variable of other OSs, which may interleave the EU, on the same Lifeline. See figure 1b for an example. On Lifeline *L3*, the sending OS of Message *m6* takes the negation of *isCritical* for the EU on Lifeline *L3* as an enabling condition.

Branching. Collectively, we call Alternatives, Option, and Break branching constructs. In an Alternatives CF, each Operand must have an explicit or an implicit or an "else" Constraint. An implicit Constraint always evaluates to *True*. The "else" Constraint is the negation of the disjunction of all other Constraints in the enclosing Alternatives. The chosen Operand's Constraint must evaluate to $True$. If none of the Operands whose Constraints evaluate to $True$, the Alternatives is excluded. For each Operand, a boolean variable *exe* indicates the execution status of the applicable Operand, *i.e.*, *exe* is set to *True* if the Operand is chosen to execute. The variable *exe* for each Operand is initialized and declared in the CEU module on the Lifeline where the Operand's Constraint is located. The Constraint under INVAR restricts that an Operand's *exe* can be set to *True* only if the Operand's *cond* evaluates to *True*. It also restricts that at most one Operand can be chosen to execute, *i.e.*, at most one *exe* can be set to *True* at a time, or all Operand Constraints evaluate to *False*. The use of *exe* guarantees that all the enclosed Lifelines choose the same Operand's EU module to execute to avoid inconsistent choices (*e.g.*, Lifeline *L1* chooses Operand *1*'s EU whereas Lifeline *L2* chooses Operand *2*'s EU). The *cond* of the chosen Operand stays *True* and those of the unchosen Operands are set to *False* and stay *False*.

The NuSMV representation of Option and Break can be derived from the one of Alternatives. The details of translation are described in [6].

Iteration. The Loop represents its sole Operand's iterations, which are connected by Weak Sequencing. To restrict the number of iterations, the Operand's Constraint may include a lower bound, *minint*, and an upper bound, *maxint*, *i.e.*, a Loop iterates at least the *minint* number of times and at most the *maxint* number of times. If the Constraint evaluates to *False* after the *minint* number of iterations, the Loop will terminate.

Bounded Loop, whose *maxint* is given, can be translated to NuSMV modules. To keep each OS and Constraint within different iterations of a Loop unique, one way to implement an OS or a Constraint is defining an array to rename the OS or the Constraint of each iteration. For each Lifeline, We use n to represent the current iteration number. In this way, an OS within the Loop's Operand, OS_r1, and Constraint *cond* in iteration n can be represented as $OS\_r1[n]$ and $cond[n]$ respectively. For example, if a Loop iterates at most three iterations, OS_r1 in different iterations are defined as $OS\_r1[1]$, $OS\_r1[2]$ and $OS\_r1[3]$. The graphical order of the OSs within the same iteration is maintained, and the OSs among iterations execute sequentially along a Lifeline, *i.e.*, OSs in iteration n take place before OSs in iteration $n+1$.

We need to evaluate the Interaction Constraint of its sole Operand after minimum number of iterations. If $n \leq minint$, the Loop executes. If $minint < n \leq maxint$, the Loop executes only if $cond[n]$ evaluates to $True$. Otherwise, the Loop terminates and the values of the Constraint of remaining iterations (*i.e.*, from $cond[n + 1]$ to $cond[maxint]$) set to *False*. The Loop no longer executes when its iteration reaches $maxint$.

Assertion. An Assertion represents that, on each Lifeline, a set of traces of its Operand are the only valid traces following the Assertion's preceding OSs. The mapping strategy of the Assertion is very similar to the one of the Critical Region. For each Lifeline, a boolean variable *inAssertion* is initialized and declared in the EU module of the Assertion's Operand, restricting the OSs within the EU from interleaving with other OSs on the same Lifeline if the OSs prior to the CEU of the Assertion finish execution.

The variable *inAssertion* is *False* initially, and is set to *True* when the OSs in the set of *pre(CEU)* have executed. Function *pre(CEU)* returns the set of OSs which may happen right before the CEU of the Assertion. If the EU of the Assertion's Operand completes execution, *inAssertion* is set to *False* and other OSs may execute. For each Lifeline, the negation of *inAssertion* is used as an enabling condition for each variable of other OSs, which may interleave the EU of the Assertion's Operand.

Negation. We translate the Operand of a Negative into NuSMV modules, deriving all possible invalid traces.

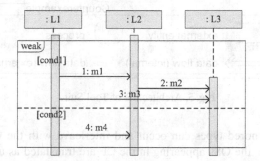

Fig. 4. Example for Weak Sequencing

Weak Sequencing and Strict Sequencing. The semantics of a Weak Sequencing enforces the total order among EUs of Operands on the same Lifeline. In any EU module of an Operand (except the first one), the first OS takes the variable *flag_final* of the EU of the preceding Operand on the same Lifeline as an enabling condition, *i.e.*, the EU cannot execute before the preceding one completes. Figure 4 is an example of Weak Sequencing. In the EU module of the second Operand on Lifeline *L2*, the first OS, *r4*, takes *flag_final* of the EU occurring immediately before this EU (*i.e.*, the EU of the first Operand) as an enabling condition.

The semantics of a Strict Sequencing enforces the total order between adjacent Operands. An EU module of an Operand (other than the first one) within a Strict Sequencing takes variable *flag_final* of every EU module within the preceding Operand as enabling conditions of the first OS. It asserts that all EUs cannot execute until its preceding Operand completes execution. We can alter the Interaction Operator of the CF in figure 4 to *strict* to make it as an example of Strict Sequencing. Comparing to the example of Weak Sequencing, OS *r4* also takes the variable *flag_final* of the EUs of the first Operand on Lifelines *L1* and *L3* as enabling conditions additionally.

Ignore and Consider. Ignore and Consider make it possible to execute the Messages not explicitly appear in the CF. To map an Ignore (Consider) into NuSMV modules, we can explore all the traces of OSs in which Messages are ignored (not considered). We assume the signature of any Message of ignored (considered) types is given, *i.e.*, the Lifelines where the sending OS and receiving OS of a Message occur are known.

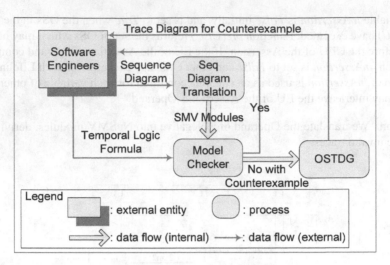

Fig. 5. Architecture of Tool Suite

The Messages of ignored types can occur and interleave with the OSs appearing in the CF. In an Ignore, the OSs appearing in the CF are translated as usual. Each OS of any ignored Message is mapped to a boolean variable in the EU module on the Lifeline where it is located. An OS of the ignored Messages can be enabled if it has not executed and the control is in the EU module. To record the status of each ignored Message's OS, an enumeration type variable *os_chosen* is introduced, which is initially *-1*. It is set to *0* if the OS is chosen to execute and is set to and stays *1* in the following steps. In each EU module of the Ignore, the OSs of ignored Messages and other OSs are interleaved, which is captured by INVAR statements using the same strategy as the implementation of Parallel.

A Consider specifies a list of message types which should be considered within the CF. It is equivalent to ignore other message types, *i.e.*, the message types not in the list cannot appear in the CF, but they may occur. If a message type is considered but does not appear in the CF, the Messages of the type cannot occur within the CF. For example, if a Consider CF considers message type *q, v,* and *w*, but only Messages of message type *q* and *v* appear in the CF. Thus, Messages of message type *w* cannot occur within the CF. In a Consider, each OS of the considered Messages can be defined as a boolean variable in the EU module on the Lifeline where it is located. If the OS does not appear in the Consider, it is defined as a derived variable, whose value is *False* to indicate the OS will never occur. For other known but not considered Messages, their OSs are defined in the same way as the OSs of the ignored Messages.

We also provide the mapping of Interaction Use, Coregion, and General Ordering to the NuSMV modules. Due to space limitation, please refer to [6] for the details of translation.

5 Tool Suite Implementation and Evaluation

As a proof-of-concept, we have developed a tool suite, implementing the techniques described in this paper. Figure 5 is a data flow diagram, illustrating the architecture of our tool suite.

The software engineer uses MagicDraw to create a Sequence Diagram, which can be converted to a textual representation in terms of XML using our MagicDraw plugin. The Sequence Diagram Translation tool takes the XML representation as input, parses it into a syntax tree, and transforms it into a NuSMV model. NuSMV model checker takes as input the generated NuSMV model and a temporal logic formula that is specified by the software engineer. If there are no property violations, the software engineer receives a positive response. If property violations exist, NuSMV generates a counterexample which is then passed to our Occurrence Specification Trace Diagram Generator (OSTDG) tool. The output from the OSTDG is an easy-to-read Sequence Diagram visualization of the counterexample to help the software engineer locate the property violation faster. Thus, the software engineer may transparently verify a Sequence Diagrams using NuSMV, staying solely within the notation realm of Sequence Diagrams.

We evaluate our technique with a case study of ISIS (Insurance Services Information System), a web application currently used by the specialty insurance industry. Our evaluation uses two Sequence Diagram examples from the design documentation of ISIS. We check the example on a Linux machine with a 3.00GHz, 8 cores CPU and 32GB of RAM. One example executed in 19 minutes 49 seconds with 3,825 reachable states out of total 3.71e+012 states, while the other example executed in 18 minutes 14 seconds with 192 reachable states out of total 4.95e+012 states. Please refer to [6] for more details of the case study and our tool suite.

6 Related Work

Verification of scenario-based notation is well-accepted as an important and challenging problem. To the best of our knowledge, our technique is the first to support all CFs and the nested CFs. Lima *et al.* provide a tool to translate UML 2 Sequence Diagrams into PROMELA-based models and verify using SPIN, with counterexample visualizations [7]. Their translation does not support Critical Region, Strict Sequencing, Negative, Assertion, Consider, Ignore, synchronous Messages and Interaction Constraint. Van Amstel *et al.* present four complementary approaches for analyzing UML 1.5 Sequence Diagrams, which do not support CFs [8]. They model check Sequence Diagrams using SPIN. Alawneh *et al.* introduce a unified paradigm to verify and validate prominent UML 2 diagrams, including Sequence Diagrams, using NuSMV [9]. Their approach supports Alternatives and Parallel.

To model check MSCs, Alur *et al.* [10,11] formalize MSC using automata. They examine different cases of MSC verification of temporal properties and present techniques for iteratively specifying requirements [12]. They focus on MSC Graph, which is an aggregation of MSCs. We extend their work to encompass more complicated aggregations using CFs. Peled *et al.* perform intensive research on the verification of MSCs

[13,14], in particular, they present an extension of the High-Level MSC [15]. They specify MSC properties in temporal logic and check for safety and liveness properties. Leue *et al.* translate the MSC specification, especially branching and iteration of High-Level MSC, into PROMELA to verify MSCs using the XSPIN tool [16]. As Sequence Diagrams have similar expressive features, our technique can be extended to work with their approach. Kugler *et al.* improve the technique of smart play-out, which is used to model check LSCs to avoid violations over computations [17]. Walkinshaw and Bogdanov [18] detail an inference technique to constrain a finite-state model with LTL. These constraints reduce the number of traces required as input to a model checker for discovery of safety counter examples. Our work can automatically model check each Sequence Diagram of a system against LTL properties separately, which helps to alleviate the state explosion problem.

Micskei and Waeselynck survey comprehensively formal semantics proposed for Sequence Diagrams by 13 groups and present the different semantic options [3]. In these groups, Knapp and Wuttke present an operational semantics for a translation of an Interaction into automata, which is used to model check UML state machines with SPIN or UPPAAL [19]. Their approach does not support all CFs and the interpretation of automata restricts the specification of Interaction Constraints. Haugen *et al.* present the formal semantics of UML 2 Sequence Diagram through an approach named STAIRS [20]. STAIRS provides a trace-based representation for a subset of CFs, focusing on the refinement for Interactions. To relate state-based behaviors with scenario-based descriptions, Bontemps *et al.* formally study the problem of scenario checking, synthesis, and verification of the LSC [21]. Their work focuses on providing an algorithm and proving the complexity for each problem. Uchitel *et al.* [22] synthesize a behavioral specification in the form of a Finite Sequential Process, which can be checked using their labeled transition system analyzer. With the semantic definition of Uchitel *et al.*, Damas *et al.* synthesize a labeled transition system model from both positive and negative scenarios, expressed in MSC [23].

7   Conclusions

In this paper, we present an approach to transform Sequence Diagrams and all CFs into NuSMV models. This enables software engineers to verify if a Sequence Diagram satisfies desired properties and visualize counterexamples as Sequence Diagrams to help user locate violations. We supplement our technique with a proof-of-concept tool suite and perform an evaluation using a case study of an industry web application.

References

1. Object Management Group: Unified Modelling Language (Superstructure), v2.4.1 (2011), Internet: http://www.omg.org
2. Cimatti, A., Clarke, E., Giunchiglia, F., Roveri, M.: NuSMV: a new symbolic model checker. Int. Journal on Soft. Tools for Tech. Transfer 2, 410–425 (2000)
3. Micskei, Z., Waeselynck, H.: The many meanings of UML 2 Sequence Diagrams: a survey. Software and Systems Modeling 10, 489–514 (2011)

4. Kugler, H., Harel, D., Pnueli, A., Lu, Y., Bontemps, Y.: Temporal logic for scenario-based specifications. In: Halbwachs, N., Zuck, L.D. (eds.) TACAS 2005. LNCS, vol. 3440, pp. 445–460. Springer, Heidelberg (2005)

5. Eichner, C., Fleischhack, H., Meyer, R., Schrimpf, U., Stehno, C.: Compositional semantics for UML 2.0 Sequence Diagram using Petri Nets. In: Prinz, A., Reed, R., Reed, J. (eds.) SDL 2005. LNCS, vol. 3530, pp. 133–148. Springer, Heidelberg (2005)

6. Shen, H., Robinson, M., Niu, J.: A logical framework for Sequence Diagram with Combined Fragments. Technical Report CS-TR-2011-015, UTSA (2011)

7. Lima, V., Talhi, C., Mouheb, D., Debbabi, M., Wang, L., Pourzandi, M.: Formal verification and validation of UML 2.0 Sequence Diagrams using source and destination of messages. Electron. Notes Theor. Comput. Sci. 254, 143–160 (2009)

8. van Amstel, M., Lange, C., Chaudron, M.: Four automated approaches to analyze the quality of UML Sequence Diagrams. COMPSAC 2, 415–424 (2007)

9. Alawneh, L., Debbabi, M., Hassaine, F., Jarraya, Y., Soeanu, A.: A unified approach for verification and validation of systems and software engineering models. In: ECBS 2006, pp. 409–418 (2006)

10. Alur, R., Yannakakis, M.: Model checking of Message Sequence Charts. In: Baeten, J.C.M., Mauw, S. (eds.) CONCUR 1999. LNCS, vol. 1664, pp. 114–129. Springer, Heidelberg (1999)

11. Alur, R., Etessami, K., Yannakakis, M.: Realizability and verification of MSC graphs. Theoretical Computer Science 331, 97–114 (2005)

12. Alur, R., Etessami, K., Yannakakis, M.: Inference of Message Sequence Charts. TSE 29, 623–633 (2003)

13. Muscholl, A., Peled, D., Su, Z.: Deciding properties of Message Sequence Charts. In: Nivat, M. (ed.) FOSSACS 1998. LNCS, vol. 1378, pp. 226–242. Springer, Heidelberg (1998)

14. Gunter, E.L., Muscholl, A., Peled, D.: Compositional Message Sequence Charts. In: Margaria, T., Yi, W. (eds.) TACAS 2001. LNCS, vol. 2031, pp. 496–511. Springer, Heidelberg (2001)

15. Peled, D.: Specification and verification of Message Sequence Charts. In: Bolognesi, T., Latella, D. (eds.) FORTE 2000. IFIP, vol. 55, pp. 139–154. Springer, Heidelberg (2000)

16. Leue, S., Ladkin, P.B.: Implementing and verifying MSC specifications using PROMELA/XSPIN. In: SPIN 1996. DIMACS, vol. 32, pp. 65–89 (1996)

17. Kugler, H., Plock, C., Pnueli, A.: Controller synthesis from LSC requirements. In: Chechik, M., Wirsing, M. (eds.) FASE 2009. LNCS, vol. 5503, pp. 79–93. Springer, Heidelberg (2009)

18. Walkinshaw, N., Bogdanov, K.: Inferring finite-state models with temporal constraints. In: ASE, pp. 248–257 (2008)

19. Knapp, A., Wuttke, J.: Model checking of UML 2.0 interactions. In: Kühne, T. (ed.) MoDELS 2006. LNCS, vol. 4364, pp. 42–51. Springer, Heidelberg (2007)

20. Haugen, O., Husa, K.E., Runde, R.K., Stolen, K.: STAIRS towards formal design with Sequence Diagrams. Soft. and Sys. Modeling 4, 355–357 (2005)

21. Bontemps, Y., Heymans, P., Schobbens, P.Y.: From Live Sequence Charts to state machines and back: A guided tour. TSE 31, 999–1014 (2005)

22. Uchitel, S., Kramer, J., Magge, J.: Synthesis of behavioral models from scenarios. TSE 29, 99–115 (2003)

23. Damas, C., Lambeau, B., Dupont, P., van Lamsweerde, A.: Generating annotated behavior models from end-user scenarios. TSE 31, 1056–1073 (2005)

A Large-Scale Elastic Environment
for Scientific Computing

Paul Marshall[1], Henry Tufo[1,2], Kate Keahey[3,4], David LaBissoniere[3,4],
and Matthew Woitaszek[2]

[1]Department of Computer Science, University of Colorado, Boulder, CO, U.S.A.
[2]CSS, National Center for Atmospheric Research, Boulder, CO, U.S.A.
[3]Computation Institute, University of Chicago, Chicago, IL, U.S.A.
[4]MCS, Argonne National Laboratory, Argonne, IL, U.S.A.

Abstract. The relatively recent introduction of infrastructure-as-a-service (IaaS)
clouds, such as Amazon Elastic Compute Cloud (EC2), provide users with the
ability to deploy custom software stacks in virtual machines (VMs) across different cloud providers. Users can leverage IaaS clouds to create elastic environments
that outsource compute and storage as needed. Additionally, these environments
can adapt dynamically to demand, scaling up as demand increases and scaling
down as demand decreases. In this paper, we present a large-scale elastic environment that extends cluster resources managers (e.g. Torque) with IaaS resources. Our solution integrates with an open-source elastic manager, the Elastic
Processing Unit (EPU), and includes the ability to periodically recontextualize
the environment with a light-weight REST-based recontextualization broker. We
deploy the Gluster file system to provide a shared file system for all nodes in
the environment. Though our implementation currently only supports Torque, we
also thoroughly discuss how our architecture can interface with different workflows, including Hadoop's MapReduce workflows and Condor's match-making
and high-throughput capabilities. For evaluation, we demonstrate the ability to
recontextualize 256-node environments within one second of the recontextualization period, scale to over 475 nodes in less than 15 minutes, and support parallel
IO from distributed nodes.

Keywords: Cloud Computing, Elastic Computing, Infrastructure-as-a-Service.

1 Introduction

With the recent introduction of infrastructure-as-a-service (IaaS) clouds [4], users can
choose to outsource computation and storage when needed. IaaS clouds offer pay-
for-use virtual infrastructure resources, such as virtual machines (VMs), to users on-
demand. On-demand resource provisioning is an attractive paradigm for users working
toward deadlines or responding to emergencies. Users in the scientific community have
begun to adopt IaaS clouds for their workflows [20], [37], [18], [43]. Additionally, the
pay-for-use charging model means that a resource provider can choose to reduce his
initial purchase of capital equipment, selecting a resource that meets the needs of his
users the majority of the time, and opt to budget for future outsourcing costs, elastically

J. Cordeiro, S. Hammoudi, and M. van Sinderen (Eds.): ICSOFT 2012, CCIS 411, pp. 112–126, 2013.

extending the resource when demand of the local resource exceeds its capacity. In previous work we developed a cloud charging model for high-performance compute (HPC) resources [44], allowing a resource provider to analyze the cost of cloud resources in the context of physical HPC resource deployments. The virtual nature of IaaS clouds allows users to customize the entire software stack, from the operating system (OS) upward, often a key requirement for complex scientific workflows.

IaaS clouds provide the underlying building blocks for elastic computing environments. However, policies are needed to ensure the environment adjusts appropriately to demand; tools to deploy and manage the environments are also needed. In [26] we propose policies for elastic environments that balance user and administrator requirements; we evaluate them using workload traces and a discrete event simulator. In [25] we developed a prototype elastic IaaS environment that extended a Torque [7] queue with Nimbus [22], [30] and Amazon EC2 clouds [1]. However, the prototype was not sufficiently scalable, scaling to 150 nodes in 60 minutes and it lacked the ability to recontextualize, preventing the environment from executing parallel jobs, or leverage multiple clouds.

In this paper, we include our previous work in [27] and expand upon it. We address the limitations of our previous prototype and present a large-scale elastic environment that is highly available, scalable, and adapts quickly to changing demand. We extend an open-source elastic IaaS manager, the Elastic Processing Unit (EPU), to support the Torque batch-queue scheduler, allowing existing scientific workflows to integrate with IaaS resources for minimal software engineering cost. To support parallel jobs, we develop a lightweight REST-based contextualization broker that recontextualizes the cluster as nodes join and leave the environment. New to this extended version of the paper, we deploy the Gluster file system [14], allowing all nodes to mount a shared file system in wide-area deployments. We also thoroughly discuss how our architecture can be adapted for other workflows, specifically Hadoop's MapReduce workflows and Condor's match-making and high-throughput capabilities. For evaluation, we deploy our solution using NSF FutureGrid [10] and Amazon EC2. Our solution leverages multiple clouds simultaneously, recontextualizes 256 node clusters within one second of the recontextualization period, scales to over 475 nodes in less than 15 minutes, and supports parallel IO from distributed nodes.

2   Approach

In previous work [25] we discuss the specifics required to extend a physical cluster with IaaS resources. Therefore, we only briefly discuss our previous prototype and its limitations before presenting our large-scale architecture and implementation.

2.1   Initial Prototype

Our initial prototype [25] implemented a standalone service that created elastic IaaS environments, providing valuable insight into the challenges faced by large-scale elastic computing environments. The prototype elastic manager service monitored a Torque queue and responded by launching or terminating cloud instances. The Nimbus context broker [23] contextualized the cloud nodes with the head node, exchanging host information and SSH keys. However, the prototype contained a number of design and implementation limitations that prevented it from scaling appropriately, using multiple cloud providers simultaneously, and recontextualizing the environment.

In particular, the prototype elastic manager service called Torque commands directly to gather information about the queue and called the Java-based Nimbus cloud client to launch instances (sometimes taking up to a few hundred seconds). This meant the system could only launch approximately a dozen nodes every few hundred seconds. Additionally, a single cluster image with preinstalled software was deployed for each cloud provider, requiring that new images had to be configured for every new cloud supported. The Nimbus context broker was used to facilitate the exchange of host information between nodes in a context, which does not allow additional nodes to join the context after the initial launch, thereby preventing the system from running parallel jobs. Lastly, the prototype elastic manager service was not highly available; it did not contain any self-monitoring or self-repairing capabilities.

2.2   Large-Scale Elastic Computing Environments

In this section we build on our prototype architecture in [25] and present an updated architecture for large-scale elastic computing environments. We address the challenges discussed in the previous section, focusing primarily on improving scalability, leveraging multiple clouds, and developing a solution for recontextualization.

Elastic Management. We extend an open-source elastic manager service, the Elastic Processing Unit (EPU) [24], under development by the Ocean Observatories Initiative [32]. The EPU aims to be a highly available and scalable service. It is publicly available on GitHub [9] as an alpha release for initial testing. It contains the necessary framework and functionality to create elastic computing environments. The EPU consists of three major components that we leverage for our elastic environments: sensors to monitor application demand, a decision engine that responds to sensor information, and a provisioner that interfaces with various cloud providers to launch, terminate, and manage the instances. The provisioner interfaces with IaaS clouds using their REST APIs. Unlike the Java-based cloud client, these operations return quickly, typically within a second or two. The decision engine loops continually, processing sensor information and executing a policy that elects to launch or terminate a specific number of instances. We refer to each loop iteration as a policy evaluation iteration. We extend the OOI EPU model to support a "push" queue model where a central scheduler, such as a batch-queue scheduler, monitors worker instances and dispatches jobs to workers instead of using the EPU's "pull" queue model where works request work from a central queue. In our model, the sensors both monitor demand and execute commands on behalf of the decision engine.

Automating Deployment and Configuration. To support multiple cloud providers seamlessly, the installation and configuration of worker nodes should be automated using a system integration framework, such as Chef [19], instead of preinstalling and preconfiguring VM images manually. With this approach, a base image that is likely available on any cloud (e.g. a Debian 5.0 image) can be used. When a new worker boots the base image, the system integration framework downloads the cluster software, installs it, and configures the worker to join the cluster head node automatically. This can be a lengthy process if a lot of software needs to be installed, therefore, software packages can either be cached on the node or they can be completely installed, allowing nodes to boot quickly and be appropriately configured.

Contextualization. Creating a shared and trusted environment, or context, is a key requirement for elastic computing environments. To support parallel jobs, all resources in the environment need to exchange information and data. However, with elastic computing environments, contextualization is a continual process since demand fluctuates constantly with nodes joining and leaving the environment. For example, a typical cluster requires that nodes exchange host information and SSH keys in order to run parallel jobs. Existing contextualization solutions, such as the Nimbus context broker, provide mechanisms to exchange host information between all nodes that are launched at the same time. However, the Nimbus context broker does not allow additional nodes to join the context at a later time.

We propose a recontextualization service that periodically exchanges information between all nodes in the context. The recontextualization service maintains an ordered list of nodes in the context. The list includes hostnames, IP addresses, SSH keys, and a generic data field for all nodes. As nodes join or leave the context, the recontextualization service updates the ordered list. Every node in the context periodically checks in with the recontextualization service. If there are updates to the context, the recontextualization service sends the updated section of the list to the node, which applies the updates in order (e.g. adding the SSH keys of nodes that joined the context to the SSH known hosts file).

3   Implementation

The earlier version of this work [27] discusses our implementation in more detail, however, we provide an overview in this section. In particular, we extend the EPU to support the Torque batch-queue scheduler, we create a set of scripts to configure worker nodes, we develop a recontextualization service that contextualizes all nodes in the context, and finally, we include support for a reliable and simple data movement. An example deployment, shown in Figure 1, consists of the main EPU components (a sensor, decision engine, and provisioner), our recontextualization service, and a deployment across multiple IaaS clouds.

3.1   EPU Extensions

The EPU currently uses the Advanced Message Queuing Protocol (AMQP) [42] to communicate between its various components. We develop a custom EPU sensor to integrate with Torque, allowing scientific workloads to use the elastic environment seamlessly. We also develop a custom decision engine to respond to the information provided by the Torque sensor. The Torque sensor, written in Python, monitors the queue and sends information to the decision engine. The pbs_python package [36], a Python wrapper class for the Torque C library, is used to gather Torque information, including both job and node information. The Torque sensor also executes commands sent to it by the decision engine, such as adding the hostname of newly launched nodes to Torque's host file. At each policy evaluation iteration, the decision engine determines whether or not to launch instances (instances that haven't joined the cluster within 10 minutes are marked as stalled and replaced), it instructs the Torque sensor to add any recently launched instances, it instructs the sensor to mark any idle Torque workers as offline in preparation to terminate them, and finally, it terminates any nodes that were previously marked offline.

3.2 Automated Worker Deployment

After the EPU launches worker instances, software packages need to be installed, the instances need to be configured as Torque worker nodes, and they need to join the cluster. We use the Chef [19] systems integration framework to download, install, and configure cluster and user software. We develop a set of Chef recipes to download, compile, and install Torque, the pbs_python package, and user software. This allows us to use any base Linux image on any IaaS cloud as a worker image, greatly reducing the time required to support additional clouds. When the base Linux node boots, a simple Python agent, bundled in the image ahead of time, automatically retrieves the Chef recipes from a GitHub repository and then executes them, installing and configuring the node from scratch. To speed up the deployment and limit possible points of failure, the recipes and software can be cached in the base image.

3.3 Recontextualization Broker

The recontextualization broker is a lightweight, REST-based recontextualization service that securely exchanges host information between all nodes in a context. All components of our recontextualization solution are written in Python and use representational state transfer (REST) over HTTPS for communication; symmetric keys are used for both user and context security. Our solution consists of three components: a client for managing contexts, an agent that runs on all nodes in the context and applies updates as it receives them, and a central broker service to facilitate the secure exchange of host information between agents. The information exchanged by nodes in the context includes the short hostname, full hostname, IP address, SSH public host key, and a generic text data field. A complete figure detailing the recontextualization process is included in our previous work [27], however, the process essentially works as follows: Recontextualization begins when a user creates a context with the client, which sends a request to the broker service. The broker responds with the newly generated context ID, a uniform resource identifier (URI) for the context and a unique context key and secret. When the user launches a cloud instance, this information is passed to the instance via the IaaS cloud's userdata field. The agent starts when the instance boots and reads the instance's userdata field to get the context information. The agent then sends its node information (hostname, etc.) to the broker. The broker maintains an ordered list of nodes that join or leave a context. After the agent sends its information to the broker, it enters into a loop

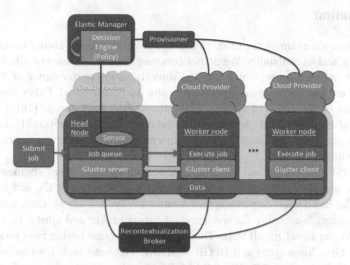

Fig. 1. Example elastic deployment with support for the Gluster file system

referred to as the recontextualization period, requesting updates from the broker and applying them. The amount of time the agent sleeps between loop iterations determines the frequency that the environment recontextualizes.

3.4 Gluster

In an earlier version of this work [27] we did not include a reliable or scalable data movement solution. Our elastic environment instead relied on Torque's ability to SCP data to and from worker nodes or common file system technologies such as NFS, which often failed in wide-area deployments. Therefore, we have updated our implementation to support the open source Gluster file system [14], shown in Figure 1. Gluster is a distributed and scalable file system with support for automatic failover. Gluster distributes data and metadata, allowing the environment to seamlessly adapt to failures or temporary outages. Furthermore, Gluster supports commodity hardware and software, making it simple to to install, configure, and deploy in cloud environments. Lastly, in addition to Gluster's native GlusterFS communication, users can also access Gluster file systems via NFS or SMB protocols.

To deploy Gluster, we developed a set of scripts to automatically download, configure, and install Gluster on both servers and clients. For our initial implementation we only deploy a single Gluster server on the cluster head node. The Gluster server exports a portion of the underlying head node file system, providing a single mount point and shared file system for all clients. We leave deployment of larger Gluster pools as well as evaluation of them for future work. We leverage the recontextualization broker to automatically install Gluster on worker nodes. When worker nodes first boot, they download Gluster, configure it, install it and then mount the Gluster server node in the context, giving them access to the shared file system.

4   Evaluation

For evaluation, we examine the reactivity of the environment, its ability to recontextualize quickly, and its scalability. We do not compare the performance of different cloud providers or instance types, which are tied directly to the performance of the underlying hardware and software configuration of the particular cloud. Other studies have examined the performance of virtual environments and IaaS clouds [16], [35], [15], [13]. And in November 2011, Amazon EC2 ranked #42 on the Top500 [31]. Users with applications that have strict performance requirements should select appropriate clouds for their environments.

We use NSF FutureGrid and Amazon EC2 for our evaluation environment. On FutureGrid we use Hotel (fg-hotel), at the University of Chicago (UC), and Sierra (fg-sierra), at the San Diego Supercomputer Center (SDSC). Both systems use Xen [6] for virtualization. We deploy the recontextualization broker and cluster head node in separate VMs on Hotel for all tests. The recontextualization broker runs inside a VM with 8 2.93 GHz Xeon cores and 16 GB of RAM. The head node runs on a VM with 2 2.93GHz Xeon cores and 2 GB of RAM. The head node contains the Torque 2.5.9 server software, Maui 3.3.1 [17], [28], as well as the EPU provisioner and decision engine. Worker nodes are deployed on both Hotel and Sierra and consist of 2 2.93 GHz Xeon cores with 2 GB of RAM. On EC2 we use 64-bit EC2 east micro instances for worker nodes, primarily due to cost (two cents per hour). Micro instances use Elastic Block Storage (EBS) and contain up to 2 EC2 compute units with 613 MB of RAM. Worker nodes use a base Linux image on each cloud and Chef installs and configures the software. For all tests, the sensor queries Torque every 60 seconds to gather job and worker information. The decision engine executes every 5 seconds, querying IaaS clouds for changes in instance state and executing its policy. Recontextualization agents send their information to the broker when they first launch and query the broker every 120 seconds for updates.

As a metric, we define the reactivity time to be the time from when the first job is submitted until the time the last job begins running for a group of jobs submitted at the same time. We also define the metric recontextualization time to be the time from when a new node attempts to join a context by sending its information to the broker until the time when all nodes in the context have received and applied the update for the new node. In addition to these metrics, we examine the ability of the elastic environment to leverage multiple clouds simultaneously and scale to hundreds of nodes, shown with a series of traces. For the reactivity and recontextualization tests, the workloads consist of a simple MPI application that sleeps for 60 minutes. For the recontextualization test, 60 minutes is more than enough time for the initial nodes to stabilize and wait for an additional node to launch and join the context. For the multi- cloud and scalability tests, the workloads consist of individual "sleep" jobs that sleep for 30 minutes, demonstrating the ability of the environment to scale up and down as demand changes.

4.1   Understanding System Responsiveness

To understand system responsiveness we consider two metrics. First, we examine the reactivity time. This includes the time to detect the change in demand, execute the

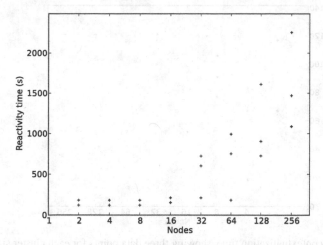

Fig. 2. Reactivity time, showing three data points for each cluster size

policy, request instances from an IaaS provider, and wait for the instances to boot and install software. To measure reactivity time, we configure the environment to launch single-core EC2 east micro worker nodes. We perform a series of tests, beginning with 2 node clusters, increasing to 256 nodes, shown in Figure 2. We run each test 3 times for each cluster size.

As we can see in Figure 2, small cluster sizes, from 2 nodes through 16, all have relatively similar reactivity times. However, interestingly, 32 and 64 node clusters each have one test with a reactivity time similar to smaller clusters while the other 2 tests are much higher. The reason for this is related to the fact that our environment detects and replaces stalled nodes after 10 minutes. In our evaluation we observed that EC2 micro instances would periodically fail (most often the instance failed to boot or access the network). Because larger cluster sizes boot more instances, they are more likely to encounter these failed instances, even when booting replacements.

The second area we explore is the recontextualization time where all nodes in the context must query the broker for updates, receive the updates and apply them. To measure the recontextualization time, we again configure the environment to use EC2 east micro instances (single core). Similar to the reactivity tests, we perform a series of tests from 2 nodes through 256, running 3 tests for each cluster size. We submit a simple MPI sleep job that requests the appropriate number of cores and allow the cluster to boot, contextualize, and begin running the job. Once the cluster stabilizes, we submit another single-core sleep job, causing an extra instance to launch and join the cluster. We measure the time from when the new instance sent its information to the broker until the time when all nodes in the environment receive and apply the update. We rely on Amazon's ability to synchronize the clocks of instances, which is done through NTP, for our time-based measurements.

As we can see in Figure 3, all clusters fully recontextualize within 1 second of the 120-second recontextualization period. The tests that recontextualize before the 120 second period do so simply because all of the existing nodes in the environment check

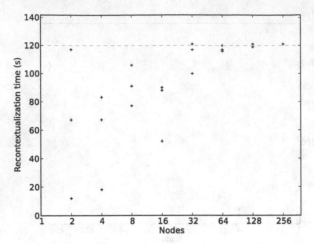

Fig. 3. Recontextualization time, showing three data points for each cluster size

in with the broker shortly after the new node has sent its information to the broker. The three 2- node cluster tests are perhaps the most interesting case. For one of the tests, both nodes check in with the broker shortly after the new node joined the context and contextualize in less than 20 seconds, whereas with another 2-node test, at least one of the nodes waits almost the full 120 second period before it queries the broker again. This is simply the result of the random timing of when nodes boot and install the required software. As the number of nodes in a context increases, the likelihood that at least one of the nodes will query the broker 120 seconds after the additional node joins the context increases.

4.2 Multi-cloud and Scalable Elastic Environments

In addition to system responsiveness, we also examine the ability of the environment to scale up and down as demand fluctuates. For our first test, we configure the environment to launch workers on Hotel and then we submit 256 single-core jobs that sleep for 30 minutes (Figure 4). The environment scales up to over 100 VMs, however, it doesn's quite reach 128 VMs (or 256 cores), because Hotel's underlying hardware is unable to deploy 128 VMs within 30 minutes.

In our second test, we configure the environment to dispatch workers on both Hotel and Sierra, shown in Figure 5. The workers from both clouds are configured to trust each other and process the same jobs from the main queue. For evaluation, we submit 512 single-core jobs that sleep for 30 minutes. In this case we observe the limited scalability of private clouds. Hotel and Sierra are not able to provide 512 cores, as both clouds reach the maximum number of instances that they can deploy at the time, shown by the horizontal line for VMs running on each cloud.

In our final test, we configure the EPU to deploy single-core EC2 east micro instances, shown in Figure 6. We submit 512 single-core jobs that sleep for 30 minutes. The environment scales to 476 instances in less than 15 minutes. Unfortunately, EC2 is not able to reach 512 instances within the first 30 minutes of the evaluation. While the

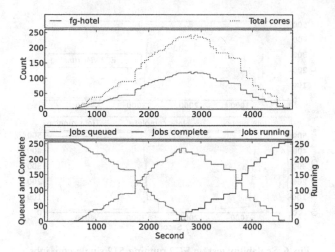

Fig. 4. Single-cloud trace running 256 single-core jobs

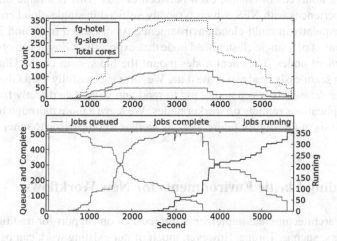

Fig. 5. Multi-cloud trace running 512 single-core jobs

environment scales quickly, it begins to trail off around 400 instances, only reaching a total of 490 instances. The remaining 22 instances fail to boot completely on EC2, thus suggesting that when using EC2 for hundreds of instances users should consider overprovisioning the deployment by a small percentage.

4.3 Data Movement

In this section we provide a brief discussion of our initial experiences with Gluster, which have been largely positive. To date we have deployed Gluster in both single-cloud and multi-cloud environments using Hotel and Sierra on FutureGrid. We have not experienced any failures with Gluster while transferring hundreds of gigabytes of

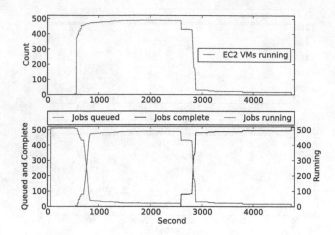

Fig. 6. Scalability test on EC2 running 512 single-core jobs

data between hundreds of clients, even between clouds. This is a huge improvement over our experiences with NFS, which typically sufficed in single-cloud environments but failed frequently in multi-cloud environments. As discussed in section 3.4, our deployment consist of a single cluster head node that exports the Gluster file system to any number of client nodes. The client nodes mount the file system on the Gluster server and can then seamlessly read and write data. We have successfully used Gluster both to transfer large datasets between nodes and to read and write data directly from parallel scientific applications running on worker nodes. We leave a more thorough benchmarking and analysis of Gluster for future work as well as a comparison to other file system technologies.

5   Extending Elastic Environments for New Workflows

Our current architecture and implementation focuses on support for traditional batch-queue clusters, such as Torque. However, much of our existing work can be used in its current form to easily support different workflows, such as Hadoop's MapReduce workflows and Condor's match-making capabilities. The sensors and policies are the most obvious components that need to be adapted. The sensors are responsible for interfacing with specific job managers and gathering information about the workload. Policies are responsible for responding to sensor information by launching additional workers, terminating existing workers, or leaving the environment unchanged. In order for environments to respond to demand more effectively, custom policies should be developed for different workflows, applications, and instance requirements.

Condor [41], recently renamed HTCondor, is a job manager for high-throughput computing workloads. Because Condor was originally developed for cycle-scavenging and emphasized high-throughput workloads, it is often used for workloads that don't have strict performance or deadline requirements and it contains substantial support for unreliable environments. HTCondor uses a match-making process to assign jobs to worker nodes where individual jobs specify attributes that they require and workers advertise attributes that they contain. Condor contains built-in support to reschedule failed jobs as well as mechanisms to checkpoint jobs and move them to different hosts. To support HTCondor, a new sensor would need to be developed in order to interface with Condor's API. New policies that understand Condor's match-making capabilities are also needed; this would allow the policies to identify job requirements and provision resources that match those requirements. Additionally, the policies should recognize Condor's ability to checkpoint, transfer, and reschedule jobs and be able to adapt accordingly. However, an HTCondor elastic environment could leverage many of the same technologies as our Torque environment, including Gluster, the recontextualization broker, and a central IaaS auto scaling and provisioning service.

Hadoop [3] is another widely-used and open source framework, primarily for MapReduce workflows. Hadoop also includes a distributed file system (HDFS) that pools together the storage capacity of individual worker nodes in the system and distributes data across the workers. Hadoop jobs are then dispatched to workers containing the data required by the job. Similar to HTCondor, new sensors and policies would need to be developed for Hadoop. As an example, Hadoop colocates tasks and data, therefore, when new workers are added to the cluster, large data sets may be distributed to them. Simply terminating idle Hadoop workers may be more problematic than Torque workers where data is stored at a central location. Therefore, it may be more beneficial to scale Hadoop clusters conservatively and avoid terminating workers whenever possible. The recontextualization broker and the central IaaS auto scaling and provisioning service, however, could all be used in their current states. Additionally, Gluster could be used without requiring any adjustments to MapReduce workflows since it includes built-in support for Hadoop.

6   Related Work

Prior to the introduction of IaaS clouds, several projects developed dynamic resource managers that adjust resource deployments based on demand [38], [39], [29]. More recently, applications have begun to add support for IaaS clouds. Specifically, Sun Grid Engine [12], now Oracle Grid Engine contains support for Amazon EC2 resource provisioning [34]. Evangelinos et al. [11] use Amazon EC2 to support interactive climate modeling. In both cases these applications only include support for Amazon EC2, and they both bundle support for EC2 directly into the application. Application-specific approaches, such as these, require that each individual application include support for all cloud providers that users may need.

Amazon CloudWatch [2] is a cloud-specific approach for elastic resource provisioning. CloudWatch can scale environments based on demand; however, it only uses Amazon EC2. OpenNebula [40], an IaaS toolkit, also provides a cloud-specific approach, bundling support for Amazon EC2. Our solution is more general than cloud-specific and application-specific approaches, allowing any application to share a single service and code base for IaaS resource provisioning. Juve et al. [21] present a generic IaaS management solution, Wrangler, that provisions IaaS resources across multiple clouds and deploys applications on those resources. Wrangler, however, is not an elastic management solution that adapts the environment based on changing demand; instead, Wrangler focuses on deploying relatively standalone environments for users. The University of Victoria's Cloud Scheduler [5] is perhaps the most similar to our solution. Cloud Scheduler monitors a Condor queue and provisions resources across Nimbus clouds and Amazon EC2. Currently, Cloud Scheduler does not contain a mechanism for recontextualizing nodes, and instead it focuses on high throughput computing (HTC) jobs.

7   Future Work

In future work we will extend our solution to support Amazon's Auto Scaling API, allowing the environment to use auto scaling services that implement Amazon's API. We will also benchmark the IO performance of Gluster in a variety of configurations, including both single-cloud and multi-cloud deployments. We will compare Gluster to other file systems, including NFS, XtreemFS [45], and ceph [8]. To demonstrate the end-to-end capabilities of the environment we will process large scientific datasets. Furthermore, we will investigate efficient data movement solutions, which are a key requirement since cloud providers may charge for data transfers, therefore, data movement solutions should avoid sending excessive amounts of data or duplicate datasets to cloud resources for both cost and performance reasons. Existing file system technologies do not include advanced policies that allow users to tailor data transfers. Such a solution would likely need to be tightly integrated with compute scheduling, allowing the environment to colocate compute processing with data.

8   Conclusions

We present a large-scale elastic computing architecture and extend an open source elastic resource manager, the Elastic Processing Unit (EPU), to support the Torque batch-queue scheduler. We also develop a lightweight REST-based recontextualization broker that periodically and securely exchanges host information between all nodes in a context, allowing the environment to support parallel jobs. To support reliable data movement over wide-area deployments we leverage the Gluster file system. In addition to our implementation, we thoroughly discuss how our architecture can support other workflows, including Condor and Hadoop. We evaluate our elastic environment by examining its ability to scale rapidly and recontextualize quickly as resources join and leave the environment. The elastic environment is able to leverage multiple clouds, recontextualize 256 nodes within one second of the recontextualization period, and scale to over 475 nodes within 15 minutes. Finally, we demonstrate that the elastic environment supports parallel IO from distributed nodes, even over wide-area networks.

References

1. Amazon Web Services, http://aws.amazon.com/
2. Amazon Web Services CloudWatch, http://aws.amazon.com/cloudwatch/
3. Apache Hadoop, http://hadoop.apache.org

4. Armbrust, M., et al.: Above the Clouds: A Berkeley View of Cloud Computing. Technical report, UC-Berkeley (2009)
5. Armstrong, P., et al.: Cloud Scheduler: A Resource Manager for Distributed Compute Clouds. J. CoRR (2010)
6. Barham, P., et al.: Xen and the art of virtualization. In: 19th ACM Symposium on Operating System Principles, pp. 164–177. ACM, New York (2003)
7. Bode, B., et al.: The Portable Batch Scheduler and the Maui Scheduler on Linux Clusters. In: 4th Annual Linux Showcase and Conference, p. 27. USENIX Association, Berkeley (2000)
8. Ceph, http://ceph.com
9. EPU, GitHub, https://github.com/ooici/epu
10. FutureGrid, https://portal.futuregrid.org
11. Evangelinos, C., Hill, C.: Cloud Computing for Parallel Scientific HPC Applications: Feasibility of Running Coupled Atmosphere-Ocean Climate Models on Amazon's EC2. In: 1st Workshop on Cloud Computing and its Applications (2008)
12. Gentzsch, W.: Sun Grid Engine: Towards Creating A Compute Power Grid. In: 1st IEEE/ACM International Symposium on Cluster Computing and the Grid, pp. 35–36. IEEE Computer Society, Washington D.C. (2001)
13. Ghoshal, D., et al.: I/O Performance of Virtualized Cloud Environments. In: 2nd International Workshop on Data Intensive Computing In The Clouds, pp. 71–80. ACM, New York (2011)
14. Gluster, http://www.gluster.org
15. He, Q., et al.: Case Study for Running HPC Applications in Public Clouds. In: 19th ACM International Symposium on High Performance Distributed Computing, pp. 395–401. ACM, New York (2010)
16. Huang, W., et al.: A Case for High Performance Computing with Virtual Machines. In: 20th Annual International Conference on Supercomputing, pp. 125–134. ACM, New York (2006)
17. Jackson, D., et al.: Core Algorithms of the Maui Scheduler. J. Job Sch. Str. for Par. Proc. 2221, 87–102 (2001)
18. Jackson, K., et al.: Seeking Supernovae in the Clouds: A Performance Study. In: 19th ACM International Symposium on High Performance Distributed Computing, pp. 421–429. ACM, New York (2010)
19. Jacob, A.: Infrastructure in the Cloud Era. In: International OReilly Conference Velocity (2009)
20. Juve, G., et al.: Data Sharing Options for Scientific Workflows on Amazon EC2. In: International Conference for High Performance Computing, Networking, Storage and Analysis, pp. 1–9. IEEE Computer Society, Washington D.C. (2010)
21. Juve, G., Deelman, E.: Automating Application Deployment in Infrastructure Clouds. In: IEEE International Conference on Cloud Computing Technology and Science, pp. 658–665 (2011)
22. Keahey, K., et al.: Virtual Workspaces: Achieving Quality of Service and Quality of Life in the Grid. J. Sci. Pro. 13, 265–276 (2005)
23. Keahey, K., Freeman, T.: Contextualization: Providing One-Click Virtual Clusters. In: eScience, pp. 301–308 (2008)
24. Keahey, K., et al.: Infrastructure Outsourcing in Multi-Cloud Environments. In: 2012 Workshop on Cloud Services, Federation, and the 8th Open Cirrus Summit, pp. 33–38. ACM, New York (2012)
25. Marshall, P., Keahey, K., Freeman, T.: Elastic Site: Using Clouds to Elastically Extend Site Resources. In: 10th IEEE/ACM International Symposium on Cluster, Cloud and Grid Computing, pp. 43–52. IEEE Computer Society, Washington D.C. (2010)
26. Marshall, P., Tufo, H., Keahey, K.: Provisioning Policies for Elastic Computing Environments. In: 26th International Parallel and Distributed Processing Symposium Workshops and PhD Forum, pp. 1085–1094. IEEE Computer Society, Washington D.C. (2012)

27. Marshall, P., et al.: Architecting a Large-Scale Elastic Environment: Recontextualization and Adaptive Cloud Services for Scientific Computing. In: 7th International Joint Conference on Software Technologies (2012)
28. Maui, http://www.clusterresources.com/pages/products/maui-cluster-scheduler.php
29. Murphy, M., et al.: Dynamic Provisioning of Virtual Organization Clusters. In: 9th IEEE International Symposium on Cluster Computing and the Grid, pp. 364–371. IEEE Computer Society, Washington D.C (2009)
30. Nimbus, http://www.nimbusproject.org
31. November 2011 Top500, http://top500.org/list/2011/11/100
32. OOI EPU, https://confluence.oceanobservatories.org/display/syseng/CIAD+CEI+OV+Elastic+Computing
33. Opscode, Chef, http://www.opscode.com/chef/
34. Oracle Grid Engine, http://www.oracle.com/us/products/tools/oracle-grid-engine-075549.html
35. Ostermann, S., et al.: A Performance Analysis of EC2 Cloud Computing Services for Scientific Computing. In: Avresky, D.R., Diaz, M., Bode, A., Ciciani, B., Dekel, E. (eds.) Cloudcomp 2009. LNICST, vol. 34, pp. 115–131. Springer, Heidelberg (2010)
36. PBS Python, https://subtrac.sara.nl/oss/pbs_python
37. Rehr, J., et al.: Scientific Computing in the Cloud. J. Com. in Sci. Eng. 12, 34–43 (2010)
38. Ruth, P., McGachey, P., Dongyan, X.: VioCluster: Virtualization for Dynamic Computational Domains. In: IEEE Cluster Computing, pp. 1–10. IEEE Computer Society, Washington D.C. (2005)
39. Ruth, P., et al.: Autonomic Live Adaptation of Virtual Computational Environments In a Multi-Domain Infrastructure. In: IEEE International Conference on Autonomic Computing, pp. 5–14. IEEE Computer Society, Washington D.C. (2006)
40. Sotomayor, B., et al.: Virtual Infrastructure Management in Private and Hybrid Clouds. J. Int. Comp. 13, 14–22 (2009)
41. Tannenbaum, T., et al.: Condor: A Distributed Job Scheduler. B. C. Comp. w. Win. 307–350 (2002)
42. Vinoski, S.: Advanced Message Queuing Protocol. J. Int. Comp. 10, 87–89 (2006)
43. Wilkening, J., et al.: Using Clouds for Metagenomics: A Case Study. In: Cluster Computing and Workshops, pp. 1–6. IEEE Computer Society, Washington D.C. (2009)
44. Woitaszek, M., Tufo, H.: Developing a Cloud Computing Charging Model for High-Performance Computing Resources. In: 10th IEEE International Conference on Computer and Information Technology, pp. 210–217. IEEE Computer Society, Washington D.C. (2010)
45. XtreemFS, http://www.xtreemfs.org

Improving Estimates by Hybriding CMMI and Requirement Engineering Maturity Models – A LEGO Application

Luigi Buglione[1,2], Jean Carlo Rossa Hauck[3], Christiane Gresse von Wangenheim[3], and Fergal Mc Caffery[4]

[1] Engineering.IT SpA - via R. Morandi 32, 00148 Rome, Italy
[2] Ecole de Technologie Supérieure (ETS) – Montréal, Canada
[3] Federal University of Santa Catarina (UFSC), Brazil
[4] Regulated Software Research Group & LERO - Dundalk Institute of Technology, Ireland
luigi.buglione@eng.it, {jeanhauck,gresse}@gmail.com,
fergal.mccaffery@dkit.ie

Abstract. Even if the 'measurement' and 'estimation' issues are one of the most relevant issues for the proper management of a project, its origin besides in a good management of its requirements. In fact, estimation is highly dependent on the quality of requirements elicitation and management. Therefore, the management of requirements should be prioritized in any process improvement program, because the less precise the requirements gathering, analysis and sizing, the greater the error in terms of time and cost estimation. Maturity and Capability Models (MCM) represent a good tool and base of experience in order to assess the status of a set of processes, but an inner limit of any model is its scope and approach for describing a certain issue and more MCM are typically available on a certain topic, dealing with it in a different way. Thus, integrating two or more models with a common area of focus can offer more information and value for an organization, keeping the best components from each model. **LEGO** (Living EnGineering prOcess) is an approach projected for this purpose. This paper proposes a LEGO application hybridizing a 'horizontal' model (a MM containing processes going through the complete supply chain, from requirements right through to delivery, e.g. CMMI or ISO 12207/15504) with a few specific 'vertical' models (MMs with focus on a single perspective or process category, e.g. TMMi or TPI in the Test Management domain, P3M3 and OPM3 in the Project Management domain) for Requirement Engineering.

Keywords: Process Appraisals, Process Improvement, CMMI, ISO/IEC 15504, LEGO, Requirement Management, Maturity & Capability Models (MCM).

1 Introduction

One of the latest neologisms from the last 5 years is 'glocal' [44], which refers to the ability to "*think* globally and *act* locally". Cultural differences among countries

J. Cordeiro, S. Hammoudi, and M. van Sinderen (Eds.): ICSOFT 2012, CCIS 411, pp. 127–139, 2013.
© Springer-Verlag Berlin Heidelberg 2013

should be taken into account more and more when designing processes, particularly as very interesting ideas may arise from a comparison among different practices. For instance, when comparing Western and Eastern worlds and behaviours, Western people 'act', Eastern people 'think' (a bit more) before acting [17, 30, 9]. But observing both perspectives and attitudes, it is possible to represent it as a sort of 'yin-yang', complementing each other [42]. Thus, there is never a better idea, but different shades to be considered when (re)designing a process and/or a technique.

Estimation is one of the core processes in any organization. According to the Webster-Merriam dictionary, it is "1. a judgment or opinion about something; 2. the act of judging the size, amount, cost, etc., of something : the act of estimating something; 3. a guess about the size, amount, cost, etc., of something". PMBOK defines estimation as "a quantitative assessment of the likely amount or outcome. Usually applied to project costs, resources, effort, and durations and is usually preceded by a modifier (i.e., preliminary, conceptual, feasibility, order-of-magnitude, definitive)" [36].

However, estimates often have a higher error rate than expected, by running a RCA (Root-Cause Analysis) for detecting issues, it is possible to remove issuing surrounding requirements. The top-10 of estimation "deadly sins" [31, 32] can be a valid starting point for improving it, noting how much the missing (or the low quality) of requirements and its related historical data as well their granularity level could largely impact on the estimation process. Using again CMMI-DEV elements, Project Planning (PP) process area – where estimation is run – in the 'Related Process Areas' includes also Requirement Management (RM) and Requirement Development (RD) for the management of requirements; PP SP1.2 affirms that "*The estimates should be consistent with project requirements to determine the project's effort, cost, and schedule*". It's the same when using the SPICE [25] language, dealing with MAN.3 (Project Management) for estimates and ENG.1 (Requirements Elicitation) plus ENG.4 (Software Requirement Analysis) [7]. Thus, there is a huge need for any organization to first reinforce the Requirement Management process (in a broader sense, not strictly in the CMMI terms, because it's a ML2 process area), starting from elicitation and analyzing (RD – Requirements Development, ML3) throughout requirements management. But what's the problem? What does not currently exist or it is not well structured in organizations?

The aim of this paper is to propose a **LEGO** (**L**iving **EnG**ineering pr**O**cess) application for the Requirements Engineering (RE) area, matching together different RE processes using a four-step process, in order to obtain a comprehensive process to be applied in an organization, which could enable better estimates to be achieved.

The paper is organized as follows: Section 2 proposes a series of specific requirements management maturity models and frameworks, for extracting any possible element of interest (EoI) for reinforcing a typical Requirements Engineering (*horizontal*) process. Section 3 summarizes the LEGO approach, with its main elements and four-step process. Section 4 shows the deployment of LEGO to the Requirements Management process, joining the CMMI-DEV RD process area with the EoI from the previously examined RE models/frameworks. Finally, Section 5 provides some conclusions and the next steps for this work.

2 Requirement Engineering: Some Maturity and Capability Models (MCM)

During the '90s the 'maturity models mania' started [12] and now many 'something-maturity-model(s)' exist in many application areas and domains, and this is also the case for (software) RE. Table 1 presents some Maturity Models in the RE arena that can represent potential "*vertical*" models to be integrated into a consolidated and well known "*horizontal*" model such as CMMI-DEV [11] or SPICE [25; 24]. The specific processes to be involved would be respectively: RD (Req. Development) and RM (Req. Management) for CMMI_DEV and ENG.1 (Req. Elicitation) and ENG.4 (Software Design) processes for SPICE. For each of the models we present: its representation types, number of MLs, process architecture type and further comments/notes.

Table 1. Some requirement engineering maturity models/frameworks

Model/ Framework	Repr. Type	ML (#)	Architect-Type	Comments/Notes
IBM RMM [19, 38]	Staged	6 [0-5]	Level-based	---
IAG RMM [20]	Staged	6 [0-5]	Matrix-based	6 dimensions (process, practices & techniques, deliverables, technology, organization, staff competency)
PRTM CRMM [18]	Staged	4 [0-3]	Level-based	---
BTH REPM [14, 15]	Continuous		Process-based	7 processes Variable number of sub-process areas per process
REAIMS Process MM [40]	Staged	3 [1-3]	Process-based	8 process areas and 66 practices (basic, intermediate, advanced)
R-CMM [34]	Staged	5 [1-5]	Process-based	'Processes' = Practices (e.g. 20 'processes' at ML2) - Adaptation of GQM for deriving practices
R-CMMi [39]	Staged	5 [1-5]	Process-based	'Processes' = Practices (e.g. 20 'processes' at ML2) - Adaptation of GQM for deriving practices using the CMMI process architecture

Some comments about those RE models that could be useful for the LEGO analysis:

- A general trend in RE is to propose staged models more than continuous ones → suggesting a 'standard' way to progress maturity within an organization more than focusing upon each single RE process. This provides interesting information   should be considered when re-modeling these models into a target model according to its process architecture.

- No particular architectural elements have been introduced/modified against well-known horizontal models, differently than in other application domain (e.g. see P3M3 [34] and OPM3 [35] in the Project Management) → there is evidence that many of those models are still maturing and evolving (e.g. [4] and [39] have deployed only details for ML2).Some possible tips about its progression could come from joining organizational and/or support processes (e.g. communication, coaching, and mentoring processes from the People CMM model [13] or from Stakeholders Engagement practices [1]).

- Documentation should be provided to fully describe the requirements and project scope → this is a point of contact with Quality Management Systems (QMS) such as ISO 9001 or 20000-1, this is typically stressed less in CMMI constellations (see also the results from Mutafeljia & Stromberg's mapping [33]) but thus is not the in SPICE related models (including a specific process on Documentation: SUP.7). Another interesting related issue concerns the quest for reducing requirements volatility (e.g. REAIMS) and defining a taxonomy of requirement attributes for properly managing them by interest groups and/or techniques (e.g. REPM), for instance, making a clear distinction between functional vs. non-functional product requirements from the outset. This is a relevant issue in the FSM (Functional Size Measurement) community, where there is often – at the practical and daily level – a misconception about the roles and relevance of NFR (Non-Functional Requirements) against FUR (Functional User Requirements) in the estimation process, where NFR are typically underestimated because not properly elicited, evidenced and sized from the requirement elicitation phase[1]. If something doesn't appear to everybody's view, it doesn't exist. If it doesn't exist, it cannot be evaluated and sized and therefore the 'nominal' effort (and costs) will be lower than expected, creating the gap in the so-called 'cone of uncertainty' in higher level SLC phases against a strong reduction of such curve progressing along the project lifetime.

The allowed choices for the "Architectural Type" column are: **Level**-based (high-level depth, generic description of needed actions per ML), e.g. [2]; **Matrix**-based (mid-level depth, indication of a series of improvement drivers with a specific text per each cell), e.g. [23]; **Process**-based (low-level depth, with a consistent process architecture and repeatable elements per each defined process), e.g. [10].

3   Experiencing LEGO to Requirement Engineering

3.1   The LEGO Approach

Recently we proposed a common-sense approach, called **LEGO** (Living EnGineering prOcess) [8] for stimulating organizations to improve their own processes, taking

---

[1] Recently IFPUG released a new method called SNAP (Software Non-functional Assessment Process) [21], sizing product NFRs moving from part of the elements composing the FPA Value Adjustment Factor (VAF) that's a complementary (but NFR-based) part of the original counting rules by Dr. Albrecht. It takes elements from the evolution of ISO/IEC 9126-1:2001 quality model [26] that now is numbered as ISO/IEC 25010:2011 [27].

pieces (such as the real LEGO bricks) from multiple, potential information sources to be integrated to form a unique, reinforced picture for a particular process or set of processes. The starting point – for this paper – is that any model/framework can represent only a part of the observed reality, not all of its possible views, simply because it needs to represent one single viewpoint at a time. Thus, through handling similar elements from different sources, we can hopefully find more 'fresh blood' for improving the organizational processes.

LEGO has four main elements, as shown in Figure 1:

1. a 'Maturity & Capability Models' (MCM) repository (www.gqs.ufsc.br/mcm), from relevant processes or MMs (meaning also the other dimensions – not yet the process dimension) can be identified;

2. knowledge about the process architecture of each model, for understanding how to transform desired elements from a certain model into the target format, especially when considering that the source models may have different architectures that need to be integrated into a single model;

3. mapping(s) & comparisons between relevant models, in order to understand the real differences or the deeper level of detail from 'model A' to import into 'model B';

4. a process appraisal method (PAM) to be applied on the target BPM (Business Process Model).

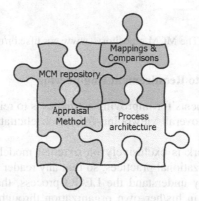

Fig. 1. The four elements of the LEGO approach

LEGO has also a related four-step process:

1. Identify your Informative/Business Goals: clearly identify your needs, moving from the current BPM version and content.

2. Query the MCM Repository: browse the MCM repository, setting up the proper filters in order to obtain the desired elements (processes; practices; etc.) to be inserted in the target BPM. The MCM is a web-based repository that enables the storage, discovery and retrieval of information on Maturity and Capability Models, providing the ability to locate models through simple and advanced searches using different attributes.

For doing this, as discussed in [16], a five-step knowledge engineering (KE)-based process needs to be run, where the steps are: Knowledge identification; Knowledge Specification; Knowledge Refinement; Knowledge Usage Knowledge Evolution[2].

3. Include the selected Element(s) into the Target BPM: include the new element(s) in the proper position in the target BPM (e.g. process group, maturity level, etc.).

4. Adapt and Adopt the selected Element(s): according to the process architecture of both process models (the target and the source one), the selected elements may need to be adapted, tailoring such elements as needed.

Fig. 2. The MCM repository (www.gqs.ufsc.br/mcm)

3.2   Applying LEGO to Requirement Engineering

One of the main requirements for improving estimates is to reinforce the management of requirements from an overall viewpoint, from their elicitation through to the day-to-day management.

The focus of this work is exclusively on external models as opposed to actual (living and active) organizational practices, so that any reader can easily access to the original sources and fully understand the LEGO process, that could (eventually, if interested) be replicated in his/her own organization through forward moving from their existing organizational Business Process Model (BPM). Our aim is to show how to hybridize ideas for obtaining a better and more comprehensive final result.

Thus, we list the preconditions, process and main results from the application of the LEGO process to the Requirements Engineering (RE) domain, in order to propose a better RE process that may be applied in an organization:

1. Identify your Informative/Business Goals: improve the estimation capability and results by a refinement in the overall management of requirements (business, technical);

---

[2] A list of techniques to apply for each of the five steps is proposed in [16], table 2.

2. Query the MCM Repository: in this paper we consider CMMI-DEV RE processes (RD; RM) as the baseline for working upon, adding eventual practices from the other RE models/frameworks listed in Table 1. After a detailed analysis, we discarded the IBM RMM, proposing only a high-level staged path with no detailed elements, and focus on the remaining ones. Table 2 proposes the list of potential elements of interest (EoI) to consider for improving CMMI processes on RE.

3. Include the selected Element(s) into the Target BPM: looking at the analysis of potential EoI in Table 2. The main improvements/suggestions seem to be mainly associated with the RD process, rather than the RM process. Table 3 shows how our suggestions were introduced in the current RD process, describing a new possible improved process that may be mapped against your own QMS internal process(es) covering that subject.

Table 2. RE Maturity & Capability Models (MCM): elements of interest

Model/ Framework	Elements of Interest (EoI)
IAG RMM	• Technology: the introduction of workflow environments for easily sharing information for keeping requirements could be useful → CMMI-DEV RD GP2.3 (Elaboration section in Part 1) • Staff competency: suggested the introduction of Bloom's levels as informative notes for all GP 2.5, not only for those two PAs
PRTM CRMM	• Level 1: link between product and customer requirements, using e.g. QFD (quality function deployment) → it could be introduced also in CMMI-DEV RD SP 3.4, not only in SP 2.1 (as currently done) for closing the analysis
BTH REPM	• RE.SI (Stakeholders and Req. Source Identification) → more specific practice to be added about Requirement Elicitation to CMMI-DEV RD SG1 • RE.GA.a2 (Qualify and Quantify Quality Requirements) → currently missing a more clear and direct link with CMMI-DEV PP SP 1.2 • DS.GA.a2 (Define Requirement Attributes) → currently less stressed (e.g. FUR vs NFR for FSM/FPA – Function Point Analysis, as requested in CMMI-DEV PP, SP 1.4
REAIMS Process MM	Basic practices: • 3.1 Define a standard document structure: missing, could be added in CMMI-DEV RD SG1, stressing the need for having an organizational 'standard' for comparing different types of requirements, having impact also on planning (different roles, productivities and schedules for different activities → PP SP 1.4). Again, it'd help also PP SP 1.2 because it'd address better the • 3.8 Make the document easy to change → criteria for writing better requirements, could be stressed more in CMMI-DEV RD SG1 / RM SG1, SP 1.3 • 6.2 Use language simply and concisely → criteria for writing better requirements could be added as a note for CMMI-DEV RD SP 1.2, sub-practice #1 Advanced practices: • 9.8 Identify volatile requirements: suggested to introduce the concept of 'volatility' also in the RD process definition by an informative note (e.g. "…verifying the new need will not be yet addressed by a formalized requirement…", with a link to RM, SP 1.3), → see also R-CMMi P20 process, same issue
R-CMM	• ML2: P19: Agree and document technical and organizational attributes specific to project → CMMI-DEV RD deals with customer and product requirements, not addressing with further informative notes about which could be possible 'constraints' such as those ones from the analysis of organizational attributes → reinforce RD SP 1.1
R-CMMi	• ML2: P20: Institute Process to Maintain Stability within Project → always about the need to minimize 'volatility', in terms of management → same comment than for REAIMS practice 9.8

4. Adapt and Adopt the Selected Element(s): after adapting the original RD process, as shown in the previous table, it should be mapped against the related QMS internal process covering that subject. Since many organizations adopt an ISO management system (e.g. ISO 9001:2008 [21]), a cross-check for validating potential improvements from the design phase could be achieved through re-applying the related mapping document to their own internal process (e.g. using the **N/P/L/F** – Not/Partially/Largely/Fully achieved ordinal scale from CMMI or SPICE). In our case, moving from CMMI-DEV, it could use Mutafeljia & Stromberg's mapping document [33] as a basis. One possible process flow for better expressing the way to do such mapping is in Figure 3. In this paper our focus was limited to only the design phase. However, a case study with the application of the hybrid-RD process will be included in a future paper.

Table 3. CMMI-DEV RD: suggestions for improvements

CMMI-DEV v1.3 RD process	Suggested Improvements
SG 1 Develop Customer Needs	• Introduce a new SP 1.0 about Stakeholders Identification and Engagement. Rationale: reinforce current formulation, before running SP 1.1. Nowadays, stakeholder engagement is the sub-practice #1 within SP 1.1. • Insert a note about possible standards (de jure/de facto) that could be consulted/useful for a better application of RD process (e.g.. [1]).
SP 1.1 Elicit Needs	• Introduce a sub-practice about the definition of requirement attributes, inserting a cross-link with PP SP 1.2 for the classification of work products (by attribute) to be sized. • Modify the current WP into: 'results of requirement elicitation activities **by entity and attribute**' (see previous comment)
SP 1.2 Transform Stakeholders needs	• Rephrase and make more general sub-practice #2: not only functional vs. quality (non-functional) attributes, but possibly establish all valuable, possible requirements taxonomies and classifications for the organization (by other criteria)
SG 2 Develop Product Requirements	• Introduce a note within the SG text about the need and relevance of define a (standard) document structure (in terms of 'documentability') and suggest – as informative note – some possible criteria to follow and appraise (e.g. readability, simple and concise language for writing requirements, etc.).
SP 2.1 Establish Product and Product components	• Sub-practice #3: refine the Example box, do no mention generic quality attributes, but be more specific about requirement classifications (e..g ISO/IEC 14143-1:1998 [24] → functional, quality, technical) → cross-link with PP 1.2 about attributes for sizing.
SP 2.2 Allocate Product Components	• ---
SP 2.3 Identify Interface Requirements	• ---
SG 3 Analyze and Validate Requirements	• ---
SP 3.1 Establish Operational Concepts and Scenarios	• ---
SP 3.2 Establish a Definition of Required …	• ---
SP 3.3 Analyze Requirements	• ---

Table 3. (*continued*)

SP 3.4 Analyze Requirements to Achieve Balance	• Introduce an informative note about the possible usage of QFD matrices also here, not only for eliciting and determining requirements in SP 2.1
SP 3.5 Validate Requirements	• ---
GP 2.3 Provide Resources	•General: stress the need and opportunity from workflow environments for an easier sharing of information among stakeholders, whatever the (CMMI) process •Specific (RD Elaboration): specific need because RD is the starting process for gathering needs to be translated into solutions
GP 2.5 Train People	• General: introduce the application of the six Bloom's cognitive levels 5 for classifying knowledge (see also IEEE SWEBOK – www.computer.org/swebok) • Specific (RD Elaboration): add 'stakeholder engagement' [1] and 'requirement sizing' [24]
GP 2.8 Monitor and Control the Process	•Specific (RD Elaboration): introduce at least one measure about the effectiveness of RD SG1 goal (e.g. % of proposed vs validated requirements)

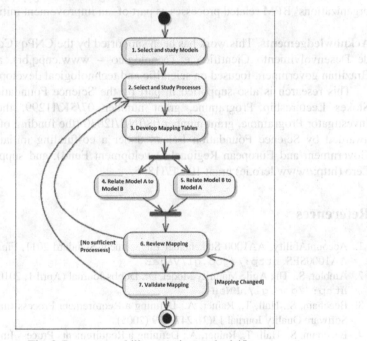

Fig. 3. Process capability mapping method 45

4   Conclusions and Next Steps

Requirements are the first step for a project and if they are not clearly and unambiguously defined this can increase the probability that project estimates will be incorrect because the project/activity scope has not been clearly documented. Even, if there are many existing requirements management models and frameworks, each model represents only one possible view of the inner reality that would be captured and reused: the '*one size doesn't fit all*' motto could be rephrased as '*one model doesn't fit all*'. Thus, at least 2 (or more) models/frameworks should be considered for improving your own processes (whatever they are), in the areas/issues needed.

In order to cope with this need, we recently proposed **LEGO** (Living EnGineering prOcess) as an open approach for improving the processes of a business process model (BPM), based upon the comparative analysis of the process architecture and elements of several concurrent models within a certain domain. Since estimation is one of the key processes for determining the success of an organization, we applied LEGO to Requirements Engineering, with the aim to improving the CMMI-DEV RD (Req. Development) process by integrating it with other requirements engineering maturity models. The final result was the design of a more encompassing hybrid-RD process that could help organizations to improve their estimates from the beginning of the value chain.

In the future, we will apply this hybrid-RD process to real case studies, proposing it as the meta-model to be used for the performing the initial gap analysis against the organizations' BPM related processes as part of an improvement initiative.

Acknowledgements. This work has been supported by the CNPq (Conselho Nacional de Desenvolvimento Científico e Tecnológico – www.cnpq.br), an entity of the Brazilian government focused on scientific and technological development.

This research is also supported in part by the Science Foundation Ireland (SFI) Stokes Lectureship Programme, grant number 07/SK/I1299, the SFI Principal Investigator Programme, grant number 08/IN.1/I2030 (the funding of this project was awarded by Science Foundation Ireland under a co-funding initiative by the Irish Government and European Regional Development Fund), and supported in part by Lero (http://www.lero.ie) grant 10/CE/I1855.

References

1. AccountAbility, AA1000 Stakeholder Engagement Standard 2011, Final Exposure Draft, AA1000SES, http://goo.gl/VajaE
2. Ambler, S.: The Agile Maturity Model, Dr. Dobbs Journal (April 1, 2010), http://goo.gl/nMNsH
3. Beecham, S., Hall, T., Rainer, A.: Defining a Requirement Process Improvement Model. Software Quality Journal 13(3), 247–279 (2005)
4. Beecham, S., Hall, T., Rainer, A.: Defining a Requirements Process Improvement Model, Technical Report 379, Hatfield, University of Hertfordshire (February 2003), http://goo.gl/6DvjY
5. Bloom, B.S., Engelhart, M.D., Furst, E.J., Hill, W.H., Krathwohl, D.R.: Taxonomy of educational objectives: the classification of educational goals. Handbook I: Cognitive Domain New York, Longmans, Green (1956)
6. Boehm, B.: Software Engineering Economics. Prentice-Hall Inc., Englewood Cliffs (1981) ISBN 0138221227
7. Buglione, L., Ebert, C.: Estimation, Encyclopedia of Software Engineering. Taylor & Francis Publisher (April 2012) ISBN: 978-1-4200-5977-9

8. Buglione, L., Gresse von Wangenheim, C., Hauck, J.C.R., McCaffery, F.: The LEGO Maturity & Capability Model Approach. In: Proceedings of the 5th World Congress on Software Quality

9. Chang, S.J.: When East and West Meet: An Essay of the Importance of Cultural Understanding in Global Business Practice and Education. Journal of International Business and Cultural Studies 2 (February 2010), http://goo.gl/OvkEw

10. CMMI Architecture Team, Introduction to the Architecture of CMMI Framework, Technical Note, CMU/SEI-2007-TN-009 (July 2007), http://goo.gl/NCPUw

11. CMMI Product Team, CMMI-DEV (CMMI for Development) v1.3, Technical Report, CMU/SEI-2010-TR-033, Software Engineering Institute (November 2010), http://goo.gl/T3okw

12. Copeland, L.: The Maturity Maturity Model (M3). Guidelines for Improving the Maturity Process, StickyMinds (September 2003), http://goo.gl/PHovg

13. Curtis, W., Miller, S., Hefley, W.: People Capability Maturity Model (P-CMM) Version 2.0 (CMU/SEI-2001-MM-001). Software Engineering Institute, Carnegie Mellon University (2001), http://goo.gl/z5jzJ

14. Gorschek, T.: Requirement Engineering Process Maturity Model (Uni-REPM), version 0.9CR, Technical Report, BTH, Sweden (January 2011), http://goo.gl/WBxos

15. Gorschek, T., Tejle, K.: A Method for Assessing Requirements Engineering Process Maturity in Software Projects, Master Thesis in Computer Science, BTH (Blekinge Tekniska Högskola), Sweden (June 2002), http://goo.gl/Tr5Dt

16. Hauck, J.C.R., von Wangenheim, C.G., Mc Caffery, F., Buglione, L.: Proposing an ISO/IEC 15504-2 compliant method for process capability/maturity models customization. In: Caivano, D., Oivo, M., Baldassarre, M.T., Visaggio, G. (eds.) PROFES 2011. LNCS, vol. 6759, pp. 44–58. Springer, Heidelberg (2011)

17. Hassan, A., Syuhada Jamaludin, N.: Approaches & Values in Two Gigantic Educational Philosophies: East and West. Online Educational Research Journal 1(2), 1–15 (2010), http://goo.gl/XQO9u

18. Hepner Brodie, C.: Are you hearing your customers' voices? In: PRTM (2006), http://goo.gl/wTz67

19. Heumann, J.: The Five Levels of Requirement Management Maturity, The Rationale Edge (2003), http://goo.gl/a7Mvj

20. Consulting, I.A.G.: Requirement Maturity Attribute Table (2009), http://goo.gl/gMgxp

21. IFPUG, Software Non-functional Assessment Process (SNAP) – Assessment Practice Manual (APM) Release 2.0 (2012)

22. ISO IS 9001:2008, Quality management systems – Requirements, International Organization for Standardization (December 2008)

23. ISO IS 9004:2009, Managing for the sustained success of an organization- A quality management approach, International Organization for Standardization (October 2009)

24. ISO/IEC IS 14143-x, Information Technology – Software Measurement – Functional Size Measurement, Parts 1-6 (2002-2011)

25. ISO/IEC IS 15504-x, Information technology – Process assessment, Parts 1-7, International Organization for Standardization (2001-2007)

26. ISO/IEC 9126-1:2001 – Software Engineering – Product quality – Part 1: Quality Model (2001)

27. ISO/IEC 25010:2011 - Systems and software engineering – Systems and software Quality Requirements and Evaluation (SQuaRE) – System and software quality models

28. Kollinger, J.: 7 Signs You Have a Bad Project Estimate (and what to do about it), Presentation (January 20, 2010), http://goo.gl/fp435
29. Koomen, T., Pol, M.: Test Process Improvement: a Practical Step-by-Step Guide to Structured Testing. Addison-Wesley (1999) ISBN 0-201-59624-5
30. Luo, P.: Analysis of Cultural Differences between West and East in International Business Negotiation. International Journal of Business and Management 3(11), 103–106 (2008), http://goo.gl/HCzTA
31. McConnell, S.: 10 Deadly Sins of Software Estimation, Presentation (2002), http://goo.gl/WjbGR
32. McConnell, Software Estimation: Demystifying the Black Art. Microsoft Press (2006) ISBN 978-0735605350
33. Mutafelija, B., Stromberg, H.: Process Improvement with CMMI v1.2 and ISO Standards, Auerbach (2008) ISBN 978-1420052831
34. OGC, P3M3: Portfolio, Programme & Project Management Maturity Model, Version 1.0, Office of Government Commerce (February 2006), http://www.ogc.gov.uk/documents/p3m3.pdf
35. PMI, Organizational Project Management Maturity Model (OPM3), 2nd edn. Knowledge Foundation. Project Management Institute (2008)
36. PMI, The Guide to the Project Management Body of Knowledge, 4th edn., Project Management Institute (2008), http://www.pmi.org
37. Schauder, J.: 8 Reasons why Estimates are too low (January 17, 2010), Schauderhaft website, http://goo.gl/F3T2f
38. Sehlhorst, S.: CMMI Levels and Requirements Management Maturity Introduction, TynerBlain (January 25, 2007), http://goo.gl/ARBLX
39. Solemon, B., Sahibuddin, S., Abd Ghani, A.A.: Re-defining the Requirements Engineering Process Improvement Model. In: Proceedings of the 16th Asia-Pacific Software Engineering Conference (APSEC 2009), Penang, Malaysia, pp. 87–92 (2009), http://goo.gl/ZpqZE
40. Sommerville, I., Ransom, J.: An Empirical Study of Industrial Requirements Engineering Process Assessment and Improvement. ACM Transactions on Software Engineering and Methodology 14(1), 85–117 (2005), http://goo.gl/xKIih
41. Standish Group, CHAOS Summary 2009. The 10 Laws of CHAOS (2009), http://goo.gl/ONXi4
42. Stawicki, J.: Principles of connecting East and West cultural differences in project management. In: XXII IPMA World Congress, Rome, Italy (2008), http://goo.gl/S81TP
43. Stellman, A., Greene, J.: Applied Software Project Management, ch. 3: Estimation. O'Reilly Publishing (2005) ISBN 978-0596009489
44. Swyngedouw, E.: Neither global nor local: 'glocalization' and the politics of scale. In: Cox, K. (ed.) Spaces of Globalization, pp. 137–166. Guilford Press, New York (1997), http://goo.gl/Lker1
45. Thiry, M., Zoucas, A., Tristão, L.: Mapping Process Capability Models to Support Integrated Software Process Assessments. Clei Electronic Journal 13(1), Paper 4 (April 2010), http://www.clei.cl/cleiej/papers/v13i1p4.pdf
46. Van Veenendaal, Test Maturity Model Integration (TMMi) version 3.1, TMMi Foundation (2010), http://www.tmmifoundation.org

Appendix

List of Acronyms

BPM	Business Process Model
CL	Capability Level
CMMI	Capability Maturity Model Integration
CMMI-DEV	CMMI for Development
ENG.1	Requirement Elicitation
ENG.4	Sw Requirement Analysis
IEC	Int. Electrotechnical Commission
ISO	Int. Organization for Standardization
LEGO	Living EnGineering prOcess
MAN.3	Quality Management process
MCM	Maturity & Capability Model
ML	Maturity Level
MM	Maturity Model
NFR	Non-Functional Requirement
OPM3	Organizational Project Management Maturity Model
P3M3	Portfolio, Programme, and Project Management Maturity Model
PAM	Process Assessment Model
PMBOK	Project Management Body of Knowledge
PMI	Project Management Institute
PP	Project Planning
PRM	Process Reference Model
QMS	Quality Management System
RCA	Root-Cause Analysis
RD	Requirement Development
RE	Requirement Engineering
REAIMS	Requirements Engineering adaptation and improvement for safety and dependability
REPM	Requirements Engineering Process Model
RM	Requirement Management
SEI	Software Engineering Institute
SPICE	Software Process Improvement Capability dEtermination (ISO/IEC 15504)
TMMi	Test Maturity Model Integration

Metamodel Independence in Domain Specific Modeling Languages

Jerónimo Irazábal[1,2] and Claudia Pons[1,3]

[1] LIFIA, Facultad de Informática, Universidad Nacional de La Plata, Argentina
[2] CONICET, Consejo Nacional de Investigaciones Científicas y Técnica, Argentina
[3] UAI, Universidad Abierta Interamericana, Buenos Aires, Argentina
{jirazabal, cpons}@lifia.info.unlp.edu.ar

Abstract. Domain-specific modeling languages can simplify the development of complex software systems by providing domain-specific abstractions for modeling the system and its evolution in a precise but simple and concise way. In this work we elaborate on the notion of domain specific model manipulation language, that is to say a model manipulation language tailored to a specific domain. In contrast to well-known model manipulation languages, such as EOL or ATL, the language syntax and semantics are directly related to a specific domain and/or kind of manipulation, making manipulation easier to write and understand. Furthermore, we show how additional languages can be defined for the same domain and we discuss about implementation alternatives achieving complete platform-independence. We illustrate the proposal through a practical example in the domain of workout plans.

Keywords: Model Driven Engineering, Model Transformation Language, Domain Specific Language.

1 Introduction

Model Driven Engineering (MDE) [31]; [28]; [18] proposes a software development process in which the key notions are models that allow engineers to precisely capture relevant aspects of a system from a given perspective and at an appropriate level of abstraction. Then, the automated development of a system from its corresponding models is realized by manipulating them. Model manipulation consists of a number of operations on the models, such as verifications, views, queries, transformations from model to model, transformations from model to code, etc.

Models can be expressed using different languages. Unlike general-purpose modeling languages (GPMLs), such us the UML, Domain-specific modeling languages (DSMLs), such as the Business Process Modeling Notation (BPMN) [34], can simplify the development of complex software systems by providing domain-specific abstractions for modeling the system in a precise but simple and concise way. DSMLs have a simpler syntax (few constructs focused to the particular domain) but its semantics is much more complex (all the semantics of the particular domain is embedded into the language).

J. Cordeiro, S. Hammoudi, and M. van Sinderen (Eds.): ICSOFT 2012, CCIS 411, pp. 140–154, 2013.

In a model-driven process, software is built by constructing one or more models, and successively manipulating them and transforming them into other models, until reaching an executable program code. A model manipulation program is a set of rules that together describe how a model can be checked (e.g. for consistency) and how a model written in the source language is mapped to a model written in the target language. Model manipulations are specified using a model manipulation language. There are already several proposals for model manipulation specification, implementation, and execution, which are being used by MDE practitioners [7]. The term "model manipulation language" comprises all sorts of artificial languages used in model manipulation development including general-purpose programming languages, domain-specific languages (DSLs) [22], modeling and meta-modeling languages and ontologies. Examples include languages such as the standard QVT [30]; ATL [1]; [10] and EOL [20].

These languages are specific for defining model manipulations but they are independent of any modeling domain; so they contain complex constructs referring to pattern matching mechanisms, control structures, etc. This can eventually compromise the primary aims for which the DSML was built: domain focus and conciseness. Consequently, an extra level of specialization should be achieved on them; we can define a manipulation language specifically addressed to a given domain, that is to say, a Domain Specific Model Manipulation Language (DSMML). For example, we can create a language dedicated to the definition of transformations between data-base models or a language addressed to the definition of transformations between business process models.

In this context, when we would like to take advantage of a very specific manipulation language we face the problem of implementing such a new language. There exist powerful frameworks for the definition of domain specific languages, such as Eclipse [12]; [14] and Microsoft DSL Tools [6]; [13].

In the present work we describe a proposal for defining domain specific model manipulation languages and also we analyze a novel way to define their semantics. Our proposal consists in using MDE tools themselves for the implementation of such languages, which improves modularity and reuse. The article is organized as follows. Section 2 presents the main features of our proposal to define domain specific manipulation languages using MDE tools. Section 3 illustrates the use of the approach to the definition of a new DSMML. Section 4 extends the example presenting an additionalDSL for the same domain. Section 5 compares our approach with related research and finally Section 6 presents the conclusions.

2   DSMML Semantics: Implementation Schema

Any language consists of two main elements: a syntactic notation (syntax) which is a set of elements that can be used in the communication, together with their meaning (semantics). The term "syntax" refers to the notation of the language. Syntactic issues focus purely on the notational aspects of the language, completely disregarding any meaning. On the other hand, the "semantics" assigns an unambiguous meaning to each syntactically allowed phrase in the language. To be useful in the computer engineering discipline, any language must come complete with rigid rules prescribing the allowed form of a syntactically well formed program, and also with formal rules pre scribing its semantics.

In programming language theory, semantics is the field concerned with the rigorous mathematical study of the meaning of languages. The formal semantics of a language is given by a mathematical structure that describes the possible computations expressed by the language. There are many approaches to formal semantics, among them the denotational semantics approach is one of the most applied. According to this approach each phrase in the language is translated into a denotation, i.e. a phrase in some other language. Denotational semantics loosely corresponds to compilation, although the "target language" is usually a mathematical formalism rather than another computer language. Formal semantics allows a clear understanding of the meaning of languages but also enables the verification of properties such as program correctness, termination, performance, equivalence between programs, etc.

Technically, a semantic definition for a language consists of two parts a semantic domain and a semantic mapping, denoted μ, from the syntax to the semantic domain. In particular, our proposal consists in using a well known manipulation language as the semantic domain for the definition of the new DSMML´s semantics. Then, the semantic function μ is defined by a transformation written in a model-to-text transformation language (such as MOFScript [25]). This M2T transformation takes a program written in the DSMML as input, and generates a program written in a general purpose manipulation language (such as EOL) as output. This schema is described in Figure 1.

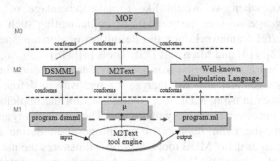

Fig. 1. Transformation scenario

The advantage of this technique is that the well-known manipulation language has already a well-defined semantics and provides an execution environment. So, the semantics of the new language becomes formally described and it is executable. Additionally, the semantic definition is understandable and adaptable because it is expressed in terms of a well-known high-level language.

3   Use Case

In this section we present a new DSMML using the proposed approach. This section is organized as follows; first we introduce the domain, then we propose different meta-models for a simplified version of the domain. Next, we present the new DSMML trough some examples. And finally we describe the most relevant issues of its implementation.

3.1   Workout Plan Domain

In websites related to running we frequently see tables such as the one showed in Figure 2. Such tables describe workout plans to help people to reach their fitness goals. The workout plan usually has a duration expressed in weeks and each day of the week contains a list of exercises that must be done with specific requirements, such as intensity and duration. Given that we are considering this domain just to exemplify our approach, we will restrict its functionality by giving to the user the possibility to specify only the time for each exercise, but without considering intensity or complex exercises.

	MONDAY	TUESDAY	WEDNESDAY	THURSDAY	FRIDAY	SATURDAY	SUNDAY
1	Run: 50	Gym: 45	Run: 50	Gym: 45	Run: 50		Run: 75
2	Run: 50	Gym: 45	Run: 50	Gym: 45	Run: 50		Run: 75
3	Run: 60	Gym: 45	Run: 60	Gym: 45	Run: 60		Run: 90
4	Run: 60	Gym: 45	Run: 60	Gym: 45	Run: 60		Run: 90

Fig. 2. A workout plan

As we said before, the DSMML is independent of the underlying meta-model. That is to say, the language syntax will remain unchanged even if we use a different but equivalent meta-model for the domain. In order to provide concrete evidence about this feature, we will present two meta-models for this domain, which are displayed in Figure 3 and Figure 4 respectively.

It is worth to mention that if we add or remove information from the meta-model, the manipulation language may get affected by these changes. For example, if we add the possibility to specify the intensity at which the exercises should be done, we might change the language to support this new feature. This fact does not mean that the language depends on the underlying meta-model; on the contrary the language just depends on the available information while how that information was represented in the meta-model is completely irrelevant.

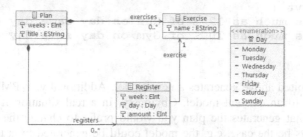

Fig. 3. Workout Plan Meta-model, version 1

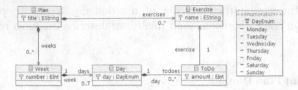

Fig. 4. Workout Plan Meta-model, version 2

3.2   WPML: A DSMML Fitting the Workout Plan Domain

In this section we introduce WPML (Workout Plan Manipulation Language). Given the high level of abstraction of WPML we consider that the code is self-explanatory. You can find detailed information about the language in [8]. The following WPML code creates the model showed in Figure 2:

```
create plan "myplan.plan"

set title "My plan"
set weeks 4

add exercise Run
add exercise Gym

on weeks 1 and 2 {
  on days Monday and Wednesday and Friday {
    do Run as much as 50 minutes
  }
  on days Tuesday and Thursday {
    do Gym as much as 45 minutes
  }
  on days Sunday {
    do Run as much as 150% of Run on day
      Monday of week same week
  }
}
from week 3 to 4 {
  on all days {
    do Run as much as 120% of Run on day same day of week 1
    do Gym as much as 100% of Gym on day same day of week 1
  }
}
```

The code exhibited above generates a new model. Additionally, WPML allows us to make changes to an existent model. Obviously, in a real situation if you have the WPML code that generates the plan you would prefer to change the code, but this may not always be the case, e.g. the model could be generated by a tool or another language. So, for example, given the model presented above, suppose we would like to increment the Running time by a 10% on the entire plan and also we would like to establish Sunday as the recovering day (day without exercises) instead of Saturday. The new plan is illustrated in Figure 5.

	MONDAY	TUESDAY	WEDNESDAY	THURSDAY	FRIDAY	SATURDAY	SUNDAY
1	Run: 55	Gym: 45	Run: 55	Gym: 45	Run: 55	Run: 82	
2	Run: 55	Gym: 45	Run: 55	Gym: 45	Run: 55	Run: 82	
3	Run: 66	Gym: 45	Run: 66	Gym: 45	Run: 66	Run: 99	
4	Run: 66	Gym: 45	Run: 66	Gym: 45	Run: 66	Run: 99	

Fig. 5. Modified workout plan

The WPML code to make those changes on the original model could be:

```
use plan "myplan.plan"

on all weeks {
on all days {
    increase Run by 10%
  }
  swap Saturday and Sunday
}
```

3.3 WPML: Implementation

This section covers the key aspects in the implementation of WPML. The organization of this section is as follows. First, the overall implementation schema is showed; then the functions and operations that are defined in the specific domain are implemented emphasizing their meta-model independence; finally, the WPML compiler is partially presented and the compilation results for the WPML are illustrated.

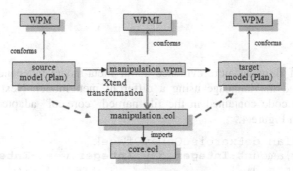

Fig. 6. DSMML implementation schema using a translational approach

Figure 6 shows an overview of the implementation schema where our domain specific manipulation language is translated to a general purpose manipulation language, in this case EOL. The EOL code generated from the WPML code imports a file named "core.eol". This file contains the implementation of all the functionality provided by the specific manipulation language, such as setting the number of weeks of the plan, adding exercises, setting the duration of each exercise per week, swapping the schedule between two days, etc.

The following code is a fragment of the file "core.eol"; it uses the meta-model showed in Figure 3:

```
operation Plan doExerciseOnDayOfWeek
(ex:String,amount:Integer,day:Integer,week:Integer) {
 if (amount = 0) {
  self.removeExerciseInDayOfWeek(ex,day,week);
 } else {
  self.getOrCreateRegister(ex,day,week).amount := amount;
 }
}

operation Plan increaseExerciseByPercentOnDayOfWeek
 (ex:String,percent:Integer, day:Integer,week:Integer) {
 var r : Register = self.getRegister(ex,day,week);
 if (r<>null) {
  r.amount = r.amount + r.amount * percent / 100;
 }
}

operation Plan swapDaysOnWeek
(day1:Integer,day2:Integer,week:Integer) {
  for (r:Register in self.registers){
    if (r.week = week) {
      if (r.day.value = day1) {
        r.setDay(day2);
      } else {
        if (r.day.value = day2) {
          r.setDay(day1);
        }
      }
    }
  }
}
```

With the aim of showing more evidence about meta-model independence we have also implemented the language using a different meta-model. Next we present a fragment of the code contained in the file named "core.eol" adapted to the meta-model showed in Figure 4.

```
operation Plan doExerciseOnDayOfWeek
 (ex:String,amount:Integer,day:Integer,week:Integer) {
  if (amount = 0) {
   self.removeExerciseInDayOfWeek(ex,day,week);
  } else {
   self.getOrCreateToDo(ex,day,week).amount := amount;
  }
}

 operation Plan increaseExerciseByPercentOnDayOfWeek
 (ex:String,percent:Integer day:Integer,week:Integer) {
  var toDo : ToDo = self.getToDo(ex,day,week);

  if (toDo<>null) {
   toDo.amount = toDo.amount+toDo.amount*percent/100;
```

```
  }
}

operation Plan swapDaysOnWeek
  (d1:Integer,d2:Integer,w:Integer) {
  for (d:Day in self.getWeek(w).days) {
    if (d.day.value = d1) {
      d.setDay(d2);
    } else {
      if (d.day.value = d2) {
        d.setDay(d1);
      }
    }
  }
}
```

Afterward, the compiler written with XTend [36] creates an EOL file from a WPML file. This file imports the core.eol file and invokes its functions according to the WPML code. The following code is a fragment of the compiler:

```
def compile(Manipulation m)
'''
import "../src/core.eol";
var p : Plan = getPlan();
«FOR c:m.metaChanges»
  «c.compileMetaChange»
«ENDFOR»
«FOR c:m.changes»
  «c.compileWeekChange»
«ENDFOR»
'''
...
def compileMetaChangeSetTitle(MetaChangeSetTitle c)
'''
  p.setTitle("«c.title»");
'''
...
def compileWeekChangeForAllWeeks(WeekChangeForAllWeeks c)
'''
for (w in Sequence{1..p.getWeeks()})
{
  «FOR dc:c.changes»
    «dc.compileDayChange»
  «ENDFOR»
}
'''
...
def compileDayChangeSwapDays(DayChangeSwapDays c)
'''
  p.swapDaysOnWeek(«c.day1.value»,«c.day2.value»,w);
'''
```

The EOL code that we show next was generated by the compiler with the WPML code given before for the creation and manipulation of a plan respectively.

```
import "../src/core.eol";
var p : Plan = getPlan();

p.setTitle("My plan");
p.setWeeks(4);
p.addExercise("Run");
p.addExercise("Gym");

for (w in Sequence{ 1,  2 }) {
  for (d in Sequence{0,2,4}) {
    p.doExerciseOnDayOfWeek("Run",50,d,w);
  }
  for (d in Sequence{1,3}) {
    p.doExerciseOnDayOfWeek("Gym",45,d,w);
  }
  for (d in Sequence{6}) {
    p.doExerciseOnDayOfWeek("Run",
((p.getAmountOfExerciseOnDayOfWeek("Run",0,w))*150/100),d
,w);
  }
}
for (w in Sequence{3..4}) {
  for (d in Sequence{0..6}) {
  p.doExerciseOnDayOfWeek("Run",((p.getAmountOfExerciseOn
DayOfWeek("Run",d,1))*120/100),d,w);
  p.doExerciseOnDayOfWeek("Gym",((p.getAmountOfExerciseOn
DayOfWeek("Gym",d,1))*100/100),d,w);
  }
}
```

The EOL code showed next is generated by the compiler with the WPML code showed before for the modification of a previously created plan.

```
import "../src/core.eol";
var p : Plan = getPlan();

for (w in Sequence{1..p.getWeeks()})
{
 for (d in Sequence{0..6}) {
    p.increaseExerciseByPercentOnDayOfWeek("Run",10,d,w);
 }
 p.swapDaysOnWeek(5,6,w);
}
```

4   Additional DSMML for the Workout Plan Domain

In this section we introduce a new language for the same domain, designed to define constraints on workout plan models.

It's worth to mention that we can use OCL to define constraints on models. However, given that OCL is a domain independent language, it cannot capture the knowledge of the subjacent domain in a smooth way, thus making the task of writing constraints harder and little intuitive. Additionally, OCL constraints are bounded to the meta model structure.

A domain specific constraint language allows us to reduce the complexity of the constraint expressions. Domain experts feel more comfortable using a specific language with constructs reflecting well-known concepts, such as exercise in our example, instead of the generic constructs provided by the OCL language. Additionally, the DSL is metamodel independent.

This section is organized in two subsections, in the first one we introduce the new DSL by examples and in the second we discuss about its implementation.

4.1 A DSL to Define Constraints on Workout Plan Models

As the knowledge of the domain is what gives sense to any DSL, we summarize a part of the knowledge we have about the workout plan domain in the next paragraph:

The duration of a workout plan is given in weeks. Each week is composed by a sequence of days. For each day, the plan establishes the point in time for each exercise. We know about the chronological order of the activities, the different kinds of exercises and the time required for their completion.

Based on that, we are able to create a language to define constraints on the particular elements in the domain, such as a given day, or week or the entire plan. The cons-traints could be as follows:

— Duration of exercises
— Sequence of exercises
— Recover time
— Relation between the different kind of exercises included in the plan

The following example specifies that the time of running shouldn't be increased more than a 10% per week:

```
use plan "myplan.plan"

on all weeks {
  ensures (minutes of Run on current week)
          lower or equal to
          110% of (minutes of Run on previous week)
}
```

Another constraint could be that whenever the person runs and does gym in the same day, he/she should finish the gym session before start running

```
use plan "myplan.plan"

on all weeks {
  on all days {
    ensures (has done (Run and Gym) today)
            then
            (end of Gym today before start of Run today)
  }
}
```

It's important to remark that as the objective of this work is to present an implementation approach to a set of DSLs for the same domain; our DSLs are illustrative and help us to present the implementation approach of multiple DSLs on the same domain. In the next subsection we discuss about how this new language could be implemented using the proposed implementation schema.

4.2   Implementation of the Constraint Language

We have identified two alternatives that can be chosen to implement this additional language. The first option and the easier to implement consists in checking the constraints on an existent model. The second implementation alternative would be to check the constraints every time a plan is modified. That is, check no constraint is invalidated with the requested change. The schemas are illustrated in figures 7 and 8 respectively.

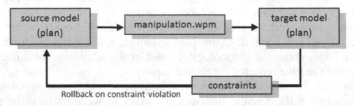

Fig. 7. Constraints checked after changes

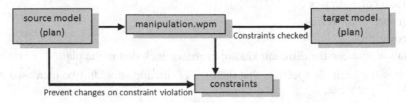

Fig. 8. Constraints checked before changes

According to the implementation approach purposed in this work, the constraints would be translated to a general transformation language such as EOL, ATL or in this case OCL would be another alternative, especially when the constraints are checked over an existent workout plan model, that is to say, when the changes were already made to the source model.

Both implementation schemas are viable, but when all the changes in the model can be undone without side effects, the first one is easier to implement.

5   Related Work

There are a number of features of our work that can be contrasted to previous works:

• The schema presented in this work is an evolution of the implementation schemas presented in [16], where the first approach covered consists in writing a transformation in a general transformation language (e.g. ATL) taking two models as input, one with the model to be manipulated and the other with the statements to be executed, and building a model as the result of applying those statements to the model given as input; the other schema consists in a two step transformation scenario, the first transformation (a model to text transformation) takes a model conforming the new DSMML and translates it to a general transformation language (e.g. ATL). Then, the generated transformation when executed on a model of the domain of interest performs the desired changes to it. In our current work, the transformation is written in a general transformation language (e.g. EOL) with the characteristic of being parameterised code. This way, the statements written in the new DSMML are translated (with a model to text transformation) to invocations to the previously written transformations, setting the parameters according to the elements to be manipulated. This way, the transformations are simpler and modularized.

• Abstraction and modularization of model transformations: Our approach can be seen as a technique for abstraction and modularization in that each high level manipulation (written in the DSMML) is associated with a lower level manipulation (written in a more general purpose language), but the users do not need to be aware of the details of the low level manipulations. In this sense, the works that propose techniques to build complex transformations by composing smaller transformation units are related to our proposal. In this category we can mention the composition technique described in [19], the Model Bus approach [4], the modeling framework for compound transformations defined in [25] and the module superimposition technique [33], among others. In contrast to these works, our approach generates the composed transformation specification in a simpler way, without introducing any explicit composition machinery.

• Creating languages that abstract from other more abstract languages: This subject has been intensely discussed in the literature on DSLs. For example, the MetaBorg [5] is a transformation-based approach for the definition of embedded textual DSLs implemented based on the Stratego framework. Similarly to our work, the MetaBorg approach defines new concepts (comparable to our notion of an abstract language) by mapping them to expansions in the host language (comparable to our notion of a concrete language). Johannes shows how to develop DSLs as abstractions of other DSLs by transferring translational approaches for textual DSLs into the domain of modelling languages [17]. The underlying notion of an embedded DSL has been discussed in [15]. The idea of forwarding has been introduced in [32]. An important distinction between these works and our work is the application to the MDE field. The AMMA framework [21] allows us to define the concrete syntax, abstract syntax, and semantics of DSLs. In [11]; [3]; [9] the reader can analyze a number of scenarios where the AMMA framework has been used to define the semantics of DSLs in terms of other languages or in terms of abstract state machines (ASMs). Our proposal is similar to the one of AMMA, but we present a novel alternative, where the language semantics is realized as the interpretation of the DSMML into a general purpose model manipulation language, by means of a transformation written in a M2T transformation language.

• Concrete-syntax-based transformations: Contrary to traditional approaches to model transformation, our approach, such as the one presented in [2], uses the concrete syntax of a language for expressing transformation rules. The claim is that this simplifies the development of model transformations, as transformation designers do not need deep knowledge of the language's metamodel. In our approach, we use the abstract DSMML with a similar purpose: users do not need to count with any knowledge of the abstract syntax of the involved modeling languages; they just use the simple syntax of the DSMML.

6   Conclusions

In this article we have explained the concept of domain specific model manipulation language, that is to say model manipulation languages tailored to a specific domain. In contrast to well-known model manipulation languages, such as EOL and ATL, the language syntax and semantics are directly related to a specific domain and/or kind of manipulation, making manipulation easier to write and understand.

In contrast to an approach where a general purpose model manipulation language is used, our approach provides the following benefits: the complexity of model manipulation programs gets reduced. A program is composed by few lines of high expressive commands. Domain experts will feel more comfortable using a specific language with constructs reflecting well-known concepts (such as, exercise and week in our example); consequently it is predictable that they will be able to write more understandable and reusable manipulation programs in a shorter time. Manipulation developers do not need to know the intricate details of the model manipulation languages, as these are encapsulated in the DSL constructs. This leads to a natural separation into a language designer and a manipulation programmer role, with a reduced learning effort for the later.

Also, we have proposed an implementation schema in which the transformation that compiles the DSMML sentences consists of invocations to previous defined operations written in a well known transformation language (e.g. EOL). This fact provides several advantages: the language semantics is formally described; it is executable; the semantics is understandable because it is written in a well-known language; the semantics can be easily modified by adding new transformation rules or even by radically changing the target language. Although this transformation may be considered as a compiler, the amount of programming skills required to create it is smaller than for creating a compiler to source code.

As an experimental example in this article we have reported the definition of a DSMML in the domain of workout plans and we have described its implementation using MDE tools. The experience was successful; showing the advantages of defining DSMML for model transformations within the same language, that is to say, transformations that locally change an existent model producing a new model that conforms to the same metamodel.

Also we have shown the implementation approach is compatible with the addition of new languages in the same domain. We've presented a new language to define constraints on training plan models and we've discussed about different alternatives for its implementation.

It is also important to take the benefits coming from the platform-independence of the model manipulation language into account; on one hand the language is independent of the underlying metamodel and on the other hand we are able to transform and execute the manipulation programs onto different model manipulation platforms, in the examples we have used EOL and ATL, but any other manipulation language can be used.

References

1. ATLAS MegaModel Management (2006), http://www.eclipse.org/gmt/am3/
2. Baar, T., Whittle, J.: On the Usage of Concrete Syntax in Model Transformation Rules. In: Virbitskaite, I., Voronkov, A. (eds.) PSI 2006. LNCS, vol. 4378, pp. 84–97. Springer, Heidelberg (2007)
3. Barbero, M., Bézivin, J., Jouault, F.: Building a DSL for Interactive TV Applications with AMMA. In: Proceedings of the TOOLS Europe 2007 Workshop on Model-Driven Development Tool Implementers Forum, Zurich, Switzerland (2007)
4. Blanc, X., Gervais, M., Lamari, M., Sriplakich, P.: Towards an integrated transformation environment (ITE) for model driven development (MDD). In: Proceedings of the 8th World Multi-Conference on Systemics, Cybernetics and Informatics (SCI 2004), USA (2004)
5. Bravenboer, M., Visser, E.: Concrete syntax for objects: Domain-specific language embedding and assimilation without restrictions. In: OOPSLA 2004: Proceedings of the 19th Annual ACM SIGPLAN Conference on Object-Oriented Programming, Systems, Languages, and Applications, pp. 365–383. ACM Press (2004)
6. Steve, C., Jones, G., Kent, S., Wills, A.C.: Domain-Specific Development with Visual Studio DSL Tools. Addison-Wesley Professional (2007) ISBN 0321398203
7. Czarnecki, H.: Feature-based survey of model transformation approaches. IBM System Journal 45(3) (2006)
8. DSMML (2011), http://www.lifia.info.unlp.edu.ar/eclipse/DSMML/
9. Di Ruscio, D., Jouault, F., Kurtev, I., Bézivin, J., Pierantonio, A.: Extending AMMA for Supporting Dynamic Semantics Specifications of DSLs (2009), http://hal.ccsd.cnrs.fr/docs/00/06/61/21/PDF/rr0602.pdf
10. Jouault, F., Kurtev, I.: Transforming Models with ATL. In: Bruel, J.-M. (ed.) MoDELS 2005. LNCS, vol. 3844, pp. 128–138. Springer, Heidelberg (2006)
11. Frédéric, J., Bézivin, J., Consel, C., Kurtev, I., Latry, F.: Building DSLs with AMMA/ATL, a Case Study on SPL and CPL Telephony Languages. In: Proceedings of the First ECOOP Workshop on Domain-Specific Program Development, Nantes, France (2006)
12. GME (2006), http://www.isis.vanderbilt.edu/Projects/gme
13. Greenfield, J., Short, K., Cook, S., Kent, S., Crupi, J.: Software Factories: Assembling Applications with Patterns, Models, Frameworks, and Tools, 1st edn. Wiley (2004)
14. Gronback, R.C.: Eclipse Modeling Project: A Domain-Specific Language (DSL) Toolkit. Addison-Wesley Professional (2009) ISBN: 0-321-53407-7
15. Hudak, P.: Modular domain specific languages and tools. In: ICSR 1998: Proceedings of the 5th International Conference on Software Reuse, Victoria, B.C., Canada, pp. 134–142. IEEE Computer Society Press (June 1998)
16. Irazábal, J., Pons, C., Neil, C.: Model transformation as a mechanism for the implementation of domain specific transformation languages. SADIO Electronic Journal of Informatics and Operations Research 9(1) (2010)
17. Johannes, J., Zschaler, S., Fernández, M.A., Castillo, A., Kolovos, D.S., Paige, R.F.: Abstracting Complex Languages through Transformation and Composition. In: Schürr, A., Selic, B. (eds.) MODELS 2009. LNCS, vol. 5795, pp. 546–550. Springer, Heidelberg (2009)

18. Kleppe, A.G., Jos, W., Bast, W.: MDA Explained: The Model Driven Architecture: Practice and Promise. Addison-Wesley Longman Publishing Co., Inc., Boston (2003)
19. Kleppe, A.: MCC: A Model Transformation Environment. In: Rensink, A., Warmer, J. (eds.) ECMDA-FA 2006. LNCS, vol. 4066, pp. 173–187. Springer, Heidelberg (2006)
20. Kolovos, D.S., Paige, R.F., Polack, F.A.C.: The Epsilon Object Language (EOL). In: Rensink, A., Warmer, J. (eds.) ECMDA-FA 2006. LNCS, vol. 4066, pp. 128–142. Springer, Heidelberg (2006)
21. Kurtev, I., Bézivin, J., Jouault, F., Valduriez, P.: Model-based DSL frameworks. In: Companion to the 21st ACM SIGPLAN Conference on Object-oriented Programming Systems, Languages, and Applications, pp. 602–616. ACM Press (2006) ISBN 1-59593-491-X
22. Marjan, M., Jan, H., Sloane Anthony, M.: When and how to develop domain specific languages. ACM Computing Surveys 37(4), 316–344 (2005)
23. Meta Object Facility (MOF) 2.0 (2003), http://www.omg.org
24. OCL (2006), http://www.omg.org/spec/OCL/2.0
25. Oldevik, J.: Transformation Composition Modeling Framework. In: Kutvonen, L., Alonistioti, N. (eds.) DAIS 2005. LNCS, vol. 3543, pp. 108–114. Springer, Heidelberg (2005)
26. Jon, O.: MOFScript User Guide (2006), http://www.eclipse.org/gmt/mofscript/doc/MOFScript-User-Guide.pdf
27. OMG (2011), http://www.omg.org
28. Claudia, P., Roxana, G., Gabriela, P.: Model Driven Software De velopment. Concepts and practical application. EDUNLP and McGraw-Hill Education, Buenos Aires, Agentina (2010)
29. Claudia, P., Jerónimo, I., Roxana, G., Gabriela, P.: On the semantics of domain specific transformation languages: implementation issues. Software Engineering: Methods, Modeling, and Teaching, ch. 13 (2011) ISBN: 9789588692326
30. QVT Adopted Specification 2.0. (2005), http://www.omg.org
31. Stahl, T., Völter, M.: Model-Driven Software Development. John Wiley & Sons, Ltd., Chichester (2006)
32. Van Wyk, E., de Moor, O., Backhouse, K., Kwiatkowski, P.: Forwarding in attribute grammars for modular language design. In: Nigel Horspool, R. (ed.) CC 2002. LNCS, vol. 2304, pp. 128–142. Springer, Heidelberg (2002)
33. Wagelaar, D.: Composition Techniques for Rule-based Model Transformation Languages. In: Procs. of ICMT2008 – Conference on Model Transformation, Zurich, Switzerland (2008)
34. Mathias, W.: Business Process Management: Concepts, Languages, Architectures, pp. 3–67. Springer (2008) ISBN 978-3-540-73521-2
35. XTend (2011), http://www.eclipse.org/Xtext/#xtend2
36. XText (2011), http://www.eclipse.org/Xtext/

Service-Oriented Integration of Metamodels' Behavioural Semantics

Henning Berg

Department of Informatics, Faculty of Mathematics and Natural Sciences,
University of Oslo, Norway
hennb@ifi.uio.no

Abstract. Metamodel composition is a central operation in model-driven engineering approaches. Composition of metamodels is not trivial. The essence of the problem is that metamodels are not defined as reusable artefacts. Moreover, most composition mechanisms focus on the structural aspects of metamodels without considering how metamodels may be composed semantically. Hence, models of different metamodels can not exchange data directly during execution at runtime. In this paper we investigate a new approach for integrating metamodels and their models by considering metamodels as reusable services at a conceptual level. In particular, the behavioural semantics of metamodels can be coupled in a loosely manner, without entanglement of semantically different concepts. This allows creating complex metamodel architectures where separation of concerns is high.

Keywords: Metamodelling, Model Composition, Behavioural Semantics, Aspect-orientation, Service-oriented Architecture, Domain-specific Language.

1 Introduction

Metamodels have an important role in *Model-Driven Engineering (MDE)* [1] where they are used, e.g. as formalisations in language and tool design. In most MDE environments, metamodels are realised as class models. Class models do not have other structure than what can be realised using simple packages, inheritance, composition and association relationships. This means that all metamodel concepts, regardless of purpose, are reified in the same modelling space without the ability to differentiate one type of concept from another. The lack of additional metamodel structure is not critical for metamodels consisting of a limited number of classes. However, as metamodels become larger and more complex, as a consequence of increasing maturity in model-driven approaches, several troubling issues emerge.

Model composition is a commonly used approach for elaborating a model or metamodel with additional concepts, e.g. [2][3][4][5][6]. Model composition is also a prerequisite for generating holistic system code, combining system views, verifying system views consistency and addressing software evolution. Model composition is performed by combining a set of models in an asymmetric or symmetric manner. Composition of metamodels is typically achieved using a variant of class merging or aspect-oriented weaving. Regardless of method, the result is a composite metamodel containing all classes from the source metamodels. There are some evident issues with many of the

J. Cordeiro, S. Hammoudi, and M. van Sinderen (Eds.): ICSOFT 2012, CCIS 411, pp. 155–170, 2013.

current model composition approaches. First, classes reflecting concepts of different concerns are all blended without inclusion of any additional metainformation describing from what source models the concepts in question originate, i.e. traceability is not semantically backed up. Second, composition of models induces conflicts that have to be resolved. E.g. class merging implies that the constituent classes do not contain equally named properties of different types, etc. Third, composition of models requires that the source models are altered intrusively. In particular, such alteration is required to integrate the constituent models' behavioural semantics. Fourth, integration of models requires explicit knowledge in metamodel design and insight into the specific environment used to realise the metamodels, e.g. *Eclipse Modeling Framework (EMF)* [7], *MetaEdit+* [8], *Generic Modeling Environment (GME)* [9], *Kermeta* [10] or similar. Fifth, the resulting models become large which makes reuse more challenging. The main problem combining proprietary metamodels is that these are not structured as reusable artefacts. In particular, there are no apparent ways metamodels should be composed. This gives a lot of flexibility since the metamodels can be combined in many different ways. However, this also induces several problematic issues as motivated.

A metamodel typically contains concepts related to one particular problem domain. By combining metamodels it is possible to increase expressiveness by extending the set of concepts that can be used in the conformant models. Composing metamodels belonging to different domains results in different concerns being tangled. This is not practical as metamodels become difficult to grasp and reason about. Even more critical is the inability to differentiate between concerns in associated tooling and editors. E.g. a *Domain-Specific Language (DSL)* made on the basis of three combined metamodels requires an associated concrete syntax where language constructs pertaining to three different concerns are all mixed together. We believe that the ability to consider one concern at the time is important to support increasingly more complex metamodels and associated tooling.

In this paper, we present the novel idea of considering metamodels as services. Specifically, we will discuss how the behavioural semantics of metamodels can be combined in a service-oriented manner, and thereby support loosely coupled integration of metamodels. Note that we do not consider every aspect of services in this paper, but use the concept of service-orientation as inspiration for defining loosely coupled metamodel components.

The paper is organised as follows. Section 2 explains the concept of metamodel components and uses *SoaML* [11] to illuminate how metamodel components are connected/composed. Section 3 delves into details on how metamodel components can be realised, while Section 4 presents an example where two metamodel components are used in concert to construct an e-commerce solution. Section 5 discusses related work, and Section 6 conludes the paper.

2   Metamodels as Services

A metamodel formalises the structure and semantics of models. We consider both static and behavioural semantics as parts of the metamodel. E.g. EMF allows defining behavioural semantics, referred to as model code, in methods of plain Java classes. Alternatively, Kermeta is a metalanguage that allows defining behavioural semantics within the operations of the metamodel classes using an action language. Hence, the conformant models are executable programs. We will not go into details on how the abstract syntax and behavioural semantics are mapped, and consider the behavioural semantics to be defined in operations within the metamodel classes.

A metamodel is constrained to a particular problem domain, and may conceptually be thought of as a service that provides structure and semantics for expressing and solving problems in this domain; in particular, behavioural semantics for performing some kind of processing. A system may be defined by using an arbitrary number of metamodels, each providing concepts for modelling of one particular system view. Metamodels are typically not related. Thus, their conformant models/programs can not exchange data at runtime in a generic manner. In this paper, we discuss how exchange of data between models can be supported by treating metamodels as services that can be connected. This allows models to send messages to each other during execution regardless of the platform on which the models execute.

Service-Oriented Architectures (SOAs) is a software engineering branch that deals with services and how they interact to realise a software system. A service is a reusable set of functionalities that provides value to its clients, e.g. other services. SOA is a broad field. In this paper, we will only use a small subset of the SOA terms and concepts to describe our approach. Specifically, we will use a service-oriented approach for integrating models at runtime. The intention is not to elaborate on all aspects of services nor give a complete definition of such.

To integrate models at runtime we need some kind of framework. Specifically, we need to formalise how the models should integrate. As mentioned, the behavioural semantics of a model can be specified as a set of operations in the model's metamodel. Hence, by creating *mappings* between metamodels' operations, we are able to formalise how their conformant models can interact. A mapping is created by using two types of interfaces: *consumer* and *provider* interfaces. A metamodel may be mapped to an arbitrary number of other metamodels through interfaces. The interfaces can be seen as an extension of the metamodel. We define a *metamodel component* as an entity consisting of three elements: a metamodel (abstract syntax and static/behavioural semantics), tools like concrete syntax and editors (optional), and one or more *service contracts*. A service contract is a SoaML concept for service specification; it specifies an agreement detailing how participants of a service fulfill roles as described by interfaces. A realised service contract is a pair of provider and consumer interfaces. SoaML is an *Object Management Group (OMG)* standardised modelling language for describing services architectures. It provides us with the modelling tool for describing *metamodel architectures*. That is, two or more metamodel components that are connected through interfaces. Note that we will not follow the SoaML specification strictly. Some additional terminology is used. A visual representation of a metamodel component is given in Figure 1. A metamodel component has a name and a platform descriptor identifying the platform on which the component is defined. In this case, the generic descriptions: *Metamodel Component* and *Platform*, respectively. Examples of platforms are EMF and Kermeta.

In SoaML, a service contract is modelled as a consumer and provider role linked by a service channel. Each role is typed with an interface that defines the role's behaviour. In our case, the roles of a service contract are fulfilled by metamodel components.

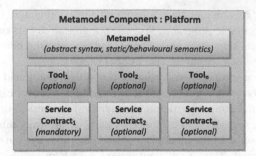

Fig. 1. Overview of a metamodel component

A metamodel architecture is created by choreographing a set of components. That is, each metamodel is bound to one or more roles of service contracts. Binding a metamodel to a service contract role is achieved by mapping each of the interface's operations to an operation found in any of the metamodel's classes. A component whose metamodel is bound to a provider role of a service contract is regarded as an *aspect* component (provider component) from the perspective of this particular service contract. Or more precisely, the component's metamodel is an aspect model since it reflects one particular aspect or concern that is utilised by a *base* component. The component whose metamodel is bound to the consumer role of the same service contract is a base component (consumer component). A metamodel component can take both an aspect and base role simultaneously, and be composed with several components in parallel. This is achieved by utilising several service contracts/interface pairs. Refer [4] for details on how the terms *aspect* and *base* are used to describe model compositions. Figure 2 gives an example where three metamodel components are composed yielding a metamodel architecture.

As can be seen, all components are connected with each other. E.g. $\mathcal{MCA}$ is connected to $\mathcal{MCB}$ through the two interfaces specified by the $\mathcal{Provide}\,\mathcal{B}_1$ service contract of the $\mathcal{MCB}$ component. Consequently, models conforming to $Metamodel\,A$ may invoke operations (operation instances) on models conforming to $Metamodel\,B$. The same architecture given as a SoaML services architecture model is given in Figure 3. The metamodel components are here participants that are related through service contracts. SoaML also operates with *service interfaces*. A service interface is a revised service contract, where the provider and consumer interfaces are elaborated with message types. We will limit the use of this term to avoid confusion. Let us focus on the $\mathcal{Provide}\,\mathcal{B}_1$ service contract and see how it is defined. The $\mathcal{Provide}\,\mathcal{B}_1$ service contract specifies two roles, here named: baseModel and aspectModel, which are linked through a service channel. The roles are associated with a consumer and provider interface, respectively. Figure 4 gives the service contract as a SoaML model.

The definitions of RequiredInterface and ProvidedInterface are given in Figure 5. The consumer interface specifies an operation named $operation_1(...)$, whereas the provider interface consists of the two operations: $operation_1(...)$ and $operation_2(...)$. We ignore types for now. Both the latter operations are mapped to operations of the B_1 class. A consumer interface may be empty if bi-directional messaging is not required.

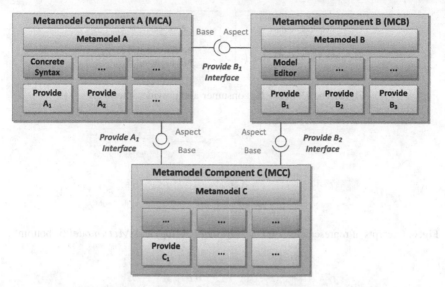

Fig. 2. Example metamodel architecture (using a simplified notation)

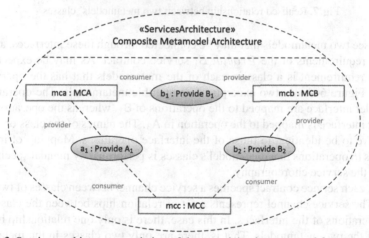

Fig. 3. Services architecture consisting of three participating metamodel components

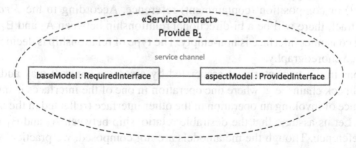

Fig. 4. The $\mathcal{P}rovide\ \mathcal{B}_1$ service contract

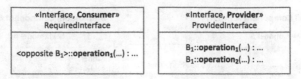

Fig. 5. The $\mathcal{P}rovide\,\mathcal{B}_1$ consumer and provider interfaces

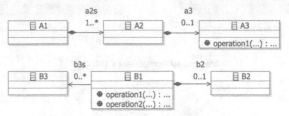

Fig. 6. Excerpts of representatives for $\mathcal{M}etamodel\,\mathcal{A}$ (top) and $\mathcal{M}etamodel\,\mathcal{B}$ (bottom)

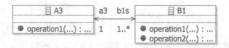

Fig. 7. Realised relationship between two metamodels' classes

Let us see two metamodels that may be connected through these interfaces, and thus fulfill the requirements of the $\mathcal{P}rovide\,\mathcal{B}_1$ service contract. As may be expected, the minimum requirement is a class in each of the metamodels that has the operation(s) specified. Figure 6 shows two excerpts of compatible metamodels. The operations of the provider interface are mapped to the operations of B_1, whereas the operation in the consumer interface is mapped to the operation in A_3. The names of the class operations do not have to be identical to those of the interface operations. Mapping of interface operations to operations in a metamodel's classes is performed by manual specification as part of the service choreography.

Hence, each service contract specifies a service channel between classes of two metamodels. The service channel represents a set of relationships between the classes that realise operations of the interfaces. In this case, there is only one relationship between classes of the two metamodels. That is, there are only two classes in the metamodels that are related. The type of relationship between classes is either an association (non-containment) or composition (containment) reference. According to the $\mathcal{P}rovide\,\mathcal{B}_1$ service contract, there will be a bi-directional relationship between A_3 and B_1. This is because the consumer interface is non-empty. The type of relationship is decided as part of the service choreography.

Operations in the two interfaces associated by a service contract may additionally relate in callback chains, e.g. where one operation in one of the interfaces is invoked as a consequence of invoking an operation in the other interface (reflected in the operation definition). Let us assume that the desirable relationship between A_3 and B_1 is an association reference. Though the metamodels are not composed, we practically end up with the scenario as illustrated in Figure 7.

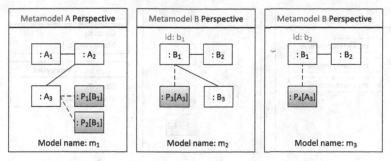

Fig. 8. Modelling separate concerns in different perspectives

3 Realising Metamodel Components

3.1 Modelling Using Proxies

So far we have seen how metamodels' operations can be related through interfaces (service contracts). Thus, the metamodels are loosely coupled which allows creating and processing of models using any kinds of proprietary tools and editors. Also important is the ability to model A and B concerns independently of each other. E.g. it is still possible to use tools compatible with $\mathcal{Metamodel\ A}$ to create models of this metamodel. Typically, this is difficult when metamodels are composed since the associated tools need to be refactored. Figure 8 illustrates how a model of $\mathcal{Metamodel\ A}$ and a model of $\mathcal{Metamodel\ B}$ can be modelled in separate perspectives (views). Notice that the A_3 object in the left perspective relates two B_1 *proxy objects*, as specified using square brackets. The B_1 object in the right perspective relates a proxy object representing the A_3 object.

A service contract specifies a connection or mapping between two metamodels' operations. As discussed, a service contract's service channel represents a set of class relationships. To realise such relationships it must be possible to navigate the operations accessible through the relationships. This is achieved using proxies. When modelling, it should be possible to refer the B_1 concept from within a model conforming to $\mathcal{Metamodel\ A}$ (and vice versa), since $\mathcal{Metamodel\ B}$ is an aspect model with respect to $\mathcal{Metamodel\ A}$. However, the metamodels are not composed together. To address this, a placeholder/proxy representing a B_1 object can be used in models of $\mathcal{Metamodel\ A}$. The proxy is linked to an actual object of the B_1 class at runtime using XML-based messages. The object of the B_1 class, as represented by the proxy, is selected from a set of previously created models conforming to $\mathcal{Metamodel\ B}$, as found in a model repository. That is, all models created using a metamodel architecture are stored in a model repository for later reference. Two B_1 proxies are used in the m_1 model of Figure 8. Each proxy represents a unique B_1 object (as found in m_2 and m_3). The proxies P_3 and P_4 represent the A_3 object in m_1.

Figure 9 shows how the B_1 proxies are linked to the m_2 and m_3 models (and objects) of $\mathcal{Metamodel\ B}$. The A_3 proxies are linked to the m_1 model in a similar manner (not shown in the figure). The four proxies realise the $\mathcal{Provide\ B_1}$ service contract at

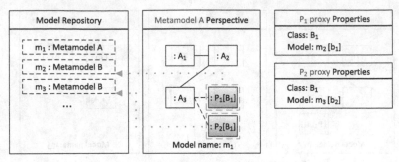

Fig. 9. Linking proxies to models/objects

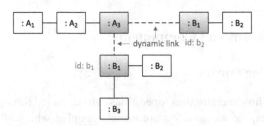

Fig. 10. The resulting model(s) as used at runtime

runtime. We will return to how the interface operations are mapped to class operations. Figure 10 shows what is achieved at runtime when executing the models.

As can be seen, links are established between the A_3 object and the B_1 objects. The links are *dynamic* since they only exist at runtime (realised using proxy runtime objects linked by XML-based messages). Dynamic links are established and maintained by a *metamodel component runtime environment*. The runtime environment acts as a super-structure on top of a metamodelling environment, like EMF. It is out of scope to go into details on how the proxies are managed by the runtime environment.

3.2 Service Choreography

Metamodel components are combined into architectures using *service choreography*. Choreography of metamodel components comprises two steps: mapping operations of service contracts' associated interfaces to class operations and selecting relationship types that the service channels represent. This includes choosing the relationship multiplicities (some constraints apply). Choreography can either be performed textually or graphically. We will illustrate choreography using an XML-based format. Figure 11 gives an excerpt of the service choreography yielding the architecture of Figure 2.

Recall that a service contract is defined using a provider and consumer interface. A service interface is a refined service contract that utilises both the provider and consumer interface to specify a service port type on a component (aspect). The conjugate service interface (defined using the same provider and consumer interfaces) specifies the type of a request port (base). We will only focus on the $\mathcal{P}rovide\,\mathcal{B}_1\,\mathcal{I}nterface$ here. The interface is a refinement of the $\mathcal{P}rovide\,\mathcal{B}_1$ service contract. The $\mathcal{MCA}$ and $\mathcal{MCB}$ components are composed by filling out three pieces of information. First, the operations

```
<interface name="Provide A1 Interface">...</interface>
<interface name="Provide B1 Interface">
  <provider component="MCB">
    <operation name="operation1" type="..." classOperation="B1::operation1" />
    <operation name="operation2" type="..." classOperation="B1::operation2" />
  </provider>
  <consumer component="MCA">
    <operation name="operation1" type="..." classOperation="A3::operation1" />
  </consumer>
  <channel baseClass="A3" aspectClass="B1" type="non-containment"
    bidirectional="true" multiplicityBase="1..1" multiplicityAspect="1..*" />
</interface>
<interface name="Provide B2 Interface">...</interface>
```

Fig. 11. Service choreography using a textual format

of the ProvidedInterface must be mapped to the operations of B_1. Second, the operation of the RequiredInterface has to be mapped to the operation in A_3. Third, the type and multiplicity of the relationship between the A_3 and B_1 classes need to be specified.

4 An E-Commerce Solution

In this section, we will illustrate metamodel components using a more pragmatic example in the domain of website design. We will use two DSLs for modelling of two different concerns: website structure and queries. Excerpts of the metamodels for the DSLs are given in Figures 12 and 13. We will refer to the metamodels as *Website* and *Query*, respectively.

As seen in Figure 12, a website comprises one or more pages that contain an arbitrary number of elements. In particular, a page may contain forms realised within a table structure. An example of a form is a list of products or similar, that can be selected by the end user. The Form behavioural semantics includes an operation addObjects(...) which accepts a list of (deserialised) objects. The operation populates a form constructed using a table element. The number of rows and columns in the table is determined automatically by the number and type of objects used as argument. We assume that the metamodels are defined in EMF, thus the behavioural semantics would be written in Java.

A simple query language is given in Figure 13. It captures concepts for expressing queries that can be used for acquisition of objects, e.g. from a database abstraction. A query consists of one or more object identifiers. An object identifier is composed of a set of property name-value pairs which is used to identify a custom set of objects. For instance, an e-commerce solution for selling computer hardware may utilise a domain model including the class Product with data fields for storing information such as product name, manufacturer, version, description, price, etc. Different types of products have unique values for the data fields. Querying for a given type of product would then be performed by using object identifiers and property name-value pairs. Describing queries that are issued to a database is a natural part of designing an e-commerce solution. However, designing the website and programming the queries represent two different concerns. It is likely that different stakeholders would model these concerns. A graphical designer could construct the website, while a programmer would define the backbone business logic including database queries. We have identified two DSLs that allow modelling these concerns. A possible approach would be to compose the metamodels of the

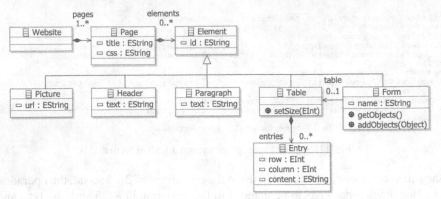

Fig. 12. Metamodel for the website design language

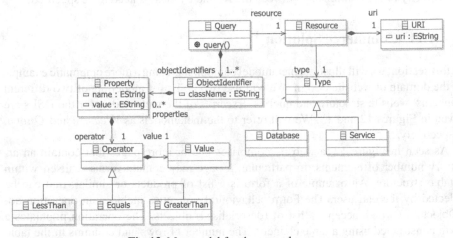

Fig. 13. Metamodel for the query language

DSLs to create a richer language that can be used to both model the website and express database queries, e.g. the Form and Query classes could be merged. First, combining Form and Query is awkward, since these classes are not semantic coherent. Second, the composition process clearly results in entanglement of concepts for expressing different concerns. A graphical concrete syntax for the composite language would yield a palette of language constructs for the entire language, whereas a textual syntax would provide the user with code completion suggestions for all the constructs. A graphical website designer would not be interested in the language constructs for performing queries as used by the programmer, and vice versa. One alternative is to manually program the concrete syntax of the composite language to differentiate the two sets of language constructs, yet the resulting model of a website and associated queries would still be expressed in the same modelling space. Providing two sets of concrete syntax concepts would require in-depth technical knowledge, which reduces the reuse value of the languages/metamodels. Additionally, the website language would typically be implemented with a graphical concrete syntax, whereas the query language is better designed using a textual syntax. Combining different kinds of syntaxes is not a trivial task.

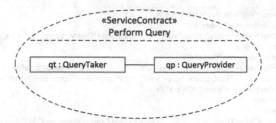

Fig. 14. The $Perform\ Query$ service contract

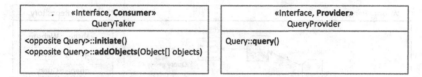

Fig. 15. The $Perform\ Query$ consumer and provider interfaces

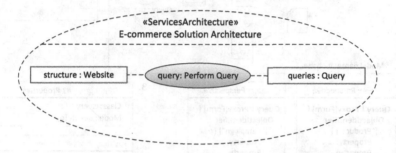

Fig. 16. The e-commerce modelling solution services architecture

Let us see how metamodel components tackle the same scenario. The behavioural semantics of Form in Figure 12 comprises the operations getObjects() and addObjects(...). The semantics of Query in Figure 13 consists of the operation query(). The operations could either be a natural part of the classes' semantics or be defined explicitly in order to construct the metamodels as reusable components. The three operations will reify the consumer and provider interfaces associated by a service contract named $Perform\ Query$.

The purpose of the example is to illustrate how models of the $Website$ and $Query$ metamodels may communicate by defining the metamodels as components. The components are named $Website$ and $Query$ as well. Only the $Query$ component will feature a service contract. The service contract of the $Query$ component is given in Figure 14. It specifies two roles, each typed with an interface. The interfaces are given in Figure 15.

As can be seen, the provider interface has one operation named query(), while the consumer interface specifies the operations initiate() and addObjects(Object[] objects). The names of the class operations that fulfill the service contract do not need to have identical names as the interface operations, however, the class operations' signatures and return types are required to match those of the interface operations. Verification of

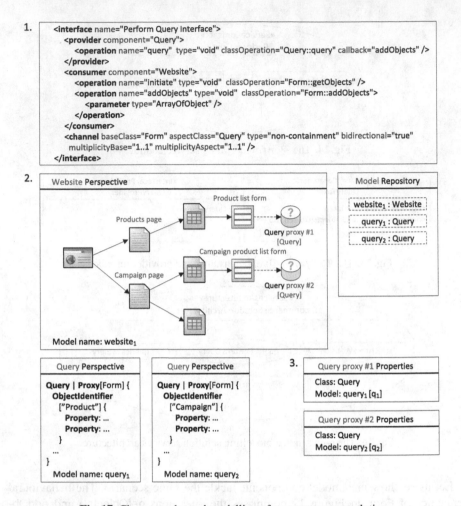

Fig. 17. Choreography and modelling of an e-commerce solution

operation mappings is out of scope of this paper[1]. We assume that each service contract has a description that informally specifies the intended semantics of the associated interfaces' operations. The services architecture describing the e-commerce modelling solution is given in Figure 16. The choreography and modelling process of the e-commerce solution consists of three steps:

1. Service choreography
2. Modelling of each concern in distinct modelling perspectives
3. Linking the base model proxies with the aspect model proxies

Figure 17 shows the three steps of choreographing and modelling of the e-commerce solution (with imagined tool support). The Form class of the *Website* metamodel and

---

[1] Assuring that an operation does what its use requires is also out of scope of this paper.

the Query class of the $Query$ metamodel realise the consumer and provider roles of the $Perform\ Query$ service contract (implicitly referred to by the $Perform\ Query$ $Interface$) (1). The initiate() operation of the consumer interface is mapped to getObjects() in the Form class ($Website$ metamodel), while the addObjects(...) operation is mapped to the equally named operation in the same class. The query() operation of the provider interface is mapped to query() in the Query class ($Query$ metamodel). I.e. the service contract is fulfilled.

The website and queries are modelled separately (2). The website model contains two forms, thus two queries have to be programmed. The website model is named website$_1$, while the query models are named query$_1$ and query$_2$. All models are stored in the model repository (when saved). Two proxies representing Query objects are used in the website model. A proxy representing a Form object is used in each of the query models. The proxies are linked to the respective models in properties panes/views (3) (only properties for the Query proxies are shown). Several proxies can be assigned to clones of the same model. E.g. if both forms required the same type of query, they could both be linked to, e.g. query$_1$. At runtime, the operations specified in the interfaces are invoked to exchange data between the models (website$_1$, query$_1$ and query$_2$) using a serialised XML-based message format. Population of a form is initiated when the behavioural semantics of the website language invokes getObjects(). This invocation is resolved by the component runtime environment and results in invocation of query() in the associated query model. Consequently, a set of objects are acquired from the database and returned to the website model via the addObjects(...) operation. addObjects(...) is specified as a callback operation for query(). This means that the query() operation's code invokes the addObjects(...) operation on the associated Form proxy, which in turn invokes the addObjects(...) operation on the actual Form object. The models are linked dynamically. That is, proxies are linked to model objects at runtime. Service choreography can to some extent be pre-defined, where information concerning consumer components is filled in according to a fixed scheme. I.e. the mappings of provider interface operations to class operations are known at design-time. These mappings are immutable properties of the provider components.

The example shows how two metamodels can be used together without using model composition. Here, only one service contract was fulfilled. A metamodel component can feature an arbitrary number of service contracts. This allows creating complex architectures with many metamodels. In addition, it is possible to connect a metamodel with other metamodels in several ways depending on what service contracts that are fulfilled. Figure 18 gives an overview of the resulting website system. We assume that the components are defined in different metamodelling environments.

5 Related Work

The work of [12] discusses how metamodel components can be realised using a graph transformation-based formalisation of MOF. In essence, a metamodel component provides export and import interfaces. Each interface identifies a submodel. A submodel of an export interface can be bound to the submodel of an import interface using graph morphisms, and thereby combining the metamodels. The work resembles the approach

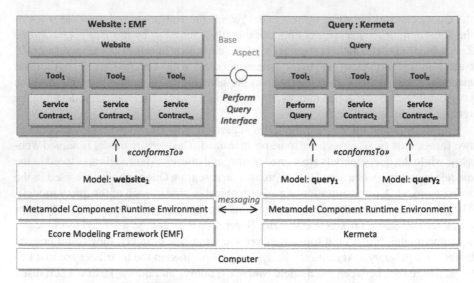

Fig. 18. Overview of the resulting website system

of this paper. The main difference is that our approach allows a higher degree of decoupling, since metamodels are connected as services.

An approach for enabling generic metamodelling is elaborated in [13]. The paper investigates how C++ concepts, model templates and mixin layers can be used to specify generic behaviour and transformations, create model component and pattern libraries and extend metamodels with new classes and semantics. A concept can be bound to models that fulfill a set of requirements specified by the concept. The binding is performed using pattern matching. Consequently, generic behaviour can be reused for instances of the compatible models. Model templates allow defining reusable patterns and components which can be instantiated with actual parameters. The parameters comprise models and model elements. Finally, mixin layer templates facilitate extending metamodels with new classes and semantics in a non-intrusive manner.

Package extension is a mechanism that allows merging equally named classes of metamodels that reside in packages [14]. A package can be defined by extending other packages. The paper also describes a package template concept. A package template is a package that can be parameterised with string arguments. The arguments support renaming of several package elements simultaneously.

An approach for loose integration of models, in the form of model sewing, is discussed in [15]. Model sewing is an operation that allows models to be both synchronised and depend on each other without utilising model composition. The discussed advantages are the ability to utilise existing GUI for the constituent models of a sewing operation, and avoidance of entanglement of concepts from different models. The approach identifies the need of mediating entities that bind the models together. The work resembles the approach of this paper. The main difference is that we utilise interfaces and treat metamodels as components that are combined in a service-oriented manner.

6 Discussion and Conclusions

Metamodel components allow using metamodels in unison without composing these explicitly together. This has apparent advantages. First, it is possible to model different concerns separately, and still support exchange of data between the resulting models at runtime by utilising model links that are maintained dynamically. This ensures a loosely coupled integration. Second, models expressing different concerns can be validated and tested independently one at the time. Specifically, the proxies can communicate with mock-ups that represent models (simulation mode). Third, choreography of metamodel components can be achieved by non-technical stakeholders since the metamodels do not need to be altered in order to connect these. The service contracts formalise the agreement between the metamodels. Fourth, a model or model fragment (clone) can be acquired from a model repository and reused, which simplifies the modelling process.

Metamodel composition usually requires that classes are merged. However, it is not always reasonable to merge two classes, particularly when the classes represent concepts of different problem domains. Using the approach of this paper, an aspect model class is instead used to type the relation between this class and a base model class (and vice versa). This resembles class refinement as discussed in [16].

A consequence of composing the abstract syntax of metamodels is the need of combining the concrete syntaxes as well. This is avoided by using components since each component independently may provide its distinct textual or graphical concrete syntax. Components also address evolution issues. *Model conformance* is a term that indicates whether a model is compatible with a metamodel. Composing metamodels breaks model conformance, which requires using model transformations to create a conformant composite model from the basis of pre-existing models. Components address this by defining a sand box/scope for each metamodel. Changing or revising the metamodel of one component will only break conformance with the existing models of this metamodel. Models of the other components' metamodels in the services architecture will still conform to their metamodels.

Two important aspects of service-oriented approaches are service repositories and service discovery, which support service reuse and availability. These concepts may be adapted for metamodel components. In particular, reusable generic metamodel patterns can be stored in searchable, distributed repositories and used as language building blocks by language engineers. A metamodel pattern may describe an aspect or requirement that is common for several metamodels/languages, e.g. a state machine or similar [17]. Analysis and validation of services are important parts of service-oriented engineering methodologies and required to ensure high quality architectures and systems. This has not been addressed in the paper.

An interesting application of metamodel components is connecting metamodels and languages (and their models) defined in different metamodelling environments. This is possible since the behavioural semantics of each metamodel can be run separately, yet integrated as specified in the service contracts. E.g. models defined in EMF could integrate with models defined in Kermeta, or similar. This is one particular application of metamodel components that justifies the high degree of separation provided by a service-oriented metamodel integration.

We believe that combining metamodels in a service-oriented manner addresses many of the limitations of model composition by increasing decoupling of models. This in turn increases reusability and scalability of metamodels and models.

References

1. Kent, S.: Model Driven Engineering. In: Butler, M., Petre, L., Sere, K. (eds.) IFM 2002. LNCS, vol. 2335, pp. 286–298. Springer, Heidelberg (2002)
2. Fabro, M.D.D., Bézivin, J., Valduriez, P.: Weaving Models with the Eclipse AMW plugin. In: Eclipse Modeling Symposium (2006)
3. Kolovos, D.S., Paige, R.F., Polack, F.A.C.: Merging Models with the Epsilon Merging Language (EML). In: Wang, J., Whittle, J., Harel, D., Reggio, G. (eds.) MoDELS 2006. LNCS, vol. 4199, pp. 215–229. Springer, Heidelberg (2006)
4. Groher, I., Voelter, M.: XWeave: Models and Aspects in Concert. In: Proceedings of the AOM Workshop 2007 (2007)
5. Morin, B., Perrouin, G., Lahire, P., Barais, O., Vanwormhoudt, G., Jézéquel, J.-M.: Weaving Variability into Domain Metamodels. In: Schürr, A., Selic, B. (eds.) MODELS 2009. LNCS, vol. 5795, pp. 690–705. Springer, Heidelberg (2009)
6. Morin, B., Klein, J., Barais, O.: A Generic Weaver for Supporting Product Lines. In: Proceedings of the Workshop on Early Aspects (EA 2008) (2008)
7. Eclipse Modeling Framework (EMF) (2012),
   http://www.eclipse.org/modeling/emf
8. Tolvanen, J.-P., Kelly, S.: MetaEdit+: Defining and Using Integrated Domain-Specific Modeling Languages. In: Proceedings of OOPSLA 2009 (2009)
9. Institute for Software Integrated Systems. Generic Modeling Environment (GME) (2012),
   http://www.isis.vanderbilt.edu/projects/gme
10. Muller, P.-A., Fleurey, F., Jézéquel, J.-M.: Weaving Executability into Object-Oriented Meta-Languages. In: Briand, L.C., Williams, C. (eds.) MoDELS 2005. LNCS, vol. 3713, pp. 264–278. Springer, Heidelberg (2005)
11. Object Management Group (OMG). Service-Oriented Architecture Modeling Language (SoaML) (2012), http://www.omg.org/spec/SoaML
12. Weisemöller, I., Schürr, A.: Formal Definition of MOF 2.0 Metamodel Components and Composition. In: Czarnecki, K., Ober, I., Bruel, J.-M., Uhl, A., Völter, M. (eds.) MODELS 2008. LNCS, vol. 5301, pp. 386–400. Springer, Heidelberg (2008)
13. de Lara, J., Guerra, E.: Generic Meta-modelling with Concepts, Templates and Mixin Layers. In: Petriu, D.C., Rouquette, N., Haugen, Ø. (eds.) MODELS 2010, Part I. LNCS, vol. 6394, pp. 16–30. Springer, Heidelberg (2010)
14. Clark, T., Evans, A., Kent, S.: Aspect-Oriented Metamodelling. The Computer Journal 46(5) (2003)
15. Reiter, T., Kapsammer, E., Retschitzegger, W., Schwinger, W.: Model Integration through Mega Operations. In: Proceedings of the Workshop on Model-Driven Web Engineering (MDWE 2005) (2005)
16. Emerson, M., Sztipanovits, J.: Techniques for Metamodel Composition. In: proceedings of the 6th OOPSLA Domain-Specific Modeling Workshop (DSM 2006) (2006)
17. Cho, H., Gray, J.: Design Patterns for Metamodels. In: Proceedings of the 11th SPLASH Domain-Specific Modeling Workshop (DSM 2011) (2011)

Fine-Grained Role- and Attribute-Based Access Control
for Web Applications

Seyed Hossein Ghotbi and Bernd Fischer

University of Southampton, U.K.
{shg08r,b.fischer}@ecs.soton.ac.uk
http://www.soton.ac.uk

Abstract. Web applications require an access control mechanism such as role-based access control to enforce a set of policies over their shared data. An access control model that is based on the desired security properties is thus a core security aspect, and the development of such models and their mechanisms are a main concern for secure systems development. Fine-grained access control models provide more customization possibilities and administrative power to the developers; however, in Web applications the corresponding policies are typically hand-coded without taking advantage of the data model, object types, or contextual information. This paper presents and evaluates ΦRBAC, a declarative, fine-grained role- and attribute-based access control model which is implemented by code generation. The generator uses a translation into logical satisfiability problems to check the ΦRBAC model for correctness and completeness, and against independently defined coverage criteria. If the model passes these tests, the generator then compiles it down to the existing tiers of WebDSL, a domain-specific Web programming language. We describe the test and code generation phases, and show the application of ΦRBAC to the development of a departmental Web site.

Keywords: Fine-grained Access Control, RBAC, Attribute Constraints, Access Control Testing, Web Application Security, Language Design.

1 Introduction

Web applications, such as Facebook, are deployed on a set of servers and are easily accessible via any Web browser through an Internet connection. As the number of users of a Web application grows, its security and the privacy of the users' data become major concerns [5], and access to shared data needs to be controlled based on a set of specific policies via one of the many types of access control such as *discretionary, mandatory*, or *role-based access control* [24].

For reasons such as maintainability and cost effectiveness [4], role-based access control (RBAC) is the most widely used [14] access control mechanism. RBAC [8] uses the notion of *role* as the central authorization element; other components of the system such as *subjects* and *permissions* (describing the allowed operations on *objects*) are assigned to one or more roles. Over the last two decades RBAC has been extended by different types of attributes, such as temporal [2] or content-based [10] attributes, which allow more secure and flexible policies [19]. For example, with time constraints such as in

J. Cordeiro, S. Hammoudi, and M. van Sinderen (Eds.): ICSOFT 2012, CCIS 411, pp. 171–187, 2013.

TRBAC [2] the developer can limit access by the users of the system to a certain period of time such as office hours. This lowers the risk of system abuse outside office hours.

Web applications typically consist of elements that have different granularity levels and are scattered throughout the application code, which makes access control more difficult. For example, a web page can contain smaller elements such as sections or even individually controlled cells of a table. Currently, developers need to hand-code the access control elements around the objects that require access control, using languages such as Scala [17], XACML [1], or Ponder [6]. However, such approaches have three main drawbacks that complicate development of fine-grained access control and can easily lead to security holes. First, they lack the right *abstraction level* to define flexible access control models that allow the specification of different policies for different individual objects. Second, they lack a *separation of concerns* [31] between access control and application [3]. If we can develop the access control components separately, we can check for potential vulnerabilities separately and mechanically, instead of manually analyzing the access control checks in the application code, which is an error-prone and time consuming process. Third, they lack a *code generation* mechanism that can automatically translate the specified abstract access control model into corresponding access control checks and weave these into the application to enforce the model without introducing coding errors.

Although testing the access control model is essential [23,20,21], testing the model on its own is not enough. Any access control is defined to cover a set of objects in an application. Therefore, the testing mechanism should also take the target application, with the woven-in access control checks, into consideration. The testing phase should thus first mechanically verify the correctness and completeness of access control model itself and then validate the application code based on a set of test cases. These test cases should cover a set of objects and policy scenarios for which a correct outcome gives the developer sufficient confidence that the deployed access control model is appropriate for the given application. For example, the system should produce more restrictive test cases for a medical application than for an internet forum.

This paper describes ΦRBAC, a fine-grained RBAC with additional attribute-based constraints for the domain of Web applications. It provides a novel mechanism for declaratively defining RBAC policies and test objectives over a range of objects with different granularity levels within a single model. This model can be formally analyzed and verified. ΦRBAC is implemented on top of WebDSL [30], a domain-specific language for Web application development. ΦRBAC uses code generation techniques weave access control checks around the objects within the application code written in WebDSL. We describe the test and code generation phases, and show the application of ΦRBAC to the development of a departmental Web site.

2   Background and Related Work

2.1   Role-Based Access Control with Additional Attributes

RBAC belongs to the *grouping privileges* class of access control models [24]. In this class privileges are collected based on common aspects, and then authorizations are assigned to these collections. The fundamental advantage of using a grouping privileges model is that it factors out similarities, and so handles changes better, which leads to an easier authorization management [11]. RBAC is used in many domains and there are number of languages that support RBAC [14,1,6]. RBAC uses the notion of *role* as the central authorization mechanism [8]. Intuitively, a role is an abstract representation of a group of subjects that are allowed to perform the same operations, on behalf of users, on the same objects. For example, in an RBAC model we can define a role supervisor and state that *any* user with this role can edit marks, while users with the role student can only read them. The other main elements of RBAC are subjects, objects, and permissions. A *subject* is the representation of an authorized user, an *object* is any accessible shared data and a *permission* refers to the set of allowed operations on objects. In the example above, the subject could actually be a session that belongs to the user after authentication and the permissions describe the allowed operations on the marks objects. Adding attributes (such as time, date, or location) to RBAC is beneficial and well studied [10,19,2], because it leads to more flexibility in the model and solves a set of the core RBAC shortcomings. Core RBAC has been standardized by the National Institute of Standards and Technology (NIST) [25], but despite a recent study trying to unify attribute-based access control models [19] there is no common ground yet.

Fine-Grained Access Control. In the existing literature, the notion of fine-grained access control refers only to models that can control access to fine-granular objects but where the policies themselves remain coarse-grained, and thus lack flexibility. For example, a number of studies [27,33] discuss fine-granular access control in the context of databases in terms of the table structure (i.e., columns, rows, etc.), while others [18,26] discuss it in the context of XML and the hierarchical structure of XML documents. Our notion is related to both objects and access control, so that the access control model itself becomes more flexible and can provide a more efficient development environment.

Typically, objects are scattered throughout the application code; therefore, if the programmer writes the access control component by hand or uses access control approaches such as XACML, the access control checks will be scattered throughout the application code as well [1]. This is not suitable from many points of views. From a design point of view, it is hard to track the access rights for each object wherever it occurs within the application, and to reason conclusively about its access control checks. From an implementation point of view, coding and maintenance of the code will be time-consuming and error-prone [32]. Finally, from a testing point of view it is hard for the tester to figure out the usage coverage of hard-coded access control checks.

Testing Access Control Models. Access control as a software component needs to be tested [28]. Testing needs to consider three aspects of an access control model, correctness, completeness and sufficiency. First, an access control model needs to be correct so that we can derive the required access control predicates for controlled objects. Since RBAC has a standard and therefore its semantics is well defined and understood, the *correctness* of any defined model should be checked based on the standard. Second, the *completeness* check of an access control model is essential. A complete access control model covers all possible outcomes of its defined policies with respect to the RBAC structure. For example, if we have student and teacher as two roles in an access control model and there is a static separation of duty between them, then the model only needs to cover three cases to be complete: first, teacher is active but not student, second, teacher is not active but student is and third, neither of them are active. The sufficiency of an access control depends on its target application and should therefore be defined by the developer. For example, a developer might define an access control model in a way that gives too much power to a user (the so-called the superuser problem [9]). In this case, the developer might check the application sufficiency against a set of objectives and discover this issue before application deployment. We will discuss the correctness, completeness and sufficiency checks of ΦRBAC in Section 3.2.

2.2 WebDSL

WebDSL [30] is a high-level domain-specific language (DSL) for creating dynamic Web applications [13]. It provides developers with the notion of entities for defining a data-model and enforcing data validation on those entities [12]. Listing 1.1 shows an example. The properties of an object are specified by their name and their type. Types can describe values, sets, and composite associations; in particular, the type of a property can be another entity. For example, in the data model shown in Listing 1.1 the tutor property is of type Teacher, and marks is a property that holds a set of Mark entities.

Listing 1.1. Student Entity in WebDSL

```
entity Student{
   studentID :: String      (name)
   courses   -> Set<Course>
   tutor     -> Teacher
   marks     <> Set<Mark>    (inverse = Mark.students)
}
```

The WebDSL compiler is implemented using SDF [15] for its syntax definition and Stratego/XT [29] for its transformation rules. It consists of a number of smaller DSLs (e.g., user interface, access control) that are structured around a core layer. It uses code transformation techniques [16] to transform the WebDSL code to mainstream Web application files (HTML, JavaScript, etc.). It uses these together with other provided layout resources (image, CSS, etc.) to compile and package to a server-deployable WAR file.

Even tough WebDSL increases the level of abstraction during development, it has two main shortcomings that our work here addresses. First, it does not support fine-grained attribute-based RBAC. WebDSL has a powerful data model, and even supports the validation of input data, but its RBAC model is oriented towards the presentational elements (i.e., pages and templates), rather than the data model, and remains coarse-grained. Moreover, if the developer wants to add attributes to the RBAC model, she needs to hardcode the policy within the application code. Second, it does not check the correctness of the defined RBAC model elements nor their implementation within the application code.

3   ΦRBAC

ΦRBAC is an approach for declaratively defining and implementing a flexible, expressive, and high-level RBAC mechanism on top of WebDSL. It generates access control elements and then weaves them into the application code in order to enforce the access control on fine-grained elements of the data model, instances of the data, and template and page elements. Moreover, it provides a testing mechanism to check the correctness of the model itself and with regard to its application. In this section we introduce the language by means of an example.

3.1   Access Control Model

As Listing 1.2 shows, a ΦRBAC model consists of three main sections: basic *RBAC* elements (lines 2-5), *policy cases* (lines 7-11) and *coverage* (lines 14-18).

Listing 1.2. ΦRBAC Example

```
1  PhiRBAC{
2    roles{teacher(10),admin(1),manager(1),advisor(10),student(*)}
3    hierarchy{advisor -> teacher}
4    ssod{(teacher,admin,advisor,manager) <-> student}
5    dsod{(and(advisor,teacher),admin)    <-> manager}
6
7    objects{G(roleAssignment),XML(address),Person.password,P(marks)}
8    policies{teacher,student,admin,advisor,Self.username == "faz",
9          This.User.location != "New York",Sys.Time(>=9:00,<=17:00)}
10   cases{ (+,-,-,?,+,?,-) -> ([r,u],[r],[s],[r,u]),
11          (-,-,+,?,-,+,+) -> ([r,u],[r],[s],[i]) }
12
13   coverage {
14     objects{P(root),student.marks}
15     policies{admin,teacher}
16     cases { (+,?) -> ([r,100],[i]), (-,+) -> ([i],[u,(>80,<=100)])}
17   }
18}
```

Basic RBAC Elements. At the core of an ΦRBAC model are the basic RBAC elements. The developer first defines roles and their cardinalities (cf. line 2), which specify the maximum number of subjects that may acquire the respective roles at any given time. The developer can also define an optional role hierarchy. In the example, the advisor role is defined as a specialization of teacher (cf. line 3). In addition, the developer can define optional *separation of duty* (SOD) constraints [25] (cf. lines 4 and 5). Static SOD (SSOD) constraints affect the role *assignment* (e.g., the roles admin and student can never be assigned to the same subject) while dynamic SOD (DSOD) constraints affect the role *activation*. For example, the DSOD constraint in Listing 1.2 states that a subject cannot activate the manager role together with either admin or both advisor and teacher roles. We then use a matrix-structure to specify the actual access control policy as well as the test case coverage. The matrix' rows and columns labels are given as the set of controlled objects and the different policy terms, while the entries of the matrix are given line-by-line as policy cases. These show the relation between the policy combinations and allowed operations on the respective objects.

Controlled Objects. *Φ*RBAC supports access control of objects with different types and granularity levels. We can divide them into *data model*, *page*, and *template* elements. The application's data structure is defined in a data model, which is then translated into a database type, such as tables in a relational database. The main benefit of using the data model as a part of controlled objects is that we can define access control on the data model elements *without* considering where or by whom they are used within the application code. *Φ*RBAC thus allow the data model elements as part of its controlled objects. It supports both coarse-grained elements such as the `student` entity shown in Listing 1.2 or more fine-grained components such as `speaker` property of an entity `Seminar`. It is important to note that *Φ*RBAC consequently supports relations, such as inheritance, between data-model components as well. For example, the type of the `speaker` property can be the `Person` entity. If this entity is access-controlled, then *Φ*RBAC automatically adds all the access control predicates from the `Person` entity to `speaker`'s predicate. However, the different properties and entities to be joined may have conflicting access control predicates, which can make a controlled object inaccessible. Such conflicts are checked during *Φ*RBAC's testing phase.

Since we do not want to force the developer to use *Φ*RBAC and the existing WebDSL access control to declare two different types of access control model, the coarse-grained components (i.e., pages and templates) are also supported within our model as controlled objects. Moreover, we support more fine-grained components of pages and templates. For page elements the developer can use *G(GroupNames)* to define a set of group names and *B(BlockNames)* to define the block names which are used by an external CSS style. In WebDSL we can use XML hierarchies within the template code, and the developer can use *XML(NodeNames)* to declare a set of XML node names as controlled objects.

Policy Terms. A policy term is an atomic access control check which can be used as building block in more complex policies. In *Φ*RBAC there are two types of policy terms. First, the developer can use a subset of the roles that were defined. Second, *user*, *data*, or *system* attributes can also be used as policy terms. In our example, the policy term `Self.username == "faz"` defines an access control check based on the current user (which is represented in *Φ*RBAC as `Self`) with the `username` property *faz*. The policy term `This.User.location != "New York"` defines an access control check based on a data attribute: for every object (represented by `This`) of the given type `User` that is used in the application, the property `location` is checked against the given value (i.e., *New York*). *Φ*RBAC allows the usual comparison operators, including a range restriction. For example in 1.2 the last policy (cf. line 9), creates an access control check for the system's office hours. The actual policy is then defined case-by-case, dependent on the logical status of the policy terms. The logical status is either *activated* or *true* (represented as + in *Φ*RBAC), *not activated* or *false* (-) or *don't care* (?). Note that *don't care* is not required but simplifies the specification of complex policies.

Policy Cases. As shown in Listing 1.2 (see lines 10 and 11), the developer can specify an arbitrary number of cases. Each case defines a logical combination of policy terms for creating an access control predicate. There are five different operations on the controlled objects. The developer can use c to denote that users with the appropriate roles (or satisfied attribute checks) are allowed to create an instance of the controlled objects or a set of objects that are embedded within the controlled objects. For example, if the controlled object is an entity, this case controls the create operations of this entity throughout the application; if the controlled object is a page, we look at the embedded objects within the page, and see if there is any create operation related to them. The developer can use r to allow read operations on the controlled object itself or its embedded objects (i.e., properties as sub-elements). Similarly, to allow update or delete operations on the controlled object itself or its embedded objects, u and d are used. s ("secret") can be used to hide the content of the object itself or its embedded objects. For example, if the controlled object is User.username then its instance will be hidden to the user, regardless of any other specified operations (i.e., create, read, update, delete). Finally, i ("ignore") can be used for defining a policy that does not effect the predicates on the controlled objects.

Note that all of these operations are guarded by the defined access control predicates. For example, Listing 1.2 line 10 shows that outside the office hours, when the authorized user with the username faz has the role teacher but not student or admin, then she cannot see any Person's password.

Coverage Cases. This part of the model (see lines 13-17 in Listing 1.2) helps the developer to define a set of independent cross checks on the ΦRBAC model and thus get assurance about the functional coverage of access control predicates over the controlled objects. In particular, we allow the developer to specify for each combination of policy terms to which extend the occurrences of an object within the target application are controlled. This can be seen as a summary that is independent of the actual access control mechanism. We allow the developer to define the coverage cases by hand because *only* the developer knows about the context of the target application, its security goals, and in what granularity level both defined ΦRBAC and the target application need to be checked.

The developer defines a number of cases, which each check the relative coverage of a set of controlled objects and their related operations for a combination of logical states (similar to Section 3.1). For example, in Listing 1.2 the first case in line 16 states a user with the activated role admin must have *read* access to all the controlled objects defined in the root page. In other words, all predicates that are derived from the policy cases (see line 11 in Listing 1.2) and will be woven around the objects within the root page, must be true for a user with the role admin activated. If we for example assume that the controlled object user.password is defined in the root page; then our first coverage case fails: based on the second defined policy case, a user with the activated role admin cannot see the instances of user.password. The coverage cases help the developer to check the defined ΦRBAC model, based on a different view, with respect to the target application. For example, in Listing 1.2, the policy cases do not directly cover the controlled object student.marks. However, in the second coverage case, we check its coverage range based on a case where the user has an activated role teacher.

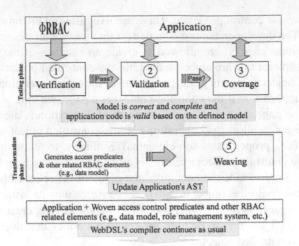

Fig. 1. An overview of the ΦRBAC generation pipeline

3.2 Code Generation from ΦRBAC Models

The ΦRBAC code generation process is divided into a *testing* and a *transformation* phase (see Figure 1). The aim of the testing phase is to validate and verify the access control model itself and its integration into the target application. As the ΦRBAC model is defined separately from the application code, the aim of the transformation phase is to first generate the access control elements (e.g., data model, access control predicates, etc.) and then to weave them into the target application code.

Testing Phase. A number of studies [23,20,21] highlight the fact that developing an access control mechanism is error-prone and the result therefore needs to be tested. Unlike the prior approaches, we emphasize the fact that correctness and completeness of the access control model on its own is *not* enough and the target application must be considered as well, based on the defined access control model. The access control predicates are derived from the access control model and need to be implemented (in our case generated) and inserted around the desired objects. Even a partial failure of doing so will result in application code that is compilable but has a number of security holes that need to be handled *after* the application deployment phase. This leads to high testing and maintenance costs after the deployment of the application. It is ideal to give a full guarantee to the developer for the defined access control model and its target Web application before deployment phase. The testing phase consists of three consecutive white-box testing steps (see Figure 1). Failure of each step will terminate the rest of the compilation and its related error messages will be given. In the first step, the defined ΦRBAC model is verified using model checking. Second, the application code is validated with respect to the defined ΦRBAC model. Third, the coverage is checked against the defined objectives.

Model Verification. This step mechanically verifies the correctness and completeness of an ΦRBAC model using SMT solver, *Z3* [7]. Here, we first verify the correctness of the defined basic RBAC elements and of each individual case defined in the policy and coverage cases with respect to the defined attributes. Second, we check the completeness of the policy and coverage cases. Since Z3 takes a representation of the model in first-order logic (FOL) and decides its satisfiability, our verification approach is to generate a number of FOL formulas from the given ΦRBAC model, and let Z3 check them individually. We then mechanically analyze Z3's output results to come to a conclusion about the correctness and completeness of the original model.

The basic RBAC elements can already create conflicts in the model. For instance, if a role `supervisor` inherits from a role `teacher` but there is also a (dynamic or static) SOD relation between them, then this specification creates a conflict and consequently an error in the model, because these two roles must be activated (due to the inheritance relation) and deactivated (due to the SOD) at the same time. To check the correctness of the basic RBAC elements, we first mechanically check if there are any undefined roles in inheritence, SSOD, and DSOD relations. Second, we check for possible conflicts between the hierarchy and SSOD (respectively DSOD) constraints by generating two FOL formulas to check with Z3. If the result is unsatisfiable (UNSAT), then there is an error in the defined basic RBAC structure. However if all the results are satisfiable (SAT) then the structure of basic RBAC elements is correct and we consequently go to the next step to check the correctness and completeness of the individually defined policy and coverage cases.

The defined cases can cause three types of errors that need to be checked:

- *Incorrect Case.* The policy terms and the policy signs specified in each case can be inconsistent with the other RBAC elements. For example, if there is a SSOD relation between the `teacher` and `student` roles, a case should not define a predicate in which both roles are active (i.e., have a "+" as policy sign), because the case can then never apply. is an error in the model if each has + for their policy sign. Similarly, we have an inconsistency if there is an inheritance relation between a parent and a child role, and a case states the parent role is not active but the child role is active.

- *Overlap.* If two cases overlap, then the respective access control predicatas can be true at the same time; if the specified access rights are then different, the model is inconsistent. An overlap between two cases can be detected by comparing the corresponding pairs of policy signs: if the signs for at least one policy term are complementary (i.e., one is active ("+") while the other is not ("-")), then there can be no overlap.

- *Incompleteness.* If the defined policy or coverage cases do not fully cover all the possible cases, then we have *incompleteness*.

The correctness of each case is checked in two steps. First, we need to check the defined `Time` and `Date` attributes and their intervals (if any). For example, we have an error, if the policy terms `Sys.Time(>=7:00,<=9:00)` and `Sys.Time(>=6:00, <=6:30)` are both activated in a single case, because this policy can never be true (i.e., the time can not be between 6 and 6:30am *and* between 7 to 9 am at the same time). Such error are checked during compile time by a set of custom Stratego strategies. In the second step we check the basic RBAC elements by generating a FOL formula from these elements, using the truth values corresponding to the policy signs for each policy term. Then, Z3 is called to check the satisfiability of the formula; a SAT result means that we have a correct case, and UNSAT means that we have an error. For example, to check the correctness of the RBAC elements defined in Listing 1.2 Line 11, in addition to the defined RBAC structure (Listing 1.2 lines 2-5), we derive a FOL formula that states admin must be *true* and teacher and student must both be *false*. In this case, Z3 gives us a SAT result, which means that there is no conflict in the defined RBAC model.

For overlap checks, we pair any two cases and generate a FOL formula in which there is a conjunction between these two cases and their sub-elements. Then we check each pair for satisfiability; (UN)SAT means that the two cases are (not) overlapping. Then, the overlapping check is repeated until all combinations are covered. For example for a policy set {teacher, student}, if we have two cases (+,-) and (+,?), then their FOL formula will be (teacher && not student) && (teacher), in which the SMT solver will give a SAT message that results in an error message because these two cases are overlapping. In case of *incompleteness* checks, we disjunctively link the negation of *all* of the cases and conjunction with the policy signs of each negated case. We then call Z3 to check the model for satisfiability. If the result is SAT, then there is a missing case and Z3 gives a counterexample for it. Since this produces the missing cases one-by-one, we need to respectively update and re-check the model, until Z3 finds no more missing cases. All steps mentioned above happen during compile-time. Since the developer does not know about Z3 and its results, we need to interpret these results for the user in terms of the ΦRBAC elements. During the last step, we parse the model checking results (UNSAT, SAT) and by retrieving its representation elements in the abstract syntax tree (AST) we give the error during the compilation based on the ΦRBAC elements.

Web Application Validation. In our approach, the access control predicates are woven into the application code around the controlled objects. The controlled objects and consequently their predicates may be nested within each other and can so create a set of conflicts. For example, in Listing 3, we have two different controlled objects, in which the instances of all users' username are embedded within the sub-element of the page UserList. We have P1 that protects UserList and P2 that protects the instances of users' username. Moreover, P1 indirectly protects P2 as P2 is nested within P1. Let us assume that P1 and P2 can conflict, e.g., P1 is true for users with the role teacher activated and P2 is true for users with the role admin activated but in the access control model there is also an SSOD relation between role teacher and admin. It is clear that users with the role admin activated can *never* access the instances of users' username, even though they have a right to do so. We call these situations *dead authorization code* and the following steps are used for finding such situations.

Listing 1.3. Nested controlled objects and their related predicates may create a set of conflicts

```
1 if(P1){ group(" UserList ") {
2    if(P2){ for(u:  User){
3          output(u.username ) // could be unreachable
4    }}
5 }
```

- *Sorting and Pairing.* First, we sort all policy cases based on the controlled objects, their related operations and predicates. Then, for each possible pair of objects, we create a list that is the union of all related predicates for that pair.
- *Potential Conflicts.* We check for conflicts between the predicates of each pair with respect to the defined RBAC structure. For this reason, for each pair, we transform their predicates and the defined RBAC structure into a FOL formula and check its satisfiability by using Z3; in case of *UNSAT*, we have a conflict.
- *Conflict Detection.* Now, we have a list of pairs in which the predicates create a conflict. We finally check whether the paired objects are embedded within each other in the application, and if so, we have found an error.

Coverage. The aim of this step is to check the required access control coverage based on the defined policy and coverage cases, and to provide feedback to the developer about the potential shortcomings of the defined ΦRBAC model. A coverage percentage shows what percentage of an object's occurrences in the application is protected *directly* or *indirectly* by the derived access control predicates that are defined in the policy cases. For each controlled object used in the coverage cases, the coverage percentage is calculated. The following three steps sketch the calculation of the coverage percentage for each controlled object:

- *Sorting and Pairing.* We sort *both* coverage and policy cases into two lists. We then combine each coverage case with all the policy cases.
- *Finding Related Cases and Partial Coverage.* We then need to find all the related policy cases for each coverage case based on the access control predicate. For this, we transform each pair of cases into a FOL formula such that the policy case's predicate is used as it is but we transform the negation of the coverage predicates. Then we call Z3 to check the *satisfiability* of the formula. If it is SAT, we omit the paired cases from the coverage computation, as they are not related; however in case of UNSAT, the predicates are related and we use the corresponding object and operation to calculate the coverage of the object based on that particular related predicate.
- *Overall Coverage.* We continually repeat the last step to find out all the *direct* and *indirect* coverage of each *(object,operation)* pair based on the defined policy cases. Then, we divide the total value of the computed coverage by the total number of the occurrences for the object throughout the application.

If the computed coverage is outside the specified range we give an error that describes the ΦRBAC elements that fail the coverage check, and terminate the compilation. The developer can then fix the coverage errors based on the defined ΦRBAC model and/or the target application.

Transformation Phase. As Figure 1 shows, the transformation phase is divided into *generating* the required elements and then *weaving* them throughout the Web application code. These elements are related to the RBAC and access control predicates of the system that are defined in the ΦRBAC model.

RBAC Generation. First, elements generated from the ΦRBAC model have to be added to the Web application's data model, in order to provide the data manipulation mechanisms for roles and their associated activities, such as maintaining list of assigned roles for each user. Second, these generated elements have to provide a *role management mechanism* for the authenticated users of the application. This mechanism consists of the *role assignment* and *activation* modules that are based on the overall RBAC structure defined within ΦRBAC model.

To extend the Web application's data model, we need to find the entity that represents the *users* of the system. In WebDSL, the developer uses the notion of *principal* to define the users' authentication credentials. For example, in Listing 1.4, the authentication is based on the username and password properties of the Person entity which represents the user of the system. We also use this entity type to represent that users have a given role (Listing 1.5, line 4) and extend it to store a set of assigned roles for each user (line 12). In addition, the session element must be extended to hold the activated roles for each user. In this we extend the data model of the application by generating the role entity (lines 2-9), extending the Person entity (lines 10-13); and extending the Web application session (lines 15-17).

Listing 1.4. WebDSL authentication credentials

```
principal is Person with credentials username, password
```

Listing 1.5. Generated data model elements

```
1  // Generated Role entity
2  entity Role {
3    name          :: String (name)
4    users         -> Set<Person>
5    inheritency   -> Set<Role> (optional)
6    ssod          -> Set<Role> (optional)
7    dsod          -> Set<Role> (optional)
8    cardinality   -> Int
9  }
10 // Extending 'Person' entity for role assignment
11 extend entity Person{
12   assignedRoles -> Set<Role> (inverse=Role.users)
13 }
14 // Extending session for activated roles
15 extend session securityContext{
16   activatedRoles -> Set<Role>
17 }
```

We already checked the correctness of the RBAC structure defined within the ΦRBAC model (see 3.2) and as shown in the generated role entity, we store each role's characteristics (e.g., SSOD) for the RBAC management component. The SSOD relations between the roles is used in the *role assignment* component which during the run-time of the system must not allow the administrator to assign conflicted roles to any users of the system. The DSOD relation between roles is used in the *role activation* module of the system, to ensure that two roles in the DSOD relation cannot be activated in any user's session. The *inheritance relation* between roles is used for both role assignment and role activation modules. These relations must be considered for the overall structure of the defined RBAC; in particular, we need to consider more than the directly defined relations for each role. For example, if a role advisor inherits from the role `teacher`, and `teacher` has an SSOD relation to `manager`, the roles `advisor` and `manager` can *never* be assigned to one user, even if the defined model did not explicitly state any SSOD relation between `advisor` and `manager`. In order to get all direct and indirect relations of each role, we translate the RBAC structure into a FOL formula, where we give a *true* value to the role whose relations, we want to check and use the SMT solver to get a counterexample in which the related roles are either true (due to inheritance relation) or false (due to SSOD or DSOD).

Predicate Generation. At this stage, we know that all specified cases are non-overlapping and correct. Each case then represents a predicate that is used to protect the controlled objects and their related operations. Before starting to generate the access control predicates, we first sort the cases based on controlled objects and operations, by joining their predicates where there is a same operation on the controlled object. For example, in Listing 1.2, for the controlled object `Person.password` both defined cases result in a `secret` operation. Therefore, the access control predicate that protects the instances of `Person.password` is equal to: `(teacher && not student && not admin) || (not teacher && not student && admin)`. These sorted cases will be parsed into an AST which is used by the predicate generator to generate a set of predicates that can be woven around the controlled objects in the Web application's AST.

Weaving Stage. Weaving is the last step in the ΦRBAC transformation phase. In this step, we first get the result of the RBAC and predicate generators. For the RBAC generator, the result is an AST that represents a number of modules that hold the generated data model and RBAC management component of the system. We weave these modules into the Web application's AST and we add a navigator to the authentication code to redirect the user to the role management component after successful authentication. Any user has access to their *role activation* component, however the *role assignment* component is protected, based on the access rights that are defined in ΦRBAC model (as shown in Listing 1.2). We then repeatedly traverse the Web application's AST, and iteratively weave in the generated access control predicates around any occurences of the controlled objects. In terms of predicates, the generated AST holds all the predicates sorted based on operations on the controlled objects. We finally pass the updated AST to the next step within the WebDSL compiler.

4   Case Study

The aim of this section is to show the benefits and limitations of the ΦRBAC modeling language and its code generation mechanism, based on the evaluation of a case study. The main objective of the evaluation is to check the efficacy of ΦRBAC during the *development phase* of a target application with a reasonably large data model, based on a rich set of policies. We chose a departmental Web site as a target application. Moreover, the goal of the evaluation is to derive a set of findings that can be used to improve *any* RBAC-based access control model, including ΦRBAC, that is intended to be used in the Web application domain.

We implemented our case study using WebDSL for the Web elements and ΦRBAC for the access control elements of the application. This case study is created and deployed for a language research group to cover their internal (e.g., organization of vivas) and external (e.g., publications) needs and to provide a fine-grained access control over the objects.

4.1 Web Application Description

In this case study, the Web application consists of three main elements, data model, pages, and access control. We divided the data model elements into two categories; users and activities. Users' entities belong to different types of users in the system such as academics or visitors. The second set of entities are related to the available activities such as adding an interest. The access control data model is generated at compile time. The size of the data model is quit large. We have nine different entities for the different types of users (e.g., `academic`, `student`) and 13 entities that cover the objects involved in activities (e.g., `publications`). Overall, we have 189 properties that are associated with 22 entities. These are the fine-grained objects that are used throughout the application code for a number of times. We divided the pages based on the different types of users and activities, regardless of the operations used for the system objects. Hence, there is only one page for each type of data and in that page all the available operations exist, but each part of the page will be access-controlled based on the policies defined in the ΦRBAC model. The access control elements for this case study are derived from the needs of the different types of users in a research group. For example, an `academic` can be a `supervisor` of a `PhD student`; however, she cannot be an examiner of a `PhD student` who she is supervising.

4.2 Evaluation and Findings

To evaluate the ΦRBAC model and mechanism, we looked at three aspects: modeling, testing, and transformation phases. The errors in the model were divided into attribute, RBAC, and the application errors, respectively. These errors were discovered before the transformation phase and consequently application deployment. The transformation strategies that were used in testing and transformation phase were tested, in a white-box manner, during their development. The woven AST was inspected manually to make sure all objects were correctly covered by the corresponding access control predicates, and conversely, that no unguarded objects were accidently covered directly or indirectly by any predicates.

The benefits are divided into development efficiency on one side, and correctness and completeness of the model and target application, respectively, before its deployment on the other side. During our case study, the ΦRBAC model was developed separately from the application code. So, in case of errors the developer did not need to search through the access control definitions scattered through the application code. Moreover, the ΦRBAC is developed at the right abstraction level: the developer did not need to use any specific object or agent-oriented terminology to define the access control components and just used the access control concepts such as roles, as they are . ΦRBAC is also a cost effective solution. In our case study the compilation time of our access control model was just 4.5 seconds on a machine with 4GB RAM and 2.3GHz CPU, to cover instances of 189 unique objects throughout the application. The correctness and completeness checks on the ΦRBAC model give an insurance to the developer about the access control of the system, so any security failure of the system during its run-time is not related to its access control element but to the other security elements of the system such as data encryption.

ΦRBAC's weakness originat in the RBAC approach itself; in particular, RBAC does not support an ownership notion. For instance, if in a research group we have a policy that states that the supervisor can edit their students' travel allowance, then any user with the role supervisor can edit the travel allowance of any student in the group regardless of who is the supervisor of those students. In order to overcome this flaw, the developer needs to introduce a number of unnecessary roles such as `supervisorOfStudentA` to enforce the mentioned policy. So ΦRBAC would be more efficient if the developer could use the ownership notion as a policy term.

5 Conclusions and Future Work

This paper introduced ΦRBAC, a declarative and fine-grained role- and attribute-based access control model for the Web application domain that enforces separation of concerns between application and access control model at the right abstraction level. ΦRBAC is defined and implemented as an extension to a domain-specific language, WebDSL, and its compiler. Its architecture is divided into a testing phase and a subsequent transformation phase. The testing phase uses a fast mechanism to check the correctness and completeness of the model and the application via code transformation and model-checking techniques. We showed how dead authorization code could occur in a fine-grained access control model, and how we check for this before the generation phase. We evaluated the approach and its mechanism based on an application example. The example demonstrated the efficacy and benefits of ΦRBAC in terms of defining a fine-grained access control model and checking correctness, completeness and sufficiency. Furthermore, it showed the applicability of ΦRBAC model for large data models based on a rich set of policies.

For future work we like to introduce the notion of ownership [22], as a policy term, to improve the ΦRBAC model and its mechanism. Also, we plan to integrate other well-known access control models, to achieve access control integration for Web applications that are constructed from mixed sources and require different access control models for different parts of the application. Moreover, in terms of the ΦRBAC architecture, we like to explore the possibility of generating our access control predicates on top of the database tier so that the application can retrieve access control settings from the database at run-time and take advantage of the database tier's security options. Furthermore, we will introduce authorization management systems for defined access control models within an application.

References

1. Abi Haidar, D., Cuppens-Boulahia, N., Cuppens, F., Debar, H.: An extended RBAC profile of XACML. In: SWS 2006, pp. 13–22. ACM (2006)

2. Bertino, E., Bonatti, P., Ferrar, E.: TRBAC: A temporal role-based access control model. ACM Trans. Inf. Syst. Secur. 2011, 191–233 (2001)
3. Chen, K., Huang, C.-M.: A practical aspect framework for enforcing fine-grained access control in web applications. In: Deng, R.H., Bao, F., Pang, H., Zhou, J. (eds.) ISPEC 2005. LNCS, vol. 3439, pp. 156–167. Springer, Heidelberg (2005)
4. Connor, A., Loomis, R.: Economic analysis of role-based access control. Technical report, National Institute of Standards and Technology (2010)
5. Dalai, A.K., Jena, S.K.: Evaluation of web application security risks and secure design patterns. In: CCS 2011, pp. 565–568. ACM (2011)
6. Damianou, N., Dulay, N., Lupu, E., Sloman, M.: The Ponder policy specification language. In: Sloman, M., Lobo, J., Lupu, E.C. (eds.) POLICY 2001. LNCS, vol. 1995, pp. 18–38. Springer, Heidelberg (2001)
7. de Moura, L.M., Bjørner, N.: Z3: An Efficient SMT Solver. In: Armando, A., Baumgartner, P., Dowek, G. (eds.) IJCAR 2008. LNCS (LNAI), vol. 5195, pp. 337–340. Springer, Heidelberg (2008)
8. Ferraiolo, D., Kuhn, R.: Role-Based Access Control. In: NIST-NCSC 1992, pp. 554–563 (1992)
9. Ferraiolo, D.F., Barkley, J.F., Kuhn, D.R.: A role-based access control model and reference implementation within a corporate intranet. In: ISS 2009, pp. 34–64. ACM (1999)
10. Giuri, L., Iglio, P.: Role templates for content-based access control. In: Workshop RBAC 1997, pp. 153–159 (1997)
11. Gorodetski, V.I., Skormin, V.A., Popyack, L.J. (eds.): Information Assurance in Computer Networks: Methods. In: Gorodetski, V.I., Skormin, V.A., Popyack, L.J. (eds.) MMM-ACNS 2001. LNCS, vol. 2052, Springer, Heidelberg (2001)
12. Groenewegen, D., Visser, E.: Integration of data validation and user interface concerns in a DSL for web applications. In: van den Brand, M., Gašević, D., Gray, J. (eds.) SLE 2009. LNCS, vol. 5969, pp. 164–173. Springer, Heidelberg (2010)
13. Groenewegen, D.M., Hemel, Z., Kats, L.C.L., Visser, E.: WebDSL: A domain-specific language for dynamic web applications. In: OOPSLA 2008, pp. 779–780. ACM (2008)
14. Groenewegen, D.M., Visser, E.: Declarative access control for WebDSL: Combining language integration and separation of concerns. In: ICWE 2008, pp. 175–188. IEEE (2008)
15. Heering, J., Hendriks, P.R.H., Klint, P., Rekers, J.: The syntax definition formalism SDF - reference manual. SIGPLAN Notices 24(11), 43–75 (1989)
16. Hemel, Z., Kats, L.C.L., Groenewegen, D.M., Visser, E.: Code generation by model transformation: a case study in transformation modularity. Software and System Modeling 9(3), 375–402 (2010)
17. Hortsmann, C.: Scala for the Impatient. Addison-Wesley Professional (2012)
18. Hsieh, G., Foster, K., Emamali, G., Patrick, G., Marvel, L.M.: Using XACML for embedded and fine-grained access control policy. In: ARES 2009, pp. 462–468. IEEE (2009)
19. Jin, X., Krishnan, R., Sandhu, R.: A Unified Attribute-Based Access Control Model Covering DAC, MAC and RBAC. In: Cuppens-Boulahia, N., Cuppens, F., Garcia-Alfaro, J. (eds.) DBSec 2012. LNCS, vol. 7371, pp. 41–55. Springer, Heidelberg (2012)
20. Martin, E., Xie, T., Yu, T.: Defining and measuring policy coverage in testing access control policies. In: Ning, P., Qing, S., Li, N. (eds.) ICICS 2006. LNCS, vol. 4307, pp. 139–158. Springer, Heidelberg (2006)
21. Masood, A., Bhatti, R., Ghafoor, A., Mathur, A.P.: Scalable and effective test generation for role-based access control systems. Software Eng. 35(5), 654–668 (2009)
22. McCollum, C., Messing, J., Notargiacomo, L.: Beyond the Pale of MAC and DAC Defining new forms of access control. In: RSP 1990, pp. 190–200. IEEE (1990)
23. Montrieux, L., Wermelinger, M., Yu, Y.: Tool support for UML-based specification and verification of role-based access control properties. In: ESEC 2011, pp. 456–459. ACM (2011)

24. Samarati, P., di Vimercati, S.D.C.: Access control: Policies, models, and mechanisms. In: Focardi, R., Gorrieri, R. (eds.) FOSAD 2000. LNCS, vol. 2171, pp. 137–196. Springer, Heidelberg (2001)

25. Sandhu, R., Ferraiolo, D., Kuhn, R.: The NIST Model for Role-Based Access Control: Towards a Unified Standard. In: Workshop on RBAC 2000, pp. 47–63. ACM (2000)

26. Steele, R., Min, K.: Healthpass: Fine-grained access control to portable personal health records. In: AINA 2010, pp. 1012–1019. IEEE (2010)

27. Sujansky, W.V., Faus, S.A., Stone, E., Brennan, P.F.: A method to implement fine-grained access control for personal health records through standard relational database queries. Journal of Biomedical Informatics 5(suppl. 1), S46–S50 (2010)

28. Tondel, I., Jaatun, M., Jensen, J.: Learning from software security testing. In: ICSTW 2008, pp. 286–294. IEEE (2008)

29. Visser, E.: Program transformation with Stratego/XT: Rules, strategies, tools, and systems in Stratego/XT 0.9. In: Lengauer, C., Batory, D., Blum, A., Odersky, M. (eds.) Domain-Specific Program Generation. LNCS, vol. 3016, pp. 216–238. Springer, Heidelberg (2004)

30. Visser, E.: WebDSL: A case study in domain-specific language engineering. In: Lämmel, R., Visser, J., Saraiva, J. (eds.) GTTSE 2007. LNCS, vol. 5235, pp. 291–373. Springer, Heidelberg (2008)

31. Win, B.D., Piessens, F., Joosen, W., De, B., Frank, W., Joosen, P.W., Verhanneman, T.: On the importance of the separation-of-concerns principle in secure software engineering. In: Workshop AEPSSD 2002 (2002)

32. Wurster, G., Van Oorschot, P.C.: The developer is the enemy. In: NSP 2008, pp. 89–97. ACM Press (2009)

33. Zhu, H., Lu, K.: Fine-grained access control for database management systems. In: Cooper, R., Kennedy, J. (eds.) BNCOD 2007. LNCS, vol. 4587, pp. 215–223. Springer, Heidelberg (2007)

An Approach to Context Modeling
in Software Development

Bruno Antunes, Joel Cordeiro, and Paulo Gomes

Centre for Informatics and Systems of the University of Coimbra, Coimbra, Portugal
{bema,jfac,pgomes}@dei.uc.pt

Abstract. The contextual information associated to the work of a developer can be used to identify the source code artifacts that are more relevant at a specific point in time. This information is essential to reduce the effort spent by developers when searching for needed source code artifacts. We propose a context model that represents the focus of attention of the developer at each moment. This context model adapts automatically to changes in the focus of attention of the developer by detecting context transitions. We have developed a prototype that was submitted to an experiment with a group of developers. The results collected show that the use of our context model to rank, elicit and filter relevant source code elements for the developer is very promising.

Keywords: Context Modeling, Context Capture, Context Transitions, Software Development, IDE.

1 Introduction

The interest in the many roles of context comes from different fields such as literature, philosophy, linguistics and computer science, with each field proposing its own view of context [1]. The term context typically refers to the set of circumstances and facts that surround the center of interest, providing additional information and increasing understanding. The context-aware computing concept was first introduced by Schilit and Theimer [2], where they refer to context as *"location of use, the collection of nearby people and objects, as well as the changes to those objects over time"*. In a similar way, Brown et al. [3] define context as location, identities of the people around the user, the time of day, season, temperature, etc. In a more generic definition, Dey and Abowd [4] define context as *"any information that can be used to characterize the situation of an entity. An entity is a person, place, or object that is considered relevant to the interaction between a user and an application, including the user and applications themselves"*.

With the increasing dimension of software systems, software development projects have grown in complexity and size, as well as in the number of features and technologies involved. During their work, software developers need to cope with a large amount of contextual information that is typically not captured and processed in order to enrich their work environment. Especially, in the IDE, developers deal with dozens of different artifacts at the same time. The software development process requires that developers repeatedly switch between different artifacts, which often depends on searching for these artifacts in the source code structure. The workspace of developers frequently

J. Cordeiro, S. Hammoudi, and M. van Sinderen (Eds.): ICSOFT 2012, CCIS 411, pp. 188–202, 2013.

comprises hundreds, if not thousands, of artifacts, which makes the task of searching for relevant artifacts very time consuming, especially when repeated very often. The contextual information associated to the work of a developer can be used to identify the source code artifacts that are more relevant at a specific point in time. Although the work of a developer is typically task oriented, it is too complex and dynamic to be easily sliced into simple tasks. The developer often addresses more than one task in a short period of time, or even at the same time, and the transitions between these tasks are not explicit. This behaviour makes it difficult to identify the context of a task and to know when the developer switches between tasks. We believe that more important than identifying the context for each one of the tasks the developer has at hands, is to understand what is the focus of attention of the developer at each moment and adapt as it changes.

We propose a context model that represents the focus of attention of the developer at each moment. This context model comprises a structural and a lexical dimensions. The structural context focus on the source code elements and their structural relations, while the lexical context focus on the terms used to represent these elements. This context model adapts to changes in the focus of attention of the developer, automatically detecting context transitions, either to a new context or a previous one. We have implemented a prototype, named SDiC[1] (Software Development in Context), in the form of a plugin that integrates the context modeling and transition mechanisms in Eclipse[2]. The prototype was submitted to an experiment with a group of developers, in order to collect statistical information about the context modeling process and to manually validate the context transition mechanism.

The remaining of the paper starts with an overview of related work. Then we introduce the developer context model and section 4 explains how the context transition is processed. The prototype developed is described in section 5. The experimentation and results discussion is presented in section 6. Finally, section 7 concludes the paper with some final remarks and future work.

2   Related Work

Kersten and Murphy [5] have been working on a model for representing tasks and their context. The task context is derived from an interaction history that comprises a sequence of interaction events, representing operations performed on a software program's artifact. They then use the information in a task context either to help focus the information displayed in the IDE, or to automate the retrieval of relevant information for completing a task. Although our structural context was inspired by their work, we have expanded this model with a lexical dimension. Also, we do not attach the context of the developer to tasks, we see the context model as a continuous and dynamic structure that adapts to the behaviour of the developer. Instead of requiring developers to explicitly define where a task starts and ends, our approach automatically adapts to the changes in the focus of attention of the developer, identifying which artifacts are more relevant for the activities of the developer in each moment.

---

[1] http://sdic.dei.uc.pt
[2] http://eclipse.org

In the same line of task management and recovery, Parnin and Gorg [6] propose an approach for capturing the context relevant for a task from a programmer's interactions with an IDE, which is then used to aid the programmer recovering the mental state associated with a task and to facilitate the exploration of source code using recommendation systems. Their work is essentially focused on methods, while our approach also covers classes and interfaces, and they do not take into consideration the interest value of these methods to the developer.

More recently, Piorkowski et al. [7] have implemented an algorithm that takes into account a list of the last methods visited by the developer to produce a list of recommendations, including methods previously visited and not previously visited by the developer. The recommendations are retrieved and ranked according to a spread-activation algorithm based on a graph representing the source code structure and the words shared between methods. The recency information was also taken into account, by applying a greater activation to more recently accessed methods. Their approach is comparable with that proposed by Parnin and Gorg [6], as they also focus the methods recently visited by the developer.

Holmes and Murphy [8] proposes Strathcona, an Eclipse plugin that allows to search for source code examples. The process consists of extracting the structural context of the code on which a developer is working, when the developer requests for examples. The search is based in different heuristics, such as inheritance relations and method calls, by matching the structural context with the code in the repository. The contextual information is explicitly provided by the developer when searching for source code examples, while our context model is automatically built from the interactions of the developer in the IDE.

Ye and Fischer in [9], propose a process called information delivery, which consists in proactively suggesting useful software engineer's needs for components. The process is performed by running continuously as a background process in Emacs, extracting reuse queries by monitoring development activities. They use the JavaDoc comments as context to create a query for retrieving relevant components. With the idea that code fragments using similar terms in the identifiers also use similar methods, Heinemann and Hummel [10] proposes the use of the knowledge embodied in the identifiers as a basis for recommendation of methods. They use the identifiers of a few source lines preceding a method call as context. These approaches focus on the identifiers and comments used in the source code to complement a query used to retrieve relevant artifacts. They do not take into consideration the focus of attention of the developer or the relative relevance of a specific artifact manipulated by the developer.

Warr and Robillard [11] developed a plugin for the Eclipse IDE to provide program navigation, by suggesting potentially relevant elements for the current context. The context is created by the user by dragging and dropping elements of interest into a view. It retrieves and ranks all the elements in the project's source code by taking into account their structural relations to any of the elements in the context. The contextual information is provided by the developer through a set of elements of interest, while our approach automatically identifies these elements of interest and how their interest evolves over time.

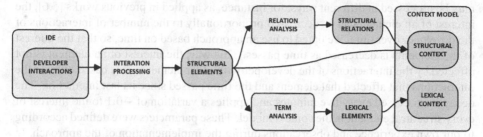

Fig. 1. Abstract representation of the process used to build the context model

3   Context Modeling

The context model we have defined aims to represent the context of the developer in relation to the source code elements that are more relevant to the work of the developer at each moment. The model is built from the interactions of the developer with the source code elements and evolves over time, as the focus of attention of the developer changes. It comprises a structural and a lexical dimensions, representing both the source code elements and the terms used to represent these elements. The process of building the context model from the developer interactions is illustrated in figure 1 and will be described in more detail on the following sections.

3.1   Structural Context

The structural context focuses on the structural elements and structural relations that are more relevant for the developer in a specific moment. The relevance of these elements and relations is derived from the interactions of the developer with the source code and is represented as an interest value. The structural context was inspired by the work of Kersten and Murphy [5], which have used a similar model to represent the context associated to a task. Next, we describe the structural context in more detail, including the structural elements and structural relations.

Structural Elements. The structural elements represent the source code elements with which the developer is interacting, including classes, interfaces and methods. Associated to each element is an interest value that is derived from the analysis of the interactions of the developer with that element. The impact of each interaction in the interest of an element has been defined based on our experience and some empirical tests, reflecting how that interaction contributes to increase or decrease the relevance of the element in the context of the developer. When an element is opened, or accessed for the first time, it is added to the structural context and its interest is increased by 0.4. When the element gains focus or is edited, its interest is increased by 0.2 and 0.1, respectively. The more the developer accesses or edits an element, the more relevant it becomes in the context model. When an element is closed, its interest is decreased by −0.4.

As time passes, the interest of the elements must be decayed, so that the relevance of an element in the context of the developer decreases if it is not used over time. The decay may be processed in different ways, for instance, as applied in previous works [5,6], the interest of an element can be decreased proportionally to the number of interactions of the developer over time. We opted to use an approach based on time, so that the interest of the elements is decreased as time passes. This way, the interest of an element is not affected by the interactions of the developer with other elements, it is based only on the interactions that affected that element and the time passed since its last interaction. The decay is processed every five minutes and applies a variation of -0.1 to the interest of every structural element in the context model. These parameters were defined according to our own experience and observations during the implementation of the approach. In order to prevent loosing context when the developer is distracted, or away for some reason, the decay is executed only if the developer has been active in the IDE since the last decay. When the interest of an element reaches zero, that element is finally removed from the structural context.

Consider SE the set of structural elements stored in the workspace of the developer. Let $I(se)$ be the interest associated to an element se, then the structural elements represented in the context model would be the subset of structural elements in the workspace with a positive interest ($CSE \subseteq SE$), as defined in equation 1.

$$CSE = \{se_1, se_2, \ldots, se_n \mid I(se_i) > 0\} \tag{1}$$

Consider E an event that affects an element se, including interactions and decays, and E^Δ the variation applied to the interest of the element se affected by the event E. Then, the interest of an element is computed using equation 2, where $I'(se)$ denotes the interest associated to the structural element se, before normalization, and E_i^Δ represents the ith event of the n events that affected element se.

$$I'(se) = \sum_{i=1}^{n} E_i^\Delta \tag{2}$$

As the developer interacts with the source code elements, their interest grows without restriction. This could lead to a situation in which an element could obtain a disproportionate interest in relation to the remaining elements. This would make it difficult to compare the relative relevance of such an element in relation to the relevance of other elements. Taking this into account, the final interest of an element is always normalized to the interval $[0, 1]$. The normalized interest $I(se)$ is computed using an inverted exponential function, as shown in equation 3, assuring that the interest of an element has an exponential growth, becoming very close to 1 for values over 5.

$$I(se) = 1 - \left(\frac{1}{e^{I'(se)}} \right) \tag{3}$$

As shown in figure 2, the structural elements `ContextModel`, `ContextElement`, `setInterest` and `getInterest` were added to the structural context because they were manipulated by the developer at some point in time. The relevance of these elements to the developer is given by their interest values, which evolved according to the different interactions of the developer with that elements over time.

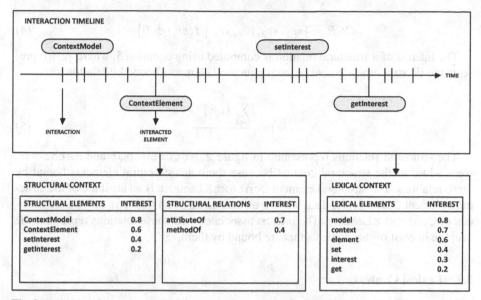

Fig. 2. Example of how the context model is derived from a set of interactions in the interaction timeline

Structural Relations. The structural relations represent the relevance of the relations that exist between the source code element that are being manipulated by the developer. These relations represent the structural relations that exist in the Java programming language, but are common to most of the object oriented programming languages, and can be categorized in three groups: inheritance (`extensionOf` and `implementationOf`), composition (`attributeOf` and `methodOf`) and behaviour (`calledBy`, `usedBy`, `parameterOf` and `returnOf`). The relevance of the structural relations can be used to measure the relevance of source code elements that are not being used by the developer, but are structurally related with the elements that are in the context model.

Because the structural relations are not directly affected by the interactions of the developer, their relevance is derived from the structural elements that exist in the structural context. When two, or more, structural elements are bound by one of these relations, that relation is added to the structural context. Associated with each relation is an interest value that represents the relevance of that relation in the context of the developer. The interest of a relation is computed as an average of the interest of all structural elements that are bound by that relation. This way, the relevance of a structural relation reflects the relevance of the structural elements that brought it to the structural context. The structural relations and their interest are updated whenever the structural context changes. When no more structural elements are bound by a relation, it is removed from the structural context.

Consider SR the set of relations defined before. Let $I(sr)$ be the interest associated to relation sr, then the structural relations represented in the context model would be the subset of structural relations with a positive interest ($CSR \subseteq SR$), as defined in equation 4.

$$CSR = \{sr_1, sr_2, \ldots, sr_n \mid I(sr_i) > 0\} \qquad (4)$$

The interest of a structural relation is computed using equation 5, where se_i^{sr} represents the ith structural element of the n structural elements bound by relation sr.

$$I(sr) = \frac{\sum\limits_{i=1}^{n} I(se_i^{sr})}{n} \qquad (5)$$

The structural relations represented in figure 2, `attributeOf` and `methodOf`, were added to the structural context because there are structural elements bound by these relations. The structural element `ContextElement` is an attribute of the structural element `ContextModel`, while `setInterest` and `getInterest` are methods of `ContextElement`. The interest associated with these relations represents the average interest of the elements that are bound by them.

3.2   Lexical Context

The lexical context focus on the terms that are more relevant in the context of the developer. It comprises a list of terms that are extracted from the names of the source code elements that are manipulated by the developer. The name of source code elements in the Java programming language typically follow the *CamelCase*[3] naming convention, resulting in one or more terms joined without spaces and with the first letter of each element capitalized. We use this characteristic to extract the different terms associated with a structural element. The lexical context comprises all the terms extracted from the structural elements in the structural context. Similarly to the elements and relations in the structural context, the relevance of each term is given by an interest value. The interest of a term is computed as an average of the interest of the structural elements from which the term was extracted. The more relevant is a structural element, the more relevant become the terms used to reference that element. The relevance of these terms can be used to identify source code elements that are lexically related with the source code elements that are currently relevant for the developer. When the structural elements change, the lexical context is updated accordingly.

Consider LE the set of all lexical elements used to reference the source code elements in the workspace of the developer. Let $I(le)$ be the interest associated to the lexical element le, then the lexical elements represented in the context model would be the subset of lexical elements in the workspace with a positive interest ($CLE \subseteq LE$), as defined in equation 6.

$$CLE = \{le_1, le_2, \ldots, le_n \mid I(le_i) > 0\} \qquad (6)$$

The interest of a lexical element is computed using equation 7, where se_i^{le} represents the ith structural element of the n structural elements from which the lexical element le was extracted.

---

[3] `http://en.wikipedia.org/wiki/CamelCase`

$$I(le) = \frac{\sum\limits_{i=1}^{n} I(se_i^{le})}{n} \tag{7}$$

The terms in the lexical context of figure 2, `model`, `context`, `element`, `set`, `interest` and `get`, were extracted from the elements in the structural context. Their interest represents the average DOI of the structural elements referenced by them.

Because terms are not explicitly related as the source code elements, the terms used in the names of all the source code elements that exist in the workspace of the developer are analyzed in order to identify terms that are related by co-occurrence. The co-occurrence relation is created when two terms are found in the name of a source code element. In a linguistic sense, co-occurrence can be interpreted as an indicator of semantic proximity [12]. We use co-occurrence as a measure of proximity between two terms, assuming that if the terms are used together to represent the same entity, that means they are related. These relations are then used to understand how the source code elements are related with each other from a lexical point of view. We also identify terms that are very frequent, such as `get`, `set`, etc. These very frequent terms co-occur with a variety of other terms and end up connecting almost every term in a distance of three relations. To avoid this, we chose to ignore all the terms that would fall in the top 30% of all term occurrences.

4 Context Transitions

As the focus of attention of the developer changes, the notion of what is relevant to the work of the developer also changes and the context model must be adapted accordingly. The context model described was designed to represent the focus of attention of the developer at each moment, but does not provide, by itself, the mechanisms needed to adapt as the focus of attention changes, which sometimes happens very fast. Because the developer commonly addresses more than one task in a short period of time, or even at the same time, the focus of attention is dispersed through different parts of the source code structure. This means that, in fact, more than one context model exist in parallel, and they must be activated and deactivated as the focus of attention changes. This issue has been addressed with a mechanism to deal with context transitions, as the focus of attention of the developer changes. This way we may have several context models, that are stored in a context model pool, with only one context model active at each moment. The system automatically detects the changes in the focus of attention of the developer and decides whether a new context should be created or an existing one should be activated.

4.1 Transition Detection

To detect changes in the focus of attention of the developer, we use the way source code elements added to the context model are related with those that are already in the context model. When the attention of the developer shifts to a different part of the source code structure, it is expected to see, in a short period of time, a reasonable number of interactions with source code elements that have no relation with those in the current

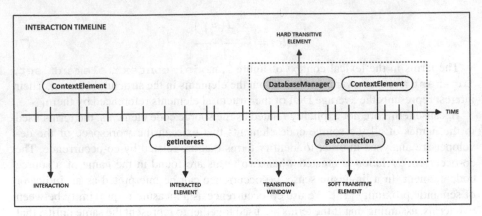

Fig. 3. Example of how the context transition window is applied to the interaction timeline

context model. We assume that in such a situation, the system must adapt to the change that is occurring in the behaviour of the developer and make a transition to a new context, or an existing one. To detect these situations we have defined a mechanism based on a transition window and a set of transitive elements (see figure 3). The transition window is a fixed time window that represents the time span within which a certain number of elements, having no relation with the current context, will start a context transition. We call these elements of transitive elements, and they can be either hard or soft transitive. The hard transitive elements are those that have no close relation with the elements in the current context, whereas the soft transitive elements are those that have some kind of relation with only hard transitive, or other soft transitive, elements. The time window moves along the interaction timeline as time passes. The hard or soft transitive elements that reach the limit of the time window are no longer marked as transitive elements. When the number of hard transitive elements reaches a threshold of 3, or the number of soft transitive elements reach a threshold of 6, within a context transition window of 3 minutes, a context transition is initiated.

As illustrated in figure 3, the transition window is located at the head of the interaction timeline. There are three elements that were accessed within the transition window, one is a hard transitive element, one is a soft transitive element and the other is an element that was already in the context model. The DatabaseManager class is considered a hard transitive element because it has no relation with any of the previously manipulated elements, while the getConnection element is considered a soft transitive element because it is a method of the DatabaseManager class but is not related with the remaining elements in the context model. The ContextElement method is not considered a transitive element because it was manipulated before and was already in the context model.

4.2   Transition Processing

When a context transition is detected, the system must remove the transitive elements from the current context, deactivate it and decide if a new context should be created or an existing one should be activated. To activate an existing context, one must assure that the developer is changing the focus of attention to a part of the source code structure that originated the existing context. The system decides if an existing context should be activated by comparing its elements with the transitive elements, those that were used to detect the context transition in the first place.

For an existing context to be activated it has to contain all the transitive elements. A context model that contains all the transitive elements assures that the new focus of attention of the developer will be properly represented. Also, such a context model increases the odds that the remaining elements in that context model are also relevant, because they are very likely to be related with the transitive elements. In case that the activated context model does not correctly represent the new focus of attention of the developer, the context transition process will be there to detect this situation and process a new context transition, if necessary. When there are no other context models, or when the condition for activating an existing context model is not satisfied, a new context is created. The transitive elements are added to this new context and then it is activated.

5   Prototype

We have implemented a prototype in the form of a plugin, that integrates the context modeling and context transition mechanisms in the Eclipse IDE. The activity of the developer is monitored in the background in order to build the context model and detect context transitions.

The prototype provides an interface where all the information related with the context modeling and context transition processes can be consulted (see figure 4). The interface shows a list of all the context models that have been created (see 1 in figure 4). When one of these context models is selected, all the information related with the selected context model is presented, including information about the structural and lexical contexts. A list of events (Added, Removed, Activated and Deactivated) associated with the context model is presented (see 2 in figure 4). Concerning the structural context, we can see the structural elements (see 3 in figure 4) and structural relations (see 4 in figure 4) that exist in the selected context model, as well as a visual representation of their current interest value. The hard and soft transitive elements are shown in gray, with the soft transitive elements having a lighter grey than the others. When one of the elements or relations is selected, a list of the events (Added, Removed, Interest Incremented and Interest Decremented) that affected that element are presented (see 5 in figure 4) and a chart representing the evolution of its interest over time is shown (see 6 in figure 4). Concerning the lexical context model, we can see the terms that exist in the current context model. Similarly to the structural context interface, when a term is selected, the list of events that affected the term is presented and a chart representing the evolution of its interest over time is shown.

6   Experimentation

We have created an experiment to validate our approach in the field, with developers using the prototype during their work. The experiment was conducted with a group of 21 developers, from both industry and academia. The developers used the prototype

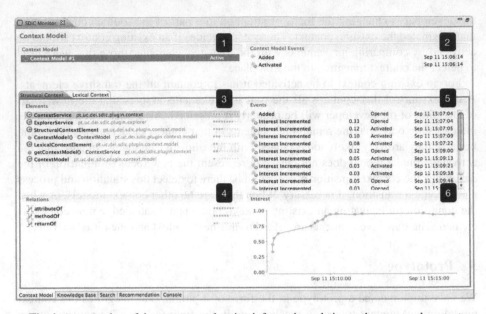

Fig. 4. A screenshot of the prototype, showing information relative to the structural context

during different time periods, with an average of 38 days per developer, using Eclipse to develop source code in the Java programming language. The objective of the experimentation was to collect statistical data about the context modeling and transition mechanisms, as well as to manually validate the context transitions processed by the system.

Concerning the context modeling mechanism, we have collected statistical data about new elements added to the context model and how they were related with the elements that were already in the context model. This information would allow us to better understand how the source code elements manipulated by developers are related with each other and how this could be used to improve the context modeling and transition processes. We have analyzed a total of $48,044$ elements added to the context model. To evaluate how these elements were related with existing elements, we have verified if they were related within a distance of 3 relations with the top 15 elements with higher interest of both the structural and the lexical contexts. About 88% of the elements were structurally related with at least one structural element, with an average distance of 2.3 relations, and about 86% were lexically related with at least one lexical element, with an average distance of 2.0 relations. These numbers show that most of the source code elements needed by developers were related with at least one of the elements manipulated before, within a distance of about two relations. Based on this, we believe that the use of our context model to rank, elicit and filter relevant source code elements for the developer is very promising. Assuming that a source code element needed by the developer is likely to be related with the elements being manipulated, we can use the proximity between this artifact and the context model to assess its relevance to the developer.

Table 1. The average number of structural and lexical elements in the context model

Average Structural Elements	11.69
Average Structural Related Elements	4.64
Average Structural Unrelated Elements	5.05
Average Lexical Elements	14.26
Average Lexical Related Elements	22.60
Average Lexical Unrelated Elements	3.82

Table 2. The percentage of times each relation appeared in the relations between added and existing context elements

Relation	Percentage
extensionOf	8.57%
implementationOf	1.38%
attributeOf	36.62%
methodOf	90.73%
parameterOf	10.37%
returnOf	3.07%
calledBy	49.75%
usedBy	31.19%

In table 1 we present the average number of structural and lexical elements, as well as the average number of elements related and unrelated with the added element. The lexical related elements have an higher average due to the fact that the name of a source code element typically comprises more than one term, and each match between one of these terms and the terms in the lexical context was considered. The results show that the source code elements added to the context model were structurally related with a an average of about 40% of the elements that were already in the context model. The results of the lexical elements are even more expressive. This reinforces the idea that the source code elements manipulated by developers are highly correlated. We have also analyzed the types of relations that are more common between the added elements and the existing elements. The percentage of times each relation appeared is shown in table 2. The composition and behavior relations are by far the most common, as expected.

With respect to the context transition process, we have collected statistical information about 109 context transitions, presented in table 3. All the context transitions led to the creation of a new context. We could conclude that a transition to a previous context is something very uncommon, but the problem may also reside in the rules we have defined for switching to an existing context. At first, the similarity between the two sets of elements was computed using the Jaccard index [13], also known as the Jaccard similarity coefficient, which is a statistical measure used for comparing the similarity between sample sets. When the similarity between the two sets was greater than a threshold of 0.5, the existing context would be activated. After some time, we verified that the context transitions to existing context models were not happening and realized that using the Jaccard metric would not be adequate for our purpose. The two sets being compared

Table 3. The statistical information collected about the context transition process

Context Transition	Percentage
New Context	100%
Existing Context	0%
Hard Transition	73%
Soft Transition	27%

were very often disproportionate, because the number of transitive elements tends to be small compared to the number of elements in a context model. Hence, the threshold was never reached and none of the existing contexts would be activated.

Being aware of this problem, we have refined the conditions to activate an existing context, focusing only in the transition elements. Because the transition elements are more relevant for the context transition process than the others, we may assume that if an existing context contains all the transition elements, then this context model is a good candidate to be activated. Despite this change, there were no context transitions to an existing context. This way, we tend to believe that the transitions to an existing context are rare, but the process must be better studied in order to draw stronger conclusions. With respect to the transitive elements, we could conclude that context transitions are more often caused by reaching the hard transitive elements threshold, than by reaching the soft transitive elements threshold. This was expected, because the hard transitive elements are more relevant to the process and therefore have a lower threshold. But, it also shows that the soft transitive elements have their role in detecting context transitions.

Finally, we asked the developers to evaluate how each context transition detected by the system could be identified as change in their focus of attention. They were presented with the structural elements that were in the context model before the transition and the elements that were used to detect the transition (both hard and soft transitive). They were asked to rate how the context transition would be related with a change in their focus of attention in a scale from 1 (Poorly Related) to 5 (Highly Related). The average score for the 55 context transitions evaluated was 3.00, with a confidence interval of ± 0.33, for a confidence level of 95%. The average score obtained is not conclusive, but is encouraging, at least. One of the problems we have faced is that developers have some difficulties understanding the concepts of context transition and focus of attention, which can have lead to misjudgment in the evaluation process.

7   Conclusions

We have presented an approach to context modeling and context transition detection in software development. The context model combines a structural and a lexical dimensions, to represent the source code elements, structural relations and terms that are more relevant for the developer in a specific moment in time. The context transition detection mechanism allows the context model to automatically adapt to the changes in the focus of attention of the developer. We have implemented a prototype that integrates our approach in Eclipse. This prototype was submitted to an experiment with a group of developers to collect statistical information about the context modelling process and to manually validate the context transition mechanism. The statistical information collected shows that the source code elements manipulated by the developer are highly correlated, leading us to believe that the use of a context model to assess the relevancy of a source code element to the developer is very promising. The human evaluation of the context transition mechanism was not conclusive, but the results are nevertheless encouraging, considering the fact that developers have some difficulties in understanding the concept of context transition. An early version of our context model was already applied to support the context-based search of source code in the IDE [14], showing that the use of context contribute positively to the ranking of search results. A similar version of this context model was also applied to the recommendation of relevant source code in the IDE [15].

With respect to future work, there are a set of processes and parameters of special interest that could be studied in more detail. For instance, the decay applied to the interest of a structural element in the context model follows a linear function of time. But, the interest of an element be decayed differently, for instance using a logarithmic function of time. Additionally, it would be interesting to understand if different decay rates should be applied to different source code elements. For instance, the interest of a class could decay at a different rate of the interest of a method. The context transition detection is another point that requires further research. The parameters that regulate this process were defined based on our own experience and observations, and the results obtained through the developers evaluation of context transitions were not conclusive. Also, our context transition mechanism is entirely based on the structural relations between source code elements. But, it would be interesting to evaluate what is the role of lexical relations in this process.

Acknowledgements. Bruno Antunes is supported by a FCT scholarship grant SFRH/BD/43336/2008, co-funded by ESF (European Social Fund).

References

1. Mostefaoui, G.K., Pasquier-Rocha, J., Brezillon, P.: Context-Aware Computing: A Guide for the Pervasive Computing Community. In: Proc. of the IEEE/ACS International Conference on Pervasive Services (ICPS 2004), pp. 39–48. IEEE Computer Society, Washington, DC (2004)
2. Schilit, B., Theimer, M.: Disseminating Active Map Information to Mobile Hosts. IEEE Network 8(5), 22–32 (1994)
3. Brown, P.J., Bovey, J.D., Chen, X.: Context-Aware Applications: From the Laboratory to the Marketplace. IEEE Personal Communications 4, 58–64 (1997)
4. Dey, A.K., Abowd, G.D.: Towards a Better Understanding of Context and Context-Awareness. In: Proc. of the CHI Workshop on the What, Who, Where, When, and How of Context-Awareness, The Hague, The Netherlands (2000)
5. Kersten, M., Murphy, G.C.: Using Task Context to Improve Programmer Productivity. In: Proc. of the 14th ACM SIGSOFT International Symposium on Foundations of Software Engineering (SIGSOFT 2006/FSE-14), pp. 1–11. ACM, New York (2006)
6. Parnin, C., Gorg, C.: Building Usage Contexts During Program Comprehension. In: Proc. of the 14th IEEE International Conference on Program Comprehension (ICPC 2006), pp. 13–22. IEEE Computer Society, Washington, DC (2006)

7. Piorkowski, D., Fleming, S., Scaffidi, C., Bogart, C., Burnett, M., John, B., Bellamy, R., Swart, C.: Reactive Information Foraging: An Empirical Investigation of Theory-Based Recommender Systems for Programmers. In: Proc. of the ACM Annual Conference on Human Factors in Computing Systems (CHI 2012), pp. 1471–1480. ACM, New York (2012)
8. Holmes, R., Murphy, G.C.: Using Structural Context to Recommend Source Code Examples. In: Proc. of the 27th International Conference on Software Engineering (ICSE 2005), pp. 117–125. ACM, New York (2005)
9. Ye, Y., Fischer, G.: Supporting Reuse by Delivering Task-Relevant and Personalized Information. In: Proc. of the 24th International Conference on Software Engineering (ICSE 2002), pp. 513–523. ACM, New York (2002)
10. Heinemann, L., Hummel, B.: Recommending API Methods Based on Identifier Contexts. In: Proc. of the 3rd International Workshop on Search-Driven Development: Users, Infrastructure, Tools, and Evaluation (SUITE 2011), pp. 1–4. ACM, New York (2011)
11. Warr, F.W., Robillard, M.P.: Suade: Topology-Based Searches for Software Investigation. In: Proc. of the 29th International Conference on Software Engineering (ICSE 2007), pp. 780–783. IEEE Computer Society, Washington, DC (2007)
12. Harris, Z.: Distributional Structure. Word 10(23), 146–162 (1954)
13. Jaccard, P.: Étude comparative de la distribution florale dans une portion des Alpes et des Jura. Bulletin del la Société Vaudoise des Sciences Naturelles 37, 547–579 (1901)
14. Antunes, B., Cordeiro, J., Gomes, P.: Context-Based Search in Software Development. In: Proc. of the 7th Conference on Prestigious Applications of Intelligent Systems (PAIS 2012) of the 20th European Conference on Artificial Intelligence (ECAI 2012), pp. 937–942. IOS Press (2012)
15. Antunes, B., Cordeiro, J., Gomes, P.: An Approach to Context-Based Recommendation in Software Development. In: Proc. of the 6th ACM Conference on Recommender Systems (RecSys 2012), pp. 171–178. ACM Press, New York (2012)

Linear Software Models Are Theoretical Standards of Modularity

Iaakov Exman

Software Engineering Department, The Jerusalem College of Engineering, Jerusalem, Israel
iaakov@jce.ac.il

Abstract. Modularity is essential to obtain well-composed software systems from COTS (Commercial Off-The-Shelf) components. But COTS components do not necessarily match the modules of the designed software system. A clear-cut procedure is needed for the choice of the necessary and sufficient components providing the required functionalities. Linear Software Models are rigorous theoretical standards of modularity. These models are proposed as formal criteria for well-composed software systems. The paper lays down theoretical foundations – upon linear independence and reducible matrix concepts – providing precise meanings to familiar software concepts, such as coupling and the single responsibility theorem. The theory uses a Modularity Matrix – linking linearly independent software structors to composable software functionals. The theory has been tested by applying it to small canonical systems and to large software systems found in the literature.

Keywords: Modularity, Theoretical Standards, Software Composition, Linear Software Models, Well composed Systems, Modularity Matrix.

1   Introduction

Significant progress since Parnas' classical paper [13] – which posed the modularity issue in the software context and treated it by informal reasoning – paved the way for run-time system composition/update from COTS software components. Yet there remain fundamental obstacles to make this vision concrete.

Modularity's wisdom of low dependency among modules has been informally stated in innumerable ways: recommendations such as single responsibility, source-code dependency metrics, design patterns and tools. But recommendations, metrics, patterns and tools never crystallized into a systematic theoretical approach.

This is exactly the problem dealt with by this paper: to provide a solid and generic basis to treat software composition in a rigorous and consistent way, enabling theoretical models against which to check real systems. To this end, Linear Software Models are proposed upon well-established linear algebra techniques.

1.1   The Software Composition Problem

The software composition problem, analysed by this paper, is how to build a well designed modular software system from available COTS components that were not designed specifically for a particular system.

J. Cordeiro, S. Hammoudi, and M. van Sinderen (Eds.): ICSOFT 2012, CCIS 411, pp. 203–217, 2013.
© Springer-Verlag Berlin Heidelberg 2013

Components are deployment units needed to actually run software systems. They are loaded to the computer memory as indivisible wholes. Typical examples are a C++ dll (dynamically linked library), a jar (Java archive) or a C# assembly.

On the one hand, the software engineer, by using best practices, designs a modular software system in terms of desirable architectural units. Architectural units describe the structure and behaviour of a particular software system.

On the other hand, *components* are assumed to be mainly purchased as COTS (Commercial Off-The-Shelf) components from several manufacturers, and less frequently to be produced in-house. It is realistic to expect variability among COTS from distinct sources.

1.2   Linear Software Models: Structors and Functionals

This paper describes Linear Software Models as a theory of software composition. In this theory, the architecture of a software system is expressed by two kinds of entities: structors and functionals.

Structors – a new term reminding vectors – are structural architectural units. Structors generalize the notion of structural unit to cover diversity of types (structs, classes, interfaces, aspects) and hierarchical collections (sets of classes, as design patterns). Structors refer to types, not instances. Structors are loadable within components.

Functionals are architectural system units from a behavioral point of view. These are *potential functions* that can be, but are not necessarily invoked. Typically these are Java or C# methods, related functions (e.g. a set of trigonometric functions) or roles – supplying the functionality of a design pattern, cf. Riehle [14]. Note: we use *Functional* as a noun, similarly to the mathematical concept with this name in the calculus of variations, and to the grammatical use of *Potential* in physics.

Structors contain a finite set of functionals and are represented by finite vectors.

Modules are architectural units in a higher hierarchical level of a system. Modules are composed of grouped structors and their corresponding functionals.

Both components and systems contain structors. But the respective logics are different. Structors contained in a COTS component are fixed by the core technology of the component manufacturer and such structors must be assumed indivisible.

Structors within a system are determined by the system purpose. Not all structors of a component may be required by a system. Similarly, not all functionals within structors are needed by a system, and some of them may never be invoked. The numbers of structors or functionals provided by a component are not constrained. Analysis starts with a list of structors and a list of functionals that must be in a system. If two structors provide distinct functionals, both are needed. If they provide the same functionals, one of them is redundant. For partial overlap, either one may be complemented by a third structor. But which one is preferable? Within a Linear Software Model the answer is clear: choose a linearly independent set of structors.

Linear models are usually formulated in terms of matrices. The Modularity Matrix is a Boolean matrix with columns standing for structors and rows for functionals. A matrix element is 1-valued for a functional-structor link and 0-valued for no link.

1.3   Modularity Matrix: An Introductory Example

A simple useful system is here described in terms of a Linear Software Model to illustrate concepts found along the paper. It refers to OFB (Output Feed-Back) encryption of a long message (Fig. 1) before network transmission – e.g. Kaufman, et al. [9]. A message is cut into N blocks of fixed length and each one is treated separately.

A random Initial Vector is generated. Each block of the message is pre-processed. A corresponding vector is also pre-processed to the size of a block, and then encrypted. The encrypted output vector is fed back into the encryption function, through the vector pre-processing. Feedback is done N times, obtaining one vector for each message block. The kth encrypted vector is then Xored with the kth message block.

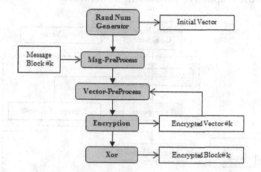

Fig. 1. OFB encryption of long message. This is a functional calling dependency graph for a generic k^{th} message block. Functionals are displayed as (blue) rounded rectangles. Some of the input/output dataflow is shown in regular rectangles.

Table 1. OFB functionals

#	Functional	Description
1	Random number generator	from a distribution
2	Encryption function	e.g. RSA encryption
3	Xor	a logical function
4	Vector-Pre-Process	Fetch(vector,size)
5	Message-Pre-Process	fetch & pad message

The OFB software system has five functionals (Table 1) and the following four structors: S1) Rand - offers random distributions; S2) Crypto structor - offers encryption protocols; S3) Logical - provides logical functions, say AND, OR, XOR; S4) Proc - a processor structor provides pre-processing functions.

The resulting OFB modularity matrix (Table 2) has 2 identical lowest rows. The matrix reflects that the pre-processing functionals are not independent. Both functionals are provided by the same structor, thus they are not distinguishable.

Table 2. OFB rectangular Modularity Matrix with linear dependencies

		S1=Rand	S2=Crypto	S3=Logical	S4=Proc
Rand Num Gen	F1	1	0	0	0
Encryption Func	F2	0	1	0	1
XOR	F3	0	0	1	1
Vector-Pre-Proc	F4	0	0	0	1
Msg-Pre-Proc	F5	0	0	0	1

An interesting feature of OFB encryption is that one can prepare all encrypted vectors in advance, before there are any message blocks to be sent. Therefore, one can rearrange the functional calling graph, enabling totally separate execution.

Two modules naturally appear, one dealing with vectors and the other with message blocks – see Fig. 2. In each module, the processing structor, besides pre-processing, invokes the respective processing functional.

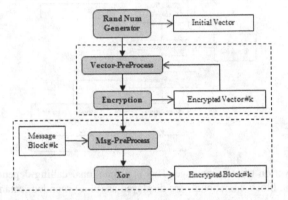

Fig. 2. OFB functionals modularized. Rearranged functional calling graph of Fig. 1. The upper dashed lines module pre-processes vectors, encrypts and saves them. The lower module fetches message blocks, pre-processes them and Xors each block with its saved vector.

Table 3. OFB strictly linear model – Modularity Matrix

		S1= Rand	S2= Crypt	S4=Vec Proc	S3= Logical	S5=Msg Proc
Rand Num Gen	F1	1	0	0	0	0
Encryption Func	F2	0	1	1	0	0
Vector-Pre-Proc	F3	0	0	1	0	0
XOR	F4	0	0	0	1	1
Msg-Pre-Proc	F5	0	0	0	0	1

Independent pre-processing functionals which are able to run in parallel in distinct machines need independent structors. So, one has a VectorProc structor and a separate MsgProc structor. These structors are aware – by means of associations – of the respective processing functionals which they are able to invoke.

Row and column swap operations lead to a block-diagonal matrix (Table 3). The diagonal blocks in this matrix match the modules in Fig. 2.

The system matrix in Table 3 strictly obeys a Linear Software Model. This means that all its modules have linearly independent rows and columns. Thus, each of its functionals is distinguishable. For instance, according to the matrix in Table 3 functional F_2 is provided by structors $\{S_2, S_4\}$.

The independent execution of VectorProc and MsgProc, in time and space, clarifies the sense of an independent software structor. It must be: a) *Loadable/Runnable* – in a virtual or real machine; b) *Separable* – i.e. able to run in *separate* machines.

The remaining of the paper is organized starting from the basic theory (section 2), through concrete case studies (section 3), to a discussion (section 4).

2   Linear Software Models of Composition

The aim of this section is to describe the new theoretical approach – the Linear Software Models of Composition.

Linear Software Models are the simplest theoretical models of software composition. Systems obeying such a model are composed just by addition of independent modules.

2.1   Modularity Matrices' Linear Independence

A Linear Software Model contains a list of software structors and another of software functionals. Its Modularity Matrix is defined as:

Definition 1 – Modularity-Matrix

A fully expanded Modularity-Matrix is a Boolean matrix asserting links (1-valued elements) between software functionals (rows) and software structors (columns). The absence of a link is marked by a 0-valued element.

By definition, software structors are elementary artifacts, which the software engineer decides to look at them as indivisible into smaller structors. Say, the OFB crypto structor (section 1.3) is not split into – prime factorization or modulo arithmetic – although decomposition is obviously possible. The same holds true for functionals.

Besides being indivisible, only structors with unique roles, as the OFB VectorProcessor and MsgProcessor needed for parallelism, are in the Matrix. Multiple structor copies, say by fault tolerance reasons, are not included in the Matrix.

Independent structors must be represented by distinct vectors. But, sets of differing vectors may still be dependent. The generic criterion for independent structors in any system subsets is linear independence:

Definition 2 – Independent Structor

A software structor is independent of other structors in the system, if it provides a non-empty proper sub-set of functionals of the system, given by the 1-valued links in the respective column, and is linearly independent of other columns in the Modularity Matrix.

We now look at the links from the functional point of view. In order to be able to distinguish a functional, its set of links in the functional row must be unequivocal. Again linear independence is the relevant criterion:

Definition 3 – Composable Functional
A software functional is independently composable or just composable in terms of structors, if it corresponds to a non-empty proper sub-set of system structors, given by the 1-valued links in the respective row, and is linearly independent of other rows in the Modularity-Matrix.
  This set is the composition set of the functional.

For instance, for OFB (Table 3) the XOR functional composition set is {S3, S5}.

2.2   Well-Composed Modularity Matrices Are Square

A well-composed modularity matrix has additive properties, i.e. it has composable functionals from independent structors. Then:

Theorem 1 – Well-Composed Modularity-Matrix
If in a Modularity-Matrix all its functionals are composable with independent structors, the Modularity-Matrix number of structors Ns is equal to its number of functionals NF. The matrix is Square.
  Such a matrix is called a Well-Composed Modularity-Matrix.

A proof sketch is (detailed proofs will be given in a longer paper): Assume a matrix without empty rows/columns. First, structors are used as a basis for functional vectors. Then, functionals are a basis for structor vectors. By linear independence, in each case vector numbers cannot be greater than the basis. As both cases must be simultaneously true, follows the equality NS=NF. The matrix is square.

  The theorem assumptions are very intuitive. An analogy is the symptom sets to diagnose illnesses. Say, high temperature, a very common symptom, is not enough to identify a disease. Diseases with the same symptom sets are indistinguishable. To unequivocally diagnose an illness one needs independent sets of symptoms.

  This theorem does not force a one-to-one functional/structor match. It is obeyed by matrices with NVAL 1-valued elements greater than NS and NF (see e.g. Table 4).

Table 4. Abstract square Modularity Matrix with N_{VAL}=6, while N_S=N_F=3

	S1	S2	S3
F1	1	0	1
F2	0	1	1
F3	1	1	0

  Algebraically, there are simple criteria for well-composed matrices: non-zero matrix determinant or matrix rank equal to the number of rows/columns.

2.3   Reducible Modularity Matrices

When a Modularity Matrix has disjoint dependency sets, structors and their functionals can be grouped into modules, such that vector sets in different modules are linearly independent. This reduces the matrix to block-diagonal (fig. 3), i.e. with smaller squares of any size along the diagonal, see e.g. Rowland, Weisstein, [16]. All off-block elements are zero.

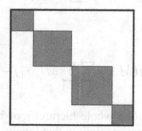

Fig. 3. Schematic Block-Diagonal Matrix

A "union-set" is the union of composition sets for a set of functionals. Then:

Theorem 2 – Modularity Matrix Reducibility
Any well-composed Modularity Matrix in which the union-set for a given set of functionals is disjoint to the other functional union-sets is reducible, i.e. it can be put in block-diagonal form.

A proof sketch is: apply row and column exchanges to bring the disjoint union-set to the upper-left matrix corner. As the whole Modularity Matrix is Well-composed, the disjoint union-set is itself square (by Theorem 1) and its diagonal is along the whole Matrix diagonal. The residual 1-valued elements are thus also square bounded, along the whole Matrix diagonal. This reasoning is extensible to any number of blocks.

The previous theorems naturally lead us to define linear software system models of composition. The two theorems are combined in the Linear-Reducible model, in the strict sense.

Definition 4 – Linear Reducible Model
The Linear-Reducible model of software system composition, in the strict sense, is characterized by a well-composed and reducible Modularity Matrix having at least two disjoint blocks.

We identify modules with disjoint diagonal blocks of structors/functionals, corresponding to the intuitive notion of modular software systems. One can express modularity quantitatively by the diagonality of a Modularity-Matrix M, telling how close its 1-valued elements are to the main diagonal. It is the difference between the Trace, the diagonal elements' sum, and offdiag, a new term dealing with off-diagonal elements:

$$Diagonality(M) = Trace(M) - offdiag(M) \qquad (1)$$

Offdiag sums over 1-valued Mjk off-diagonal elements, times the absolute value of the difference of the element's column k and row j indices. For each row j and column k:

$$RowOffdiag(M,j) = \sum_{k=1}^{N} M_{jk} \cdot |j-k|$$

$$ColOffdiag(M,k) = \sum_{j=1}^{N} M_{jk} \cdot |j-k| \tag{2}$$

The overall matrix offdiag is:

$$offdiag(M) = \sum_{j=1}^{N} \sum_{k=1}^{N} M_{jk} \cdot |j-k| \tag{3}$$

The next operations may unfold a whole hierarchy of block levels, where a level is defined by the matrix components explicit in that level:

a) Block collapse – transforms a block into a single element *black-box*.

b) Block expansion – restores a collapsed black-box back into a *white-box*.

To assure that these operations preserve diagonality, black-boxes are labeled by the <Trace, offdiag> diagonality value, of the original white-box. To be able to restore the white-box, hidden rows/columns should be stored elsewhere.

The modularity hierarchy is thus given by:

Definition 5 – Number of modules at a level
The number of modules of a software system at a hierarchy level is the number of blocks from the modularity matrix partition into disjoint union-sets at that level.

2.4   The Single Responsibility Theorem

The last theoretical piece of the Linear Models is a linear algebraic formulation of the single responsibility principle (see e.g. Martin, [11]). It is valid after one obtains a block-diagonal matrix:

Theorem 3 – Single Responsibility
In a strictly block-diagonal modularity matrix each structor column intersects a single module. Similarly, each functional row intersects a single module.

This theorem is easily verified. It means that a single module is responsible for providing each functional exclusively by its structors. This is a plausible interpretation of the familiar principle, since related structors and functionals are grouped in a single module.

3   Case Studies

The goal of this section is to demonstrate the power of Linear Software models, showing by case studies a range of concrete software systems obeying such a model.

We have chosen representative software systems of disparate purposes and sizes to illustrate the Linear Models. It turns out that all systems are well-composed. Small systems are strictly Linear-Reducible – i.e. obey a model with a linearly independent and reducible matrix – and larger systems are bordered Linear-Reducible. In each case, a modularity matrix is obtained, block-diagonalized and analysed in terms of Linearity.

3.1   Small Systems Are Strictly Linear Reducible

Small systems and intermediate reusable building blocks strictly obey the Linear-Reducible Software model. These are Parnas' KWIC index and the Observer pattern. KWIC was thoroughly analysed by Parnas to be a canonical example. The Observer pattern was deliberately designed to be reused.

Parnas' KWIC Index. The 1972 Parnas paper [13] described two KWIC index modularizations. The system outputs an alphabetical listing of all circular shifts of all input lines. Functionals were extracted from Parnas' own system description. Structors are explicit in the paper – where they are called modules.

The Modularity Matrix of Parnas' 1st modularization is in Table 5 (0-valued elements are omitted for clarity; blocks have a darker background). It is almost block-diagonal, but two features are problematic:

a) the Master Control column vector is not a proper subset of the functionals;

b) non-zero outliers break block-diagonality.

Table 5. Parnas' 1st modularization – Modularity Matrix

Structors → Functionals		Input 1	Circular Shifter 2	Master Control 3	Alpha-betizer 4	Output 5
Input = ordered set of lines	1	1		1		
Does circular shift on a line	2		1	1		
Line= store line in word order	3	1	1	1	1	
Sort lines in alphabetical order	4			1	1	
Outputs circular shifted lines	5			1		1

The matrix clearly hints to couplings to be resolved: the notably higher RowOffdiag=4 of the 3rd row, contains all outliers, besides the master control ones. The solution is: a- to delete the master control, as quoting Parnas, it "does little more than sequencing", it is not a real structor; b- to add a new Line-Storage structor, as Parnas informally argued, to decouple the 3rd row "Line" functional from the Input, Circular-shifter and Alphabetizer. The 2nd Parnas' modularization fits the strictly diagonal 5-module matrix in Table 6.

Table 6. Parnas' 2nd modularization – Modularity Matrix

Structors →		Input	Circular Shifter	Line Storage	Alpha-betizer	Output
Functionals		1	2	3	4	5
Input = ordered set of lines	1	1				
Does circular shift on a line	2		1			
Line= store line in word order	3			1		
Sort lines in alphabetical order	4				1	
Outputs circular shifted lines	5					1

We use decouple in a precise new meaning, viz. linearly independent composition.

The matrices in Tables 5 and 6 are not equivalent, having different non-zero element numbers. Which one is more modular? The 1st matrix diagonality has a value –5. The 2nd diagonality equals the Trace and is 5. Thus, the 2nd is more modular.

We arrived at the same Parnas conclusions, by formal Modularity Matrix arguments. This system strictly obeys the Linear-Reducible Model.

Observer Design Pattern. The Observer Design Pattern abstracts one-to-many interactions among objects, such that when a "subject" – changes, all the "observers" – are notified and updated.

The Observer Modularity Matrix is based upon the Design Patterns' GoF book [6]. Its sample code refers to an analog and a digital clock, the "concrete observers", changing according to an internal clock – the "concrete subject".

The system structors are:

• generic Observer pattern entities, directly taken from the pattern list of "Participants": abstract subject, abstract observer, concrete subject and concrete observer.

• specific application structors – a subject resource, a GUI for each external clock and an initiator which constructs the clocks.

The Observer functionals were extracted from the complete set of functions that may be invoked in the sample code. These functions were trimmed by elimination of linear dependencies. *Keep-observers-list* attaches/detaches observers.

State is not maintained in the same way in the subject and in the observers. The unique subject sets the state ("ticks") by means of a *Keep-Global-state* functional, while observers, are updated at unrelated times by *Keep-Local-state*.

Table 7. Observer linear reducible – Modularity Matrix

Structors →		subject	Concrete subject	subject resource	concrete observer	Observer	Gui analog	Gui digital	Init
Functionals		1	2	3	4	5	6	7	8
Keep observer list	1	1							
Notify observers	2	1	1						
Keep-global-state	3		1	1					
Keep-local-state	4				1				
Update observers	5				1	1			
Draw-analog	6						1		
Draw-digital	7							1	
Constructor	8								1

Row/column reordering of a quite arbitrary initial matrix causes modules to emerge in a strictly Linear-Reducible matrix. (Table 7). The modules are a subject and an observer, the generic module roles [14] for this design pattern, each one with the respective abstract/concrete structors and the specific clock modules.

In Table 7, subject and observer modules emerged from basic structors. Alternatively one can deal with black-box collapsed modules (as defined in subsection 2.3) in a higher hierarchical level matrix shown in Table 8.

Table 8. Observer higher level Modularity-Matrix

Structors →		Subject	Observer	Clock Appl.
Functionals		**1**	**2**	**3**
Keep-global-state & Notify observers	1	<3.2>		
Keep-local-state & Update observers	2		<2,1>	
construct, draw clocks	3			<3,0>

The Observer analysis illustrates that, despite arbitrary initial order, automatic reordering brings about a matrix accurately reflecting the pattern functionality.

The Observer pattern is a prototypical example. It would be desirable to have all reusable building blocks as the Observer, strictly obeying the Linear-Reducible Model, to allow linearly independent composition into larger software systems.

3.2   Larger Software Systems Are Bordered Linear Reducible

We have shown the Linear Model applicability to real systems, viz. larger projects from the literature. The novel result: these systems are bordered Linear-Reducible.

NEESgrid Modularity Matrix. The NEESgrid "Network Earthquake Engineering Simulation" project enables network access to participate in earthquake tele-operation experiments. The system was designed by the NCSA at University of Illinois. Modularity Matrix functionals were extracted from a report by Finholt, et al. [5] with exactly 10 upper-level structors.

Table 9. NEESgrid initial Modularity Matrix

Structors →		chef	Data Rp	Data Vu	Data Str	Data Dis	Telepre	Data Ac	Hyb Exp	Sim Rep	Grid Infr
Functionals		1	2	3	4	5	6	7	8	9	10
Collect_Data	1		1		1			1			
Search_Data	2					1					
Manage_Data	3		1	1							
HybridExper	4								1		
Data_View	5			1							
Sync_Collab	6	1					1				
Async_Collab	7	1									
Other_Collab	8	1		1				1			1
SimulCodes	9									1	
HighPerfComp	10										1

An initial modularity matrix (Table 9) was obtained by straightforward linearity considerations: eliminating empty and identical rows; an empty column, "Electronic Lab Notebook", was deleted. A column was assigned to a next-level structor *Data-Discovery* (DataDis) as it neatly fits the *SearchData* functional. The scattered non-zero elements are typical of initial matrices in this kind of analysis.

Pure algebraic row/column reorder, without semantic concerns, brings about the almost block-diagonal Matrix (in Table 10). Its modules – diagonal blocks – are:

- Data manipulation – collect, search, manage, view – the upper-left block;
- Collaboration tools – synchronous, async, other – the middle block;
- Infrastructure – grid, codes – the lower-right block.

Table 10. NEESgrid Bordered Linear-Reducible Modularity Matrix

Structors →		Data Str	Data Dis	Data Rp	Data Vu	Data Ac	Telepre	chef	Grid Infr	Sim Rep	Hybr Exp
Functionals		4	5	2	3	7	6	1	10	9	8
Collect_Data	1	1		1		1					
Search_Data	2		1								
Manage_Data	3			1	1						
Data_View	5				1						
Other_Collab	8				1		1		1	1	
Sync_Collab	6						1	1			
Async_Collab	7							1			
HighPerfComp	10								1		
SimulCodes	9									1	
HybridExper	4										1

Module interpretation is hinted by functional names – Data and Collab.

Outliers appear in the rows with maximal value RowOffDiag=6, Collect_Data and Other_Collab. The latter prefix "Other" hints at mixed functionals to be decoupled.

This case study shows that: a- algebraic reordering, without prior semantic knowledge, obtains plausible modules; b- outliers are amenable to interpretation, in particular matching project notes (e.g. the row 8, column 10 outlier, marked "not within the project scope" in project documents).

The significant result, common to large case studies, is that there are few outliers, and all of them are in columns/rows adjacent to the Linear Model blocks. This is what we call bordered Linear-Reducible.

4   Discussion: Theoretical Standards of Modularity

4.1   Main Contribution: Linear Software Models

This paper's main contribution is the Linear Software Models, as theoretical standards against which to compare real software systems. The models stand upon well-established linear algebra, as a broad basis for a solid theory of composition – beyond current principles and practices.

The analysis starts from lists of structors and functionals required by the software system architecture. In the case studies, structors and functionals were identified from the literature, apparently being a subjective informal process. In practical applications the lists are objectively constrained by the structors actually available within COTS components that may be purchased from manufacturers,

Given the lists of structors and functionals required by a system and those available in COTS components, one can assert, from the Modularity Matrix properties of the system, which structors are independent and which functionals are independently composable. This solves the practical and well-defined component matching problem. One can then infer which design improvements are desirable.

This view is very different from design models, such as UML, whose purpose is not to serve as theoretical standards. Design models freely evolve with design and system development. Design models have indefinite modifiability to adapt to any system, in response to tests of system compliance to design.

4.2   Related Work

Matrices have been used to deal with modularity. A prominent example is DSM (Design Structure Matrix) proposed by Steward [20], developed by Eppinger and collaborators e.g. [18],[19] and part of the "Design Rules" approach by Baldwin and Clark – see e.g. [1] and also Cai et al. [3], [17]. DSM and other matrices, such as Kusiak and Huang's [10] hardware modularity matrix, are meant to be evolving design models.

Linearity, not found in DSM, is the outstanding feature of our standard models. Essential distinctions of Linear Software Models from DSM are:

• Theoretical Standards vs. Design Models – our models' goal is to serve as theoretical standards for software composition, as opposed to DSM design models which emphasize design process and manufacturing.

• Functionals vs. Structures-only – our modularity matrices display structor to functional links, while both DSM matrix dimensions are labeled by the same structures.

Baldwin and Clark explicitly state in footnote 2, page 63 of their book [1]: "it is difficult to base modularity on functions... hence their definition of modularity is based on relationships among structures, not functions". See Ulrich [21] for a different view.

Usually, modularity matrices are much more compact than DSM. For instance, Parnas' KWIC DSM in [3] has 20 rows/columns instead of just 5 in our Modularity Matrix.

Although diagonality has seldom been calculated within modularity, formulas have appeared in other contexts. Clemins in [4] used for speaker identification, the Frobenius norm – the sum of the squares – of all off-diagonal elements to measure diagonality. Our *offdiag* definition is better suited to modularity, as it directly reflects distance to the diagonal, while the Frobenius norm just sums Boolean elements.

An indirect coupling metric is "similarity coefficients", cf. Hwang, Oh, [7], comparing matrix row pairs, over all columns. The similarity for each column is: both 1 elements, both 0, or different. These coefficients ignore distances from the diagonal.

The Modularity Matrix has a superficial similarity to a traceability table. But their purposes are definitely different. Traceability tables are used to *trace* code and tests to requirements, while our functionals' essence is to verify linear independence.

The module detection literature is plentiful. Tools to improve legacy code use clustering to partition graphs, by Mitchell, Mancoridis, [12], metrics to increase cohesion, by Kang, Bieman, 1999 [8] and slicing of FDGs – Functional Dependence Graphs by Rodrigues, Barbosa, [15], tools to detect modularity violations by Wong, et al., [22]. Despite the quantitative flavor, they clearly differ from our Linear Models.

4.3   Future Work

A mathematical characterization of modularity matrix outliers deserves further investigation. This relates to the broader issue of determining block sizes, after exclusion of outliers, and module refactoring.

A practical issue is to systematically obtain a broad class of basic patterns strictly obeying the Linear-Reducible Model, like the Observer, as advocated for software building blocks.

Efficiency issues concerning modularity matrix generation and reordering (cf. Borndorfer, et al. [2]) for large scale systems will be investigated.

This work has found that small software systems are strictly Linear-Reducible, and some large software systems are bordered Linear-Reducible. This poses a variety of open questions.

The larger systems shown to be bordered Linear-Reducible were developed before the proposal of the Linear Model. It is conceivable, but still unclear, that in view of this model they could be modified in a natural way to comply with the strict Linear-Reducible model. Similarly, future large scale systems developed with awareness of linearity, may show that strictly Linear-Reducibility rather than limited to certain systems, is indeed applicable to a wide variety of software systems.

4.4   Conclusions

Software has been perceived as essentially different from other engineering fields, due to software's intrinsic variability, reflected in the soft prefix. This versatility is often seen as an advantage to be preserved, even though software composition has largely resisted theoretical formalization.

We have found that Linear Software Models can be formulated, without giving up variability. Thus, software systems of disparate size, function and purpose, may have Linearity in common.

References

1. Baldwin, C.Y., Clark, K.B.: Design Rules. The Power of Modularity, vol. I. MIT Press, Cambridge (2000)
2. Borndorfer, R., Ferreira, C.E., Martin, A.: Decomposing Matrices into Blocks. SIAM J. Optimization 9(1), 236–269 (1998)

3. Cai, Y., Sullivan, K.J.: Modularity Analysis of Logical Design Models. In: Proc. 21st IEEE/ACM Int. Conf. On Automated Software Eng., ASE 2006, pp. 91–102. Tokyo, Japan (2006)

4. Clemins, P.J., Ewalt, H.E., Johnson, M.T.: Time-Aligned SVD Analysis for Speaker Identification. In: Proc. ICASSP02 IEEE Int. Conf. Acoustics Speech and Signal Proc., vol. 4, pp. IV-4160 (2002)

5. Finholt, T.A., Horn, D., Thome, S.: NEESgrid Requirements Traceability Matrix, Technical Report NEESgrid-2003-13, School of Information, University of Michigan, USA (2004)

6. Gamma, E., Helm, R., Johnson, R., Vlissides, J.: Design Patterns: Elements of Reusable Object-Oriented Software. Addison-Wesley, Boston (1995)

7. Hwang, H., Oh, Y.H.: Another similarity coefficient for the p-median model in group technology. Int. J. Manufacturing Tech. & Management 5, 38–245 (2003)

8. Kang, B.-K., Bieman, J.M.: A Quantitative Framework for Software Restructuring. J. Softw. Maint. Research & Practice 11(4), 245–284 (1999)

9. Kaufman, C., Perlman, R., Speciner, M.: Network Security – Private Communication in a Public World. Prentice-Hall, Englewood Cliffs (1997)

10. Kusiak, A., Huang, C.-C.: Design of Modular Digital Circuits for Testability. IEEE Trans. Components, Packaging and Manufacturing Technology – Part C 20(1), 48–57 (1997)

11. Martin, R.C.: Agile Software Development: Principles, Patterns and Practices. Prentice Hall, Upper Saddle River (2003)

12. Mitchell, B.S., Mancoridis, S.: On the Automatic Modularization of Software Systems Using the Bunch Tool. IEEE Trans. Software Engineering 32(3), 193–208 (2006)

13. Parnas, D.L.: On the Criteria to be Used in Decomposing Systems into Modules. Comm. ACM 15, 1053–1058 (1972)

14. Riehle, D.: Describing and Composing Patterns Using Role Diagrams. In: Mutzel, K.-U., Frei., H.-P. (eds.) Proc. Ubilab Conf., Universitatsverlag Konstanz, pp. 137–152 (1996)

15. Rodrigues, N.F., Barbosa, L.S.: Component Identification through program slicing. Electronic Notes in Theoretical Computer Science 160, 291–304 (2006); Proc. Int. Workshop Formal Aspects of Component Software (FACS 2005) (2005)

16. Rowland, T., Weisstein, E.W.: Block Diagonal Matrix. from MathWorld (2006), http://mathworld.wolfram.com/BlockDiagonalMatrix.html

17. Sethi, K., Cai, Y., Wong, S., Garcia, A., Sant'Anna, C.: From Retrospect to Prospect: Assessing Modularity and Stability from Software Architecture. In: Proc. European Conf. on Software Architecture, WICSA/ECSA, pp. 269–272 (2009)

18. Sosa, M.E., Agrawal, A., Eppinger, S.D., Rowles, C.M.: A Network Approach to Define Modularity of Product Components. In: Proc. IDETC/CIE ASME International Design Engineering Technical Conf. & Computers and Information in Engineering Conf., Long Beach, CA, USA, pp. 1–12 (2005)

19. Sosa, M.E., Eppinger, S.D., Rowles, C.M.: A Network Approach to Define Modularity of Components in Complex Products. ASME Journal of Mechanical Design 129, 1118 (2007)

20. Steward, D.: The Design Structure System: A Method for Managing the Design of Complex Systems. IEEE Trans. Eng. Manag., EM-29(3), 71–74 (1981)

21. Ulrich, K.T.: The Role of Product Architecture in the Manufacturing Firm. Res. Policy 24, 419–440 (1995)

22. Wong, S., Cai, Y., Kim, M., Dalton, M.: Detecting Software Modularity Viola-tions. In: Proc. 33rd Int. Conf. Software Engineering, pp. 411–420 (2011)

Author Index